Carlyle
and the Burden of History

Thomas Carlyle. Photograph by Julia Margaret Cameron, 1867. All rights reserved:
the Metropolitan Museum of Art, the Alfred Stieglitz Collection, 1949. (49.55.324)

£19.50

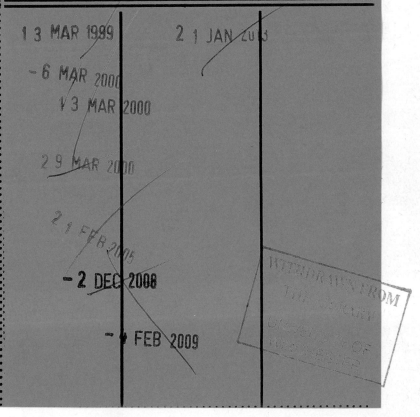

CARLYLE
and the
Burden of History

JOHN D. ROSENBERG

CLARENDON PRESS · OXFORD
1985

Oxford University Press, Walton Street, Oxford OX2 6DP
Oxford New York Toronto
Delhi Bombay Calcutta Madras Karachi
Kuala Lumpur Singapore Hong Kong Tokyo
Nairobi Dar es Salaam Cape Town
Melbourne Auckland
and associated companies in
Beirut Berlin Ibadan Mexico City Nicosia

Oxford is a trade mark of Oxford University Press

Published in the United States
by Harvard University Press, Cambridge, Mass.

British Library Cataloguing in Publication Data
Rosenberg, John D.
Carlyle and the burden of history.
1. Carlyle, Thomas—Criticism and interpretation
I. Title
828'.808   PR4434
ISBN 0-19-812846-0

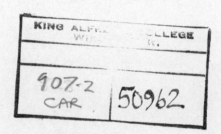
Set by DMB Typesetting, Oxford
Printed in Great Britain at
The University Press, Oxford
by David Stanford
Printer to the University

To Maurine and Matthew

Preface

History, as Carlyle understood it, is poetry, prophecy, biography, and social criticism—all in one. In the writing of history he found his vocation, and his practice of that vocation is the subject of this book.

Carlyle conceived of his histories as modern prose-epics—successors to the Bible, Homer, and Milton. In *The French Revolution* he came closest to realizing this exalted ambition. A central document of nineteenth-century culture, *The French Revolution* is my principal concern, but Carlyle's historical imagination figures importantly in almost all that he wrote: in his early essays on English culture, as in the bitter journalism of *Latter-Day Pamphlets*, he is the chronicler and critic of his own age; *On Heroes and Hero-Worship* is rooted in history; in *Reminiscences* and in the autobiographical *Sartor Resartus* he is the historian of himself.

Radical and authoritarian, compassionate and bigoted, prophetic and blind, Carlyle the man is as difficult to categorize as his works. His indictment of the brutality of *laissez-faire* capitalism inspired Dickens, Ruskin, and Engels, yet he supported slavery in the American South and was awarded the Order of Merit by Bismarck's Prussia. His moving plea for community gradually gives way to a frightened call for authority, his receptivity to new ideas hardens into intolerance of all creeds save his own.

Carlyle's estrangement from the world and from his own genius becomes increasingly apparent in the years following *The French Revolution*. *Past and Present*, his last great work, is also the first in which he loses his way. His confidence in his ability to read the design of history falters, and as the past grows unintelligible, the present becomes intolerable. He retreats within himself, and the signs of that long withdrawal are everywhere evident in *Frederick the Great*, his final meditation on history.

In the course of writing this book I was generously aided by fellowships from the American Council of Learned Societies and the National Endowment for the Humanities. My wife Maurine and friend Elliott Zuckerman read the manuscript in each of its many stages; their criticism and encouragement were vital. Joanna Gondris and Maude Meisel were the most astute and enterprising of research assistants.

My chapters on *The French Revolution* profited greatly from the keen scrutiny of Anne Prescott. Elizabeth Wheeler offered a host of helpful suggestions, substantive as well as stylistic. Louis Menand's comments unfailingly led me to tighten an argument or more nearly approximate a truth. To Margaretta Fulton and Kim Scott Walwyn I owe thanks for their confidence in this book even before it reached their editorial desks. For reasons too numerous to specify and too important to ignore, I am also indebted to Richard D. Altick, Jonathan Arac, James R. Bird, Jr., Andrew Brown, K. J. Fielding, Elizabeth Langen, Fred Kaplan, George Leonard, Peter Rudnytsky, and Joseph Slater.

My final chapters were written in the pleasant village of Peacham, in the former summer-home of Moses Hadas, the first of the great company of teachers I encountered on entering Columbia College just after the Second World War. Moses Hadas, Mark Van Doren, Lionel Trilling, Joseph Wood Krutch, F. W. Dupee, Andrew Chiappe— forty years ago they taught me much of what I know of the humane study of literature. I like to think they teach me still.

J. D. R.

New York City
October 1984

Contents

The Advent of a Prophet

1

From *Sartor Resartus* to *The French Revolution*

Late in the summer of 1833 the young Emerson rode across the desolate hills of Dumfriesshire to the Carlyle farm at Craigenputtoch. Unknown to his hosts and unexpected, Emerson journeyed into the wilderness to meet a writer whose name he had not known only a few months earlier. But before sailing from America, he had learned to recognize the voice that spoke to him with compelling urgency from the pages of Carlyle's early, unsigned essays—'by far the most original & profound essays of the day,'[1] he later wrote to Carlyle in a letter that commemorated their meeting and inaugurated their lifelong correspondence.

When Emerson appeared at Craigenputtoch, Carlyle and his wife Jane had been living for five years in self-imposed solitude. Carlyle's essays on the German Romantics and on English culture had appeared in leading periodicals, but his literary ambition far outran any recognition he had yet achieved. Two years earlier he had completed a quasi-autobiographical novel even stranger than its title, but no publisher would take *Sartor Resartus* and it did not appear in book form until Emerson, acting as Carlyle's intellectual midwife, secured its publication in America. But Emerson was in search not of celebrity but of truth and of himself, and by the end of a long day's talk he felt he had come closer to both. The two men walked over the bleak hills, looked southward 'into Wordsworth's country' and spoke of 'the immortality of the soul',[2] a subject much on their minds. (Both men had abandoned careers in the ministry, Emerson shortly before sailing to Europe, Carlyle in his early twenties.) 'Christ died on the tree', Carlyle remarked: 'that built Dunscore kirk yonder; that brought you and me together.'[3] But if Christ brought them together, so too did their rejection of His divinity and His church. Their quest for a credible gospel, for belief in themselves and in the supremacy of spirit over matter in an increasingly disbelieving world, set the seal on their sudden brotherhood, the 'sacred covenant', as Carlyle later put it, 'that exists between us two to the end . . .'.[4]

Both Emerson and Carlyle saw in their meeting a personal and historical significance that transcended the social occasion. 'A white day in my years,' Emerson noted in his *Journal* at his departure.[5] And almost fifty years later Carlyle remarked, in sending his love to Emerson via a mutual friend, 'I still think of his visit to us at Craigenputtoch as the most beautiful thing in our experience there.'[6] Jane caught the essence of the occasion in a simile: 'It was like the visit of an angel; . . . and though he staid with us hardly twenty four hours, yet when he left us I cried—I could not help it.'[7] It is difficult to imagine the large-boned Emerson as an angel, but the incongruity of Jane's simile and her untimely tears are revealing: Emerson's appearance out of nowhere must have seemed more like a visitation than a visit. His arrival was the sign that Carlyle's long sojourn in the wilderness would end, that deliverance in the form of recognition was at hand. A gifted stranger had come all the way from America, where Carlyle was venerated by the elect. The question of Jesus to the multitude—'what went ye out into the wilderness to see?'—hung unspoken over their meeting. Emerson had answered it by the very act of his pilgrimage: a prophet, a preparer of the way.

No literary creation of Carlyle's is more remarkable than his self-creation as a prophet during the years at Craigenputtoch (1828–34). In December 1829 he wrote to John Wilson, the formidable 'Christopher North' of *Blackwood's Magazine*, 'I have some thoughts of beginning to *prophecy* [*sic*] next year, if I prosper; that seems the best style, could one strike into it rightly.'[8] The new style fitted Carlyle awkwardly, and the self-conscious irony of his letters barely hides the grandeur of his ambition. To a friend he compares the austere solitude of Craigenputtoch to John the Divine's hermit-like life on Patmos, except that 'no Revelation is yet forthcoming'.[9] He is more direct in announcing his mission to his devout mother. In London, looking for a publisher for *Sartor*, he meets 'various well-disposed . . . young men, who even feel a sort of scholarship [*discipleship?*] towards me'. Gliding easily into his mother's idiom, he complains of the 'want of instruction and light in this mirk midnight of human affairs, such want as probably for eighteen hundred years there has not been: if *I* have any light to give, then let me give it . . .'[10] The letter was written in September 1831, a few weeks after Carlyle completed *Sartor Resartus*, a novelized sermon in which he tries to convert England from the old 'Mythus of the Christian Religion'[11] to the new gospel of Natural Supernaturalism.

Henry Crabb Robinson met Carlyle in London at this time and was struck by his resemblance to a 'religious zealot'.[12] Robinson recognized in Carlyle's speech and manner the outward manifestations of an inward conviction that was to determine the subsequent shape of his career. By 1833 Carlyle could step back from himself and marvel at what a 'wondrous figure' he had become in the wilderness. 'The very sound of my voice has got something savage-prophetic', he wrote to his brother John: 'I am as a John Baptist, girt about with a leathern girdle, and whose food is locusts and wild honey.'[13] Carlyle wrote this letter shortly before leaving his native Scotland in his fortieth year and ending his long literary apprenticeship. His biographer James Anthony Froude closes his account of Carlyle's years in Scotland with the comment that 'the Annandale peasant boy' was about to become 'the wonder of the London World. He had wrought himself into a personality which all were to be compelled to admire, and in whom a few recognised, like Goethe, the advent of a new moral force. . . .'[14]

   That force stemmed from Carlyle's newly won sense of having found a vocation and a subject adequate to his own genius. In *Sartor Resartus* his subject had been himself and the Universe. In *The French Revolution* he turned from himself to society and created the work that at last established his fame. In the pause between the two books, all of Carlyle's movements, intellectual and physical, have the quality of lived allegory. A career in *belles lettres* had come to seem increasingly irrelevant to his own needs and to those of society. Near the end of his stay at Craigenputtoch, in the autumn of 1833, he wrote to his brother John of his 'yearly growing . . . persuasion that all Art is but a reminiscence now, that for us in these days *Prophecy* (well understood) not Poetry is the thing wanted; how can we *sing* and *paint* when we do not yet *believe* and *see?*'[15] He was confident of his powers but uncertain of his prospects. 'A kind of *moulting* season with me', he noted in his diary: 'Almost all things go by systole and diastole, even one's spiritual progress.'[16] Hesitantly but inexorably, he moved closer to what he now called 'the subject of subjects'.[17] His new friend John Stuart Mill sent him books on the French Revolution, and, in a letter of September 1833 acknowledging the gift, Carlyle announces that the 'right *History*' of the French Revolution would be 'the grand Poem of our Time. . . . [T]he man who *could* write the *truth* of that, were worth all other writers and singers.' He again evokes the image of John the Baptist and wonders if he might not 'prepare the way' for such a work.[18]

As a trial run at mastering historical narrative in a prophetic style, he writes 'The Diamond Necklace', a 'kind of attempted *True Fiction*'[19] based on the scandal that shook the Court on the eve of the Revolution. In this last of his labours in the wilderness, Carlyle probes the elusive relations between fact and fiction, history and poetry, that he was to explore so boldly in *The French Revolution*. 'I am busy constantly studying with my whole might for a Book on the *French Revolution*', he writes in his first letter to Emerson. 'It is part of my creed that the only Poetry is History, could we tell it right. This truth (if it prove one) I have not yet got to the limitations of; and shall in no way except by *trying* it in practice. The story of the Necklace was the first attempt at an experiment.'[20]

Carlyle completed 'The Diamond Necklace' in December 1833, during his final months of austere isolation at Craigenputtoch. In the first weeks of the new year he wrote to Sarah Austin, 'I have arrived at a kind of pause in my History, so singular is the course of things without me and within me.'[21] The following day, on 22 January, he began the study of the *Iliad* in Greek, an experience of great moment for all of his subsequent writing. 'I have not written a word these many months . . .', he confided to Mill later in the spring. 'But the reading worth all other readings continues to be my *Homer*. Glorious old Book, which one would save, next after the Bible, from a universal conflagration of Books!'[22] Carlyle's enraptured reading of Homer coincides exactly with his resolve to write a modern epic on the Revolution and to uproot himself from his native Scotland. Moving to London was a brave decision—a 'burning of our ships', as Jane called it[23]—made at a low ebb in Carlyle's affairs. *Sartor* had begun to appear serially in *Fraser's Magazine* but was greeted with almost 'unqualified disapprobation'[24] by the few who read it. Vacillating between desperation and self-exaltation, Carlyle considered emigrating to the backwoods of America with a rifle and spade.[25] 'Life here is but a kind of Life-in-Death', he wrote from Craigenputtoch to John Carlyle in February 1834, yet he has 'a kind of sacred faith' in the prospect of his new life in London.[26]

Four months later the Carlyles moved into the house on Cheyne Row in which they were to pass the long remainder of their married lives. By day they could glimpse 'the summits of St. Paul's Cathedral and Westminster Abbey, and by night the gleam of the great Babylon affronting the peaceful skies'.[27] Carlyle's books are mirrors: *Sartor Resartus*, written in solitude, is the most solitary of his works, its action almost entirely interior; *The French Revolution*, written amidst the press of early Victorian London, teems with abundant life. The hero of *Sartor*, Carlyle's ungainly *alter ego* Diogenes Teufelsdröckh, is a stateless alien who wanders the wide earth in search of the archetypal Romantic communion with himself and with Nature. The hero of *The French Revolution*—if it has a hero other than its author—is the demonic Paris mob. At the end of *Sartor Resartus*, Teufelsdröckh mysteriously disappears and Carlyle conjectures that his vanished hero will soon resurface in London. In these closing lines, Carlyle, born in the same year as John Keats, signals his demise as a Romantic poet and foretells his rebirth as a Victorian prophet.

*

Some time during the Craigenputtock years, Carlyle came to distrust the sovereignty of the imagination and to exalt instead the poetry of fact. In the early essay 'Goethe' (1828), he had written that ' "the fiction of the poet is not falsehood, but the purest truth" ' (26: 251). Four years later, in the essay 'On Biography', his emphasis is starkly different:

"Fiction, while the feigner of it knows that he is feigning, partakes, more than we suspect, of the nature of *lying*. . . . All Mythologies were once Philosophies; were *believed*: the Epic Poems of old time, so long as they continued *epic* . . . were Histories, and understood to be narratives of *facts*." *

(28: 49–50)

He goes on to argue that the highest order of creativity is not 'Fiction' but the 'invention of new Truth, what we can call a Revelation'. The grandest of fictions fades before 'the smallest historical *fact*' (28: 53–4). Carlyle had begun to see in history the 'sole Poetry possible' in the disbelieving modern world (28: 45). The gods of the *Iliad* long ago lost their power to terrify us, the 'gods' of *Paradise Lost* are 'superannuated lumber' (28: 45). Modern epic, severed from its sacred roots, is altogether dead. The true heir of the epic poet is the historian. He is a scribe of the real, a kind of prophet-in-reverse who reconstructs the still-unfolding epic of the past.

---

* Here and elsewhere I have used quotation marks within quotation marks to indicate that Carlyle is speaking through one of his many fictitious personas, in this instance Professor Gottfried Sauerteig. For the importance of Carlyle's impersonations, see the footnote on p. 18, below.

This line of thought, in which Carlyle combines in the historian the roles of prophet and poet, can be traced to a notebook entry for 14 February 1831:

The old Epics are great because they (musically) show us the *whole world* of those old days: a modern Epic that did the like would be equally admired, and for us far more admirable. But where is the genius that can write it? Patience! Patience! he will be here one of these centuries.[28]

In this impatient plea for 'Patience! Patience!' the reader detects Carlyle's bold self-summons to write a great modern epic. The notebook entry ends with a crescendo of questions about history, epic, and Scripture that remind us how far from orthodoxy Carlyle had wandered since making his literary début, a trial sermon he had preached at the age of 19 to his classmates at Divinity Hall in Edinburgh. Is 'true History', he asks himself, 'the true Epic Poem?—I partly begin to surmise so.—What after all is the true proportion of St Matthew to Homer, of the Crucifixion to the Fall of Troy!'[29] The equality of authority Carlyle grants to St Matthew and Homer is surprising in a still-pious son who all his life revered the parents who had raised him in the most rigid Calvinism. A decade before this notebook entry, Carlyle lost his faith in orthodox Christianity and in the literal truth of the Bible. Yet his loss of orthodoxy only intensified the lifelong urgency of his will to believe. In Basil Willey's words, Carlyle is the classic instance of that typical phenomenon of his time, 'the religious temperament severed from "religion"'. Carlyle's need to believe and his need to be heard were the two energizing forces of his life. He ceased to be a student of divinity at Edinburgh in 1818 but was all his life an evangel of the divine, and although he renounced the pulpit of the Scottish Kirk, he succeeded in making England into his congregation.

The young Carlyle's sermon at Divinity Hall was a commentary on a line from Psalm 119, 'Before I was afflicted I went astray . . .'.[31] He remained an exegete of Scripture long after he strayed, but like so many of his anguished contemporaries, he taught himself to read God's Word in more than one text. His first text was the Bible, and although it lost its unique authority, it never lost its primacy. In *Sartor Resartus* he discovered in God's 'second book', Nature, the Divinity that had grown faint in His 'first book', Scripture. But the text which more than any other he made his own was God's 'third book', His writing in time, or History. It is this temporal scripture which Carlyle exalts as ' "that divine BOOK OF REVELATIONS, whereof a Chapter is completed from epoch to epoch, and by some named HISTORY; to which inspired Texts your numerous talented men, and your innumerable untalented men . . . are the better or worse exegetic Commentaries . . ." ' (1: 142).[32]

Much has rightly been made of the 'disappearance of God' in the literature of the nineteenth century—Carlyle himself laments that 'the Divinity has withdrawn from the Earth' (28: 30)—but the metaphor of 'displacement' rather than 'disappearance' more truly describes the wrenching shift felt in the locus of the divine. The divine energies had not been dissipated so much as transmuted, the Word not eradicated but discovered in new places. If the eighteenth century relegated God to a distant corner of the Newtonian universe, the nineteenth century, bereft of that distant Presence, learned to celebrate Him in Nature, to sense His dwelling, in Wordsworth's phrase, in 'the living air, / . . . and in the mind of man'.[33]

The faith that Carlyle lost while reading Hume, Gibbon, and the *philosophes* he rediscovered, changed into something rich and strange, in the German Romantics, whose work he helped introduce to the English public. Scepticism and materialism reduced the divine to the level of the mechanical or the 'merely' natural; Carlyle seeks to repair the damage by exalting the natural to the level of the supernatural, the human to the level of the divine. The miracle of the loaves and the fishes, he proclaims, pales before the continuing miracles of Nature and of Man. In place of the Calvinist God he inherited, he offers us in *Sartor* the divinity of Man himself, the ' "unutterable Mystery of Mysteries" '; in place of the Bible he offers us the God-written ' "Apocalypse of Nature" '; in place of the Church he offers the illimitable Temple of the Universe; and in place of the worship of Saints he gives us the Gospel of Heroes.[34]

At the same time that the Higher Criticism was undermining the authority of the Bible, Carlyle sought to elevate history into a secular scripture. 'All History', he contends in ' Jesuitism',

is an inarticulate Bible; and in a dim intricate manner reveals the Divine Appearances in this lower world. For God did make this world, and does forever govern it; the loud-roaring Loom of Time, with all its French revolutions, Jewish revelations, "weaves the vesture thou seest Him by".

(20: 325–6)

This is the gospel of Natural Supernaturalism transposed from the world of nature to the world of human events. Carlyle glides over the distinction between sacred history and secular, biblical and modern, with his easy, alliterative linkage of *French revolutions/Jewish revelations* —a triple surprise in its Jewish modifier, its heterodox plural, and lower-case 'r'. In *Sartor Resartus* he argues that, if only we could tear off our tattered clothes of habit, we would see that all nature is supernatural; in *The French Revolution* he argues that, properly interpreted, all history is *sacred* history, the unfolding of God's Providence in time. Underlying and energizing both visions is the conviction that nature and history are at bottom emblematic and will yield up their secrets to the typological scrutiny that traditionally had been applied to the Bible. ' "All visible things are emblems" ', Teufelsdröckh proclaims: ' "Matter exists only spiritually, and to represent some Idea, and *body* it forth" ' (1: 57). Language is intrinsically metaphoric; the Universe itself is 'but one vast Symbol of God' (1: 175). The critic's task is to interpret and revitalize this sacred text. Prometheus-like, he brings us ' "new Fire from Heaven" ' in the shape of ' "new Symbols" ' that reveal the divinity encoded in ' "the Volume of Nature . . . whose Author and Writer is God" ' (1: 179, 205).

We see the God-intoxicated Teufelsdröckh through the eyes of his sceptical 'Editor', as if Carlyle had split in two his doubting and believing selves. Through his verbally antic hero, he manages both to be himself and to mock himself, to be poet and anti-poet. Beneath Teufelsdröckh's outlandish dress and speech we recognize the soul of a Romantic poet, and in Carlyle's ambivalence toward his hero we detect his deeper ambivalences toward Romanticism. To the end of his life Carlyle continued to feel the dominant emotion of the Romantics—wonder over the miraculousness of the seemingly commonplace. Yet if his impulse to wonder links him to the Romantic tradition, his Calvinism, instilled by his parents and so deep as to be virtually innate, alienated him from equally powerful elements of that tradition. Seen in this light, *Sartor Resartus* may be read as Romanticism half-way down the road to renouncing itself, an early Victorian 'Two Voices', in which doubt has become the pre-condition for tenable belief. Rousseau's myth of mankind as innately good, corrupted only by society, or Wordsworth's faith in a benevolent—albeit awesome— Nature, ran counter to Carlyle's conviction, voiced most forcefully in *The French Revolution*, that our life in nature, as in society, is an incessant struggle, 'a black desperate battle of Men against their whole

Condition and Environment' (4: 205). Herr Diogenes Teufelsdröckh embodies in his name—'God-born Devil's dung'—Carlyle's sense of the mixed human condition, our ideal 'transcendental' nature, trailing clouds of glory from our celestial home, and our absurd 'descendental' nature—man the time-bound biped who lies, defecates, and commits atrocities.

*

Sartor Resartus celebrates the 'god-born' in nature and man; in *The French Revolution* the balance tips and Carlyle portrays instead the diabolic in man and society. The imaginative thrust of *Sartor* is upwards to the 'Light-sea of celestial wonder', a stripping away of the mortal clothing of Space and Time until we stand naked in our own divinity (1: 43, 210). The imaginative thrust of *The French Revolution* is downward, an infernal journey to the depths of the Terror where, in the 'dim Phantasmagory of the Pit', we again stand naked, only this time awash in human blood, our nature 'savage . . . infernal' (4: 27, 247). In *Sartor Resartus* Carlyle rebuilds, phoenix-like, a sacred world out of the ashes of eighteenth-century materialism. In *The French Revolution* the promised millennium of revolutionary justice and fraternity ends in the hacking to pieces of the Swiss Guard in Paris and in mass murder at Lyons and Nantes. Unlike Milton, his great precursor-poet of Revolution, Carlyle wrote his *Paradise Regained* before his *Paradise Lost*.

Outwardly dissimilar in subject, style, form, and feeling, *Sartor Resartus* and *The French Revolution* are linked by a remarkable inner complementarity. In *Sartor Resartus* Carlyle records a revolution within himself, his conversion from suicidal despair to the 'new Mythus' of Natural Supernaturalism. In *The French Revolution* he turns from chronicling the upheaval within himself to chronicling the larger upheaval of society—from conversion to revolution. His understanding of conversion in the former, and of revolution in the latter, was shaped by the crisis he experienced in his mid-twenties and dramatized a decade later in a single blazing moment in *Sartor Resartus*.*

---

* There is some uncertainty over the date and duration of the crisis but none over its severity or the essential autobiographical truth of Carlyle's account in 'The Everlasting No'. Of this account Carlyle later wrote:

Nothing in "*Sartor*" thereabouts is *fact* (symbolical *myth* all) except that of the "*incident* in the Rue St Thomas de l'Enfer,"—which occurred quite literally to myself in

There he describes his agony in the mechanical garden of the eighteenth century: ' "The Universe was all void of Life, of Purpose, of Volition, even of Hostility: it was one huge, dead, immeasurable Steam-engine, rolling on, in its dead indifference, to grind me limb from limb" ' (1: 133). This nadir of negation Carlyle calls 'The Everlasting No', and to its horrific yet impersonal threat of annihilation his whole being rises up and shouts its defiant protest:

> "The Everlasting No had said: 'Behold thou art fatherless, outcast, and the Universe is mine (the Devil's)'; to which my whole Me now made answer: '*I* am not thine, but Free, and forever hate thee!'
> "It is from this hour that I incline to date my Spiritual New-birth, or Baphometic Fire-baptism. . . ."

(1: 135)

The moment of conversion is clearly religious yet profoundly un-Christian. Carlyle-Teufelsdröckh experiences a sudden lifting not of sin but of *angst*; he feels no humbling of self, no sudden inrushing of Christ, but a radical aggrandizement of his own ego: ' "I was strong, of unknown strength; a spirit, almost a god." ' Embedded in this most influential nineteenth-century account of spiritual crisis, obscured by its Calvinist idiom ('Death. . . . the pangs of Tophet. . . . the Devil') is an extraordinary recasting of traditional religious experience in psychological* and political terms. Carlyle's conversion is at bottom a defiant negation of Negation, a kind of psychological revolution whereby the oppressed self casts off the oppressive Universe and exclaims, ' "*I* am not thine, but Free, and forever hate thee!" ' 'Such a Protest,' Carlyle writes, 'in a psychological point of view' is 'the most important transaction in Life' (1: 134–5). In *The French Revolution* an entire exploited under-class rises in similar protest; the result is 'the most remarkable transaction in these last thousand years' (4: 205). In *Sartor Resartus* the spring of action is 'The Everlasting No', which elicits

---

Lieth [*Leith*] Walk, during those 3 weeks of total sleeplessness, in which almost my one solace was that of a daily bathe on the sands between Lieth and Portobello. Incident was as I went *down* (coming *up* I generally felt a little refreshed for the hour): I remember it well, & could go yet to about the place.

(John Clubbe, ed., *Two Reminiscences* (Durham, NC: Duke University Press, 1974), p. 49.) Froude assumes the incident in Leith Walk occurred in June 1821, but John Clubbe and Fred Kaplan more plausibly date it in the summer of 1822. See Clubbe, p. 49, fn. 64; and Kaplan, p. 82.

---

* More ardent Freudians than I might make much of the bold-faced ' "my whole ME stood up. . . . I directly thereupon began to be a Man" ' (1: 135).

from Teufelsdröckh a counter-affirmation, 'The Everlasting Yea'. The equivalent agent of change in *The French Revolution* Carlyle calls 'transcendental despair', a societal desperation so deep and urgent that it turns upon itself and 'completes the circle, so to speak; and becomes a kind of genuine productive hope again'.[35]

Nothing is closer to the wellsprings of Carlyle's genius than this incessant dialectic of contraries by which nature and supernature, dream and history, madness and reason, turn into their seeming opposites. The most encompassing of these 'wondrous Dualisms' (10: 44) is the great cosmic contest of good and evil over arching man, who is 'a mystery to himself and others: in the centre of two Eternities, . . . in the intersection of primeval Light with the everlasting Dark' (4: 43). This ageless Manichaean struggle takes place just above the surface of human events, like Homer's gods poised over the battlefields of Troy; it also threatens to burst up like a volcanic explosion and fracture the thin crust of civilization. Suspended over us as gods, pent up within or below us as demonic forces, this cosmic contest bursts upon the stage of history at certain climactic moments, of which the French Revolution is the great modern instance. The struggle is enacted within the consciousness of the individual soul in *Sartor Resartus*; it is enacted by an entire nation, with the whole world as onlooker, in the French Revolution, which Carlyle portrays as a modern Apocalypse.

The age-old threat underlying individual stability and, by extension, the social order, figures in a passage at once tender and menacing in *Sartor Resartus*. In even the sanest of souls, Carlyle writes,

lies a whole world of internal Madness, an authentic Demon-Empire; out of which, indeed, his world of Wisdom has been creatively built together, and now rests there, as on its dark foundations does a habitable flowery Earth-rind.

(1: 207)

Sanity for Carlyle is not a natural condition but a fragile achievement, 'creatively built' and constantly imperilled. Madness is 'a mysterious-terrific . . . boiling up of the Nether Chaotic Deep' (1: 207) that threatens to engulf us all. Carlyle writes in the overblown idiom of Teufelsdröckh, but his conviction that the irrational and the unconscious are powerful determinants of individual and social life shapes his whole sense of history. Human life, he writes in *The French Revolution*, is a 'singular Somnambulism, of Conscious and Unconscious, of Voluntary and Involuntary' (3: 105).

The 'habitable flowery Earth-rind' resting on its dark foundations compresses into a single prophetic flash Carlyle's pre-space-age vision of the earth as a living organism seen from an immense distance. The phrase is at once pastoral and chilling, as if the imagination of a nature poet had turned from an English meadow to outer space. These 'cosmic pastorals' of Carlyle have nothing to do with daffodils, nightingales, or flowers hidden in crannied walls; they are tender yet cold to the touch and carry always the sense of a small habitable space set against a vast, menacing background. The thin, living crust of the earth is fragile as a flower and, like civilization itself, Carlyle implies, only skin-deep.

In *The French Revolution* that skin bursts asunder. The Revolution provides the laboratory conditions in which 'the "daemonic element" that lurks in all human things' (2: 39) can at last vent itself. Early in the first volume Carlyle describes the breakdown of the *ancien régime*, the mass hunger and impending anarchy. Without identifying his source—himself—he alludes to the passage on the Demon-Empire of Madness in *Sartor* and voices the dominant theme of *The French Revolution*. Our whole social being, he writes, is '*overarched* by Habit, as by a thin Earth-rind, laboriously built together' and stretched over an abyss:

. . . if "every man," as it has been written, "holds confined within him a *mad*-man," what must every Society do . . . [when] your "thin Earth-rind" be once *broken*! The fountains of the great deep boil forth; fire-fountains, enveloping, engulfing. . . . instead of a green flowery world, there is a waste wild-weltering chaos;—which has again with tumult and struggle, to *make* itself into a world.

(2: 38)

This is Carlyle's interior portrait of revolution, of the violence he knew within himself and believed lay suppressed just below the surface of civilization.

2

History and the Human Voice

The phrase *historical imagination* contains a seeming contradiction: *history* suggests a narrative of facts and *imagination* the invention of fictions. But for Carlyle the contrary of history is not fiction but oblivion, the unravelling of the collective human memory that holds, civilization together. History is not a record of civilization; it is civilization itself, the past speaking to the present and to the future through the voice of the historian. Without that animating voice, we would have no history—only gibberish and unmarked graves.

History and the human voice, life and speech, are virtually one in Carlyle's mind. His moving reminiscence of his stonemason father, begun while the body still lay above ground and finished just after it was laid in the grave, a memorial so spontaneous as to be the diary of the mourner as well as a portrait of the dead, is above all a tribute to James Carlyle's powers of speech. 'Never shall we again hear such speech as that was', Carlyle writes, the purest 'of all the dialects I have ever listened to', a 'full *white* sunlight'.[1]

James Carlyle died in 1832; three years later, on the occasion of another loss that Carlyle took at least as hard, his father returned to him in a dream. Carlyle had gone to sleep late on the night of 6 March 1835, after John Stuart Mill, pale and shaken, had told him that the entire first volume of *The French Revolution*, which Mill had been reading in manuscript, had been inadvertently burnt. The following morning Carlyle wrote in his *Journal*:

The night has been full of emotion; occasionally sharp pain (something cutting or hard—grasping me round the heart) occasionally with sweet consolations. I dreamed of my Father and sister Margaret alive, yet all defaced with sleepy stagnancy, swoln hebetude of the Grave,—and again dying, as in some strange rude country: a horrid dream!

Like the dream itself, in which Father and Sister die a second death in a strange country, Carlyle dies twice as he relives their deaths and, in the unvoiced language of the dream, the death of his book. Much of the horror of the dream and all of its poignancy lie in its *wordlessness*. The dead are clearly seen—their bloated features emerge all too visibly— but they cannot hear or make themselves heard: 'How I longed for some Psalm or Prayer that I could have *uttered*,' the *Journal* entry ends, 'that my loved ones would have joined me in! But there was none: Silence had to be my language.'[2]

The haunting topography of Carlyle's 'horrid dream' of 1835 returns a decade later, in his prologue to *Oliver Cromwell's Letters and Speeches* (1845). This extraordinary chapter ('Anti-Dryasdust') in a now-forgotten work is in fact a dialogue in which Carlyle dramatizes two opposing aspects of himself as a historian: 'Dryasdust', a sterile, ghoulish rummager among the dead; and an unnamed writer and friend who, Orpheus-like, descends to the underworld and returns with the living treasure of the past. Ghoul and 'sacred Poet', these are Carlyle's two familiars as he practises his art: himself as dessicated, mole-like digger among heaps of unsorted documents, a creature of night and unclean thoughts; and himself as epic-singer and prophet who aspires to write 'a modern *Iliad* as memorial of the Past' (6: 3, 8). The journey into history is for Carlyle always a double journey, back-ward in time and downward into the self, a descent simultaneously to the underworld of the historical past and to his own interior life. While reading about Cromwell, he wrote to his friend John Sterling that he was doing 'mole's work, boring and digging blindly underground; my own inner man is sometimes very busy (too busy) but the rest is all silence.'[3] The allusion to Hamlet's excited trafficking with his father's ghost[4] captures Carlyle's sense of dread and shame at being too close to the untouchable dead, an emotion that colours his letter of the same period to Emerson: 'I have again got down into primeval Night; and live alone and mute with the *Manes*, as you say; uncertain whether I shall ever more see day. I am partly ashamed of myself: but cannot help it.'[5]

In his *Journal* Carlyle is even more explicit about the downward descent that always accompanies the 'mood of creation'.[6] In the spring of 1836 he complains of writing *The French Revolution* with his 'heart's blood. The sorrow and chagrin I suffer is very great. . . . I shudder sometimes at the abysses I discern in myself, the acrid hunger, the shivering sensitiveness, the *wickedness*. . . .'[7] On these fer-tile descents into 'primeval Night' Carlyle brought along as little bag-gage as possible, taking only the sparsest of notes and storing his research in his prodigious memory.* He composed in a strange, self-induced state of hyper-alertness and somnambulance, a kind of feverish semi-consciousness: 'Partly I was busy,' he wrote to Emerson on completing *On Heroes*; 'partly too, as my wont is, I was half-asleep.'[8]

However eccentric, Carlyle's mode of composition is as old as that of the Hebrew prophets and ancient Bards, for whom memory did its labour of sorting and synthesizing in a state of inspiration or semi-trance. Carlyle's great works of imaginative synthesis—*Sartor Resartus*, *The French Revolution*, *Past and Present*—are shaped not like reasoned arguments but like controlled dreams in which recurrent symbols do the work of discursive logic. Writing, particularly the writing of history, always necessitates for Carlyle a kind of willed fellowship with the dead. Dryasdust is the dessicated archivist Carlyle fears he may become, but beyond Dryasdust—or beneath him—lies the miracle-working mole Carlyle deliberately turned himself into in order to resurrect the past. Midway through his research on *Cromwell* he complained to Emerson of having burrowed his way through mountains of dreary rubbish, but the complaint is tinged with a nervous gaiety again reminiscent of Hamlet in the company of ghosts and graves:

I even take a gowlish kind of pleasure in raking through these old bone-houses and burial-aisles now; I have the strangest fellowship with that huge genius of DEATH . . . and catch sometimes, thro' some chink or other, glimpses into blessed *ulterior* regions,—blessed, but as yet altogether silent.[9]

Silent because the heaped mounds of unsorted archives have not yet begun to speak to Carlyle, and hence he cannot yet endow them with life. His struggle to bring his hero to life figures centrally in the prologue to *Cromwell*, in which he takes his reader on a mythic voyage to the underworld of the British Museum. Some fifty-thousand pamphlets and folios lie mouldering in labyrinthine corridors, a 'shoreless chaos', unindexed, unedited, or else 'edited as you edit wagon-loads of broken bricks and dry mortar, simply by tumbling up the wagon!' (6: 2). No one has more vividly evoked the stagnant backwaters of archival research, the sheer inchoateness of the unreconstructed past:

* Compare this letter of December 1845 to the Reverend Alexander Scott: 'But as to . . . taking Excerpts, I think I universally . . . avoid writing beyond the very minimum . . . and on the whole try to keep the whole matter simmering in the *living* mind and memory rather than laid up in paper bundles or otherwise laid up in the way. . . . Only what you at last *have living* in your memory and heart is worth putting down to be printed; this alone has much chance to get into the living heart and mind of other men.' (*New Letters of Thomas Carlyle*, ed. A. Carlyle (London, 1903), 2: 11.)

"But alas . . . what is it, all this . . . inarticulate rubbish-continent, in its
ghastly dim twilight, with its haggard wrecks and pale shadows; what is it, but
the common Kingdom of Death? . . . this mouldering dumb wilderness of
things once alive. Behold here the final evanescence of Formed human things
. . . changing into sheer formlessness;—ancient human speech itself has sunk
into unintelligible maundering. This is the collapse,—the etiolation of human
features into mouldy blank; *dis*solution; progress towards utter silence and
disappearance; disastrous ever-deepening Dusk of Gods and Men!"

(6: 10)[10]

This haunting passage marks the return of Carlyle's 'horrid
dream' on the night his manuscript had sunk into the wilderness of
things once alive. But the dream of personal loss has widened into a
collective nightmare of human oblivion, a shadowy sunken continent,
'"trackless, without index, without finger-post, or mark of any
human foregoer"' (6: 3). In this Carlylean underworld of Anti-
History, presided over by the plutonic Dryasdust, the human past has
been all but eradicated under mounds of successive errors and mind-
less commentary. The sound of the fifty thousand pamphlets '"is not
a *voice*, conveying knowledge or memorial of any earthly or heavenly
thing; it is a wide-spread inarticulate slumberous mumblement, issuing as if from the lake of Eternal Sleep"' (6: 3).*

*

Despite his own great powers of recall, Carlyle repeatedly stresses the
importance of *forgetting* in the writing of history. In the prologue to
Cromwell he contends that the historian rises above a mere Dryasdust
and becomes a sacred poet as much by virtue of 'wise oblivion' as by
'wise memory' (6: 8). And in 'On History Again' (1833), he compares
Memory and Oblivion to Day and Night, each essential to the other's
existence, as are 'all other Contradictions in this strange dualistic Life

* Carlyle's evocation of the voicelessness of the unreconstructed past is itself voiced
by the main speaker of the prologue, more than half of which is set off in quotation
marks and imagined as spoken by a character other than Carlyle. The point would
not be worth making were it not that Carlyle's critics, by citing his words but omitting
his indications of direct and indirect discourse, have in effect been misquoting him
for a century and a half. Passages often cited as 'straight' Carlyle, are in fact spoken
by one of his many quirky impersonations—Dryasdust, Smelfungus, Sauerteig,
Teufelsdröckh, Plugson of Undershot, Sir Jabesh Windbag. To obscure the identity of
the speaker is to lose half of what is said, for, in Carlyle's view, no thought exists apart
from the voice that utters it, just as no historical text exists apart from the conflicting
chorus of voices that enacted it.

of ours' (28: 173). In part he is pointing to the principle of selective omission, without which history could not be written. But he is also stressing the necessity of cultivating the unconscious mind in recovering the collective past, as Wordsworth had made its cultivation essential to the recovery of the individual past. 'A like unconscious talent of remembering and of forgetting again', Carlyle asserts, is indispensable to the writing of history and of autobiography (28: 173). For Wordsworth the self preserves its continuity and sanity through a return to those early, formative experiences in nature when it first came to consciousness. The self remains open to such experiences through a 'wise-passiveness' (the equivalent of Carlyle's 'wise oblivion') that puts to momentary rest the conscious, ratiocinative mind. The epic journey inward into autobiographical time that Wordsworth began in *The Prelude* finds its analogue in the epic journey backward into historical time that Carlyle began in *The French Revolution*.

It is above all as memorialists—the one, of the continuities of the self in nature; the other, of the continuities of human society in time—that Wordsworth and Carlyle distinguish themselves in a century that was obsessed with history. Wordsworth's term for the 'binding' that holds the self together is 'natural piety';[11] for Carlyle we must invent an equivalent term such as 'historical piety'. The defining note of this piety is a piercing love of the past, a backward-glancing search by those who, in Carlyle's phrase from the *Cromwell* prologue, 'struggle piously, passionately, to behold, if but in glimpses, the faces of our vanished Fathers' (6: 3).[12] For Wordsworth, the search is for the face of his vanished self, reflected in the still waters of his past, where he can glimpse 'The Child [who] is Father of the Man'. The genius of Wordsworth and Carlyle, divergent in so many ways, coincides in the drive to escape the prison-house of time and reach those islands of consciousness in which the past coexists with the present. Wordsworth described such privileged moments in the grainy phrase 'spots of time', and his best poetry evokes them. Carlyle's finest passages are built upon spots of historical time, uncanny moments of temporal montage in which the remote past breaks through the grid of the present, or the once-present collapses into the past, as when the ancient chronicle of Jocelin of Brakelond, 'suddenly shorn-through by the scissors of Destiny, *ends*' (10: 125), and the reader is plunged back again into the noise of the nineteenth century. *Past and Present*, as its title suggests, is a gallery of these montages. History for Carlyle is the half-magical science of celebrating this 'wondrous . . . contiguity and perpetual closeness [of] the Past and Distant with the Present in time and place; all times and all places with this our actual Here and Now' (5: 160–1).[13]

Carlyle's impulse to connect past and present is untouched by the softer sentiments usually associated with nostalgia or antiquarianism. However much he feels a Tennysonian tenderness for vanished faces, he drops no idle tears over a past that he austerely refuses to romanticize. 'No age ever seemed the Age of Romance to *itself*', he writes at the start of his first historical work; Roland de Roncesvalles rode in bad weather and good, chewed on tough beef, 'was saddle-sick, calumniated, constipated' (28: 327). The whole point of 'The Diamond Necklace' is that 'Romance exists . . . in Reality alone' (28: 329).[14] Carlyle casts no soft haze over the distant past precisely because, for him, it is not distant but present and needs only our heightened consciousness to recognize its proximity. He practises a kind of hard-nosed mysticism, moving back in time in order to obliterate time. In Carlyle's eyes the past does not 'progress' in measured steps towards the present but is eerily contiguous with it, like the drowned man of Wordsworth's childhood who years later bobs up 'bolt upright' in the heightened present of his mature recollection.

Carlyle's insistence on the matter-of-factness of the past has the paradoxical effect of investing it with extraordinary mystery and vitality. The description of twelfth-century England in *Past and Present* begins in an almost palpable prosiness of ditches and cattle, but Carlyle's pictorial realism proves to be the thinnest of illusions; within a few lines we look not at but through the picture to the timeless world that lies behind it:

Behold therefore, this England of the year 1200 was no chimerical vacuity or dreamland, peopled with mere vaporous Fantasms . . . but a green solid place, that grew corn and several other things. The Sun shone on it; the vicissitude of seasons and human fortunes. Cloth was woven and worn; ditches were dug, furrow-fields ploughed, and houses built. Day by day all men and cattle rose to labour, and night by night returned home weary to their several lairs. In wondrous Dualism, then as now, lived nations of breathing men; alternating, in all ways, between Light and Dark; between . . . hope reaching high as Heaven, and fear deep as very Hell.

(10: 44)

The passage spans in miniature that great Carlylean circuit linking the mundane to the cosmic. The brief, repetitive cadences echo the

lesser rhythms of daily life—ditches dug, fields plowed, cloth woven—
until the lesser cycles compose one macrocosmic cycle, cattle linked to
men in their rising and in their return to their *lairs*, day joined to
night, season to season, all pivoting on the great axis that joins the
habitations of men to the Heavens above and the Hell below. Carlyle's
insistence on the prosaic reality of the twelfth century produces some
of the finest poetry of the nineteenth, a poetry of visionary realism
whose proper medium is prose.

Into this charged ambience of ditches and stars, rides Richard
Cœur-de-Lion, 'not a theatrical popinjay with greaves and steel-cap
on it, but a man living upon victuals' (10: 44). The jolting awkward-
ness of the writing and the plebeian *victuals*, like Roland's tough beef
and constipation, are meant to shock the reader out of the dreamy
world of historical fiction and into the world of historical fact. A few
lines later Carlyle wonders what sort of *breeches* King John wore on the
occasion of his visit to the Abbey of St Edmund. Carlyle's source is
Jocelin of Brakelond, a monk whose *Chronicle* of daily life under the
rule of Abbot Samson was published by the Camden Society in 1840.
'These clear eyes of neighbour Jocelin', Carlyle writes,

looked on the bodily presence of King John; the very John *Sansterre*, or
Lackland, who signed *Magna Charta* afterwards in Runnymead. Lackland,
with a great retinue, boarded once, for the matter of a fortnight, in St.
Edmundsbury Convent; daily in the very eyesight, palpable to the very
fingers of our Jocelin: O Jocelin, what did he say, what did he do; how looked
he, lived he;—at the very lowest, what coat or breeches had he on? Jocelin is
obstinately silent. Jocelin marks down what interests *him*; entirely deaf to *us*.
With Jocelin's eyes we discern almost nothing of John Lackland. As through
a glass darkly, we with our own eyes and appliances, intensely looking,
discern at most: A blustering, dissipated human figure, with a kind of
blackguard quality air, in cramoisy velvet, or other uncertain texture, uncertain cut, with much plumage and fringing; amid numerous other human
figures of the like; riding abroad with hawks; talking noisy nonsense;—tear-
ing out the bowels of St. Edmundsbury Convent (its larders namely and
cellars) in the most ruinous way, by living at rack and manger there. Jocelin
notes only, with a slight subacidity of manner, that the King's Majesty,
Dominus Rex, did leave, as gift for our St. Edmund Shrine, a handsome
enough silk cloak,—or rather pretended to leave, for one of his retinue borrowed it of us, and *we* never got sight of it again; and, on the whole, that the
Dominus Rex, at departing, gave us "thirteen *sterlingii*," one shilling and one
penny, to say a mass for him; and so departed,—like a shabby Lackland
as he was! "Thirteen pence sterling," this was what the Convent got from

Lackland, for all the victuals he and his had made away with. We of course
said our mass for him, having covenanted to do it,—but let impartial posterity
judge with what degree of fervour!

(10: 45)

The paragraph opens with the double-frame of Carlyle's observing
the clear-eyed Jocelin as Jocelin observes King John. It ends with the
reader drawn through the frame and into the picture. Like Carlyle,
the reader ceases to observe Jocelin and begins to think Jocelin's
bitter thoughts, to watch shabby Lackland through Jocelin's eyes.
The transition occurs about two-thirds through the paragraph, within
the sentence that starts, 'Jocelin notes only . . .'. By the time the
reader reaches the italicized 'we' a few lines later, he must cast himself
in the role of the resentful Jocelin if the passage is to make any grammatical sense. Carlyle has moved, imperceptibly but decisively, from
medieval Latin chronicle to a kind of dramatic monologue in prose.
Throughout the paragraph Jocelin functions not as an inert 'source',
but as a vocal presence within the events he narrates. Although long-
dead, he is still *our neighbour* [OE *nēahgebūr*, nigh-dweller], for even
though he lived next door in time and place to King John, he is also,
because of the 'wondrous contiguity' of past and present, neighbour
to the whole company of Carlyle's readers, living and dead. He is
near to us but deaf to our entreaties; the power of the passage depends
upon Jocelin's ghostly proximity. However passionately the historian
implores his monkish source—what did Lackland look like? how did
he live?—Jocelin of course cannot utter an iota of fact beyond what he
has already recorded. Time may be an illusion for Carlyle but mortality
is not;* Jocelin rejoins the long-dead in the pause between Carlyle's
insistent questioning and his own firm answer: 'Jocelin is obstinately
silent.' The obstinacy, of course, is not Jocelin's but Carlyle's. In
repeatedly interrogating the dead monk, Carlyle seems to awaken
Jocelin's stubborn resistance, like a sleeper tossing and struggling to
hold onto his dream. All verbs up to this point have been in the simple
past. The disruptive shift from past to present—'Jocelin marks down

---

* David DeLaura remarks that Carlyle only 'asserted (as he did in *Sartor*) that Time is
one of the "deepest of all illusory Appearances." Closer to his continuous and almost
passionate *experience* of Time is the remark made the following year, on his father's
death: "Strange Time! Endless Time, of which I see neither end nor beginning! All
rushes on; man follows man; his life is as a Tale that has been told." He only *hoped*,
"under Time does there not lie Eternity?"' ('The Allegory of Life: The
Autobiographical Impulse in Victorian Prose', in *Approaches to Victorian Autobiography*,
ed. George P. Landow (Athens, Ohio: Ohio University Press, 1979) pp. 339-40.)

what interests *him*; entirely deaf to *us*'—is doubly disorienting. It piles
the weight of seven centuries on Jocelin's grave and at the same time
brings him and shabby Lackland back to disconcerting life. Past and
present reverse themselves along with voice and point of view, as
Carlyle enacts, in virtual dumb-show, Jocelin pointing to what interests him, Carlyle beckoning in the other direction, twelfth-century
chronicler and nineteenth-century editor gesturing across the ages.

The King John who rides like an incarnate apparition through
Carlyle's paragraph is not of course the King of Jocelin's *Chronicle*.
For in Jocelin's clear but unreflective eyes, the King is as yet untinged
by the medium of time, and in the immediacy of his own concerns,
Jocelin sees both more and less than Carlyle or we can see. Carlyle
knows he cannot portray in the nineteenth century the King John
who appeared in the twelfth century; yet in forcing us to confront the
great gap in time, he seems almost to obliterate it. He portrays with
absolute fidelity not King John Lackland but his own efforts to
visualize the King through the flickering medium of time and of
Jocelin's words. The resulting picture is a piece of pure impression-
ism, precise yet triumphantly amorphous, as if Turner had painted
the King by torchlight. We see a rough confusion of colours and tex-
tures, fringes and plumes, with an equestrian figure in red velvet,
clusters of men in noisy motion, and only one hard detail, more heard
than seen, the 'thirteen *sterlingii*' whose hollow jingle signals the
departure of King Lackland:

> And in this manner vanishes King Lackland; traverses swiftly our strange
> intermittent magic-mirror, jingling the shabby thirteen pence merely; and
> rides with his hawks into Egyptian night again. It is Jocelin's manner with all
> things; and it is men's manner and men's necessity. How intermittent is our
> good Jocelin; marking down, without eye to *us*, what *he* finds interesting!
> How much in Jocelin, as in all History, and indeed in all Nature, is at once
> inscrutable and certain; so dim, yet so indubitable; exciting us to endless con-
> siderations. For King Lackland *was* there, verily he; and did leave these
> *tredecim sterlingii* if nothing more, and did live and look in one way or the other,
> and a whole world was living and looking along with him! There, we say, is
> the grand peculiarity; the immeasurable one; distinguishing, to a really
> infinite degree, the poorest historical Fact from all Fiction whatsoever.
>
> (10: 45–6)

Here we strike the bedrock of sheer wonder that underlies Carlyle's
historical writing. It is a strange emotion, this seemingly redundant
astonishment that whatever happened, did indeed happen. Yet in

Carlyle's 'vague shoreless Universe', in which we are buffeted by the 'ever-fluctuating chaos of the Actual' (2: 9, 10), it *is* astonishing that anything ever condenses out of the aboriginal flux long enough to fix itself in time, space, or human consciousness. In this shifting, illusory world, Carlyle clings to the elusive solidity of fact as if it were the last credible miracle. Hence his amazement that 'King Lackland *was* there, verily he.' The other side of Carlyle's 'green solid' England of the year 1200 is that perhaps it exists only as a picture in the historian's mind. So, too, although King John is 'palpable to the very fingers of our Jocelin', the shadow he casts is more real than his substance, just as Jocelin's obstinate silence is more expressive than his words.

Carlyle's power of endowing the past with extraordinary 'presence' is enhanced by his complementary genius for undermining the actuality of the here and now. He is the poet of the insubstantiality of the 'real' and the reality of the phantasmagoric, the one always heightened by the other. The two are deftly juxtaposed in Carlyle's portrait of the dying Louis XV at the start of *The French Revolution*. The death-scene opens in a miasma of putrid odours, whispered intrigues, thick tapestries. But the heavy-textured realism dissolves into the starkness of a medieval morality drama as Carlyle turns to the Do-Nothing King and ushers him out of life:

Yes, poor Louis, Death has found thee. No palace walls or life-guards, gorgeous tapestries or gilt buckram of stiffest ceremonial could keep him out. . . . Thou, whose whole existence hitherto was a chimera and scenic show, at length becomest a reality: sumptuous Versailles bursts asunder, like a dream, into void Immensity; Time is done, and all the scaffolding of Time falls wrecked with hideous clangour round thy soul: the pale Kingdoms yawn open; there must thou enter, naked, all unking'd. . . .

(2: 20)

As always in Carlyle's most charged moments, the actual and the spectral change places. Foreground fades into background, 'reality' dissolves into the dream it mirrors, and the chimerical King, more substantial in death than in life, slips out of time into eternity. Much of Carlyle is in the phrase *scaffolding of Time*, with its image of Time as the flimsy prop of actuality, the skeletal lattice of illusion around which we structure our fleeting lives. But the prop is weighty and crashes to earth with the clang of armour; it falls with the ring of allusion, too, for this least heroic of modern kings, a mere 'Solecism Incarnate' (2: 21), dies to an ancient Homeric formula—'He dropped forward on his face and his armor clattered upon him.'[15] Carlyle's irony is too austere to be mistaken for the mock-heroic, his compassion too controlled for sentimentality. The perspective is at once close-up ('poor Louis') and distant, almost Olympian, as it ranges across the narrow circuit of Louis's chamber to a whole spectrum of times and conditions, naked and exalted, ancient, medieval, and modern.

*

Carlyle's sense of the illusoriness of reality goes back to his earliest childhood and gives a haunting quality of doubleness to the world he grasped through his senses and reflected in his books. The feeling is epitomized in lines from *The Tempest* to which Carlyle attached special importance and which he first saw, as a young boy, on a bust of Shakespeare being hawked in the streets of Ecclefechan by a vendor of images:

> We are such stuff
> As dreams are made on, and our little life
> Is rounded with a sleep.
>   (IV. i. 156–8)

The thirty volumes of Carlyle's works are an extended gloss on these lines. In his *Journal* he calls them 'the basis of a whole poetic universe', and he took them as a kind of motto throughout his life.[16]

Carlyle's sense of the insubstantiality of matter was always most keen when he was absorbed in the anxious labours of composition. Soon after beginning research on *Cromwell* he recorded in his *Journal*:

As I live, and have long lived, death and Hades differ little to me from the earth and life. The human figure I meet is wild, wondrous, ghastly to me, almost as if it were a spectre and I a spectre.[17]

In the same spectral temper Carlyle wrote *The French Revolution*, especially those early chapters which he forced himself to rewrite with the double anxiety of having to begin again what was already completed but had gone up in flames. The sense of unreality that haunts the great death-scene of Louis XV at Versailles haunted Carlyle himself no less keenly in London as he wrote by day and walked the streets at night:

The world looks often quite spectral to me; sometimes, as in Regent Street the other night (my nerves being all shattered), quite hideous, discordant, almost infernal. I had been at Mrs Austin's, heard Sydney Smith for the first time guffawing, other persons prating, jargoning. To me through these thin cobwebs Death and Eternity sate glaring. Coming homewards along Regent Street, through street-walkers, through—*Ach Gott*! unspeakable pity swallowed up unspeakable abhorrence of it and of myself. The moon and the serene nightly sky in Sloane Street consoled me a little. . . . Woe's me that I in Meshech am! To work.[18]

The alienated Scotsman in London easily slips into the idiom of the Hebrew Psalmist lamenting his sojourn amid alien peoples. Louis XV dying at Versailles, Paris during the Revolution, early Victorian London—Carlyle bathes them all in the same phantasmal glow, sees them all through the same visionary eyes. The London street-scene combines the circumstantial and the spectral in a way that recalls the *Inferno*, which Carlyle had begun to study only a few days before describing his 'almost infernal' walk. The force of Dante's vision makes itself felt as strongly in *The French Revolution* as in the 'Unreal City' of *The Waste Land*, where 'death had undone so many'.

All through the summer of 1835 Carlyle was in a 'detestable state of enchantment' as he rewrote the first volume of *The French Revolution*.[19] The agony of composition was 'like a Nessus' shirt' and threatened to burn him 'into madness'. He rewarded himself on completing the volume with a visit to Scotland, but the return to the site of his earliest associations only heightened his sense of estrangement. 'I flew to Scotland and my Mother for a month of rest', he wrote to Emerson, but rest 'is nowhere for the son of Adam. All looked so "spectral" to me in my old-familiar Birthland; Hades itself could not have seemed stranger; Annandale also was part of the Kingdom of TIME.'[20]

In a letter to Jane occasioned by the same visit, the Scottish countryside at first glance seems solid enough, but Carlyle's perspective elongates as his sentence lengthens, until the rolling hillside in the foreground all but vanishes into the cosmic distance:

. . . I saw the "Sweet Milk Well" yesterday; flowing (for the last four thousand years) from its three sources on the hillside; the origin of Middlebie Burn; and noted the little dell it had hollowed out all the way, and the huts of Adam's Posterity built sluttishly on its course; and a Sun shining overhead, ninety millions of miles off; and Eternity all round; and Life a vision, dream and yet fact,—woven, with uproar, on the Loom of Time![21]

Nothing is more characteristic of these cosmic pastorals of Carlyle than their lack of any middle-distance, any fixed anchoring in time and place. Although he is on the actual spot and sees the brook with his own eyes, he beholds it not in his own time but in the inhumanly elongated perspective of four thousand years. And he observes on its banks not the farmers of Annandale but *Adam's posterity*, as if huddled there under a distant sun since the Creation. In the course of a single sentence, the 'I' of Thomas Carlyle has become the Eye of Eternity surveying the 'dream and yet fact' of man's life in time.

Two years later, in the exhausted pause after completing *The French Revolution* in 1837, Carlyle again returned to Scotland and his mother. 'There is no idler, sadder, quieter, more *ghost*like man in the world even now than I', he wrote from his parents' farm at Scotsbrig to John Sterling. There follows one of the most beautiful passages in all of Carlyle's letters. The ghosts of his father and sister, who had risen to haunt his dreams on the night he learned of the destruction of his manuscript, are here at last laid to rest. In place of the menace of his night-walks in London he conveys an unearthly serenity like that of Wordsworth's 'A Slumber Did My Spirit Seal':

Scotsbrig, Ecclefechan,
28th July, 1837—

. . . Men's very sorrows, and the tear one's heart weeps when the eye is dry, what is in that either? In an hour, will not Death shake it all still again?—Nevertheless the old Brook, Middlebie Burn we call it, still leaps into i[t]s "*Caudron*" here, gushes clear as crystal thro' the chasms and dingles of its "*Linn*"; singing me a song, with slight variations of score these several thousand years . . . I look on the sapphire of St Bees Head and the Solway mirror from the gable-window; I ride to the top of *Blaweary* and see all round from Ettrick Pen to Helvellyn, from Tyndale and Northumberland to Cairnsmuir and Ayrshire: *voir c'est avoir* [to see is to possess]: a brave old Earth, after all;—in which, as above said, I am content to acquiesce without quarrel. . . . One night, late, I rode thro' the village where I was born. The old "Kirkyard Tree," a huge old gnarled ash, was rustling itself softly against the great Twilight in the North; a star or two looked out; and the old graves were all there, and my Father's and my Sister's: and God was above us all.[22]

The union of living and dead, of earthly and eternal, is perfectly caught in the closing phrases: the stars *look out*, the old graves *were all there*, like half-animate presences gathered into a company. Carlyle's Father and Sister are in some strangely indeterminate state, syntactically suspended in the phrase following *all there*. Carlyle sees their graves, but the haunting capitals carry the suggestion that he also sees them. In the world of time, Father and Sister are beneath the ground and Carlyle above it. But in the last clause—*and God was above us all*—the perspective shifts, in a twinkling the distinction is obliterated, and James, Margaret, and Thomas are all seen, side-by-side, under the eye of God.

In December 1853 Carlyle returned to the farmhouse at Scotsbrig and kept vigil by his aged mother's bedside. On Christmas Day she died. That night he slept in the room next to hers, '*her* Corpse and I the only tenants upstairs'.[23] The following day he buried her beside his Father and Sister, in the ancient Ecclefechan churchyard, in the same grave in which he now lies.

3

'The Grand Poem of our Time'

In current usage the word *revolution* denotes violent political upheaval, sudden disjunctions in ways of life or modes of thought. We tend to forget an almost contrary sense of *revolution* signifying a regular rotation around a fixed point, a cycle often of great duration. Among English historians the embattled Carlyle habitually favours the first usage, the Olympian Gibbon, the second.

In the first paragraph of *The Decline and Fall of the Roman Empire*, the word *revolution* encompasses the vast thirteen-hundred-year circuit of human history that Gibbon stakes out for his subject. Opening with a panorama of the Empire at the peak of its power, he sets out to trace its 'decline and fall; a revolution which will ever be remembered, and is still felt by the nations of the earth'. Gibbon invites his readers to observe from a pleasing distance the stately march through time that commences in the age of the Antonines and ends six volumes later, as he surveys from the brow of the Capitoline the spectacle of ancient Rome spread out in grassy ruins. Carlyle in *The French Revolution* makes his reader the eyewitness to a modern Armageddon. He writes in the disturbing urgency of the present tense of the five climactic years between the start of the Revolution and the end of the Reign of Terror. Unlike Gibbon, he seeks to re-create an event close in time and place to his readers. Marat's sister, he points out in the chapter on Marat's death, was alive in Paris at the very moment Carlyle was writing of her brother's assassination at the hands of Charlotte Corday (4: 170).

The contrasting perspectives of the two works are reflected in their titles. *The History of the Decline and Fall of the Roman Empire* is preemptive in its initial article, classic in its balance, imperial in scope. In the measured parallelism of *Decline and Fall* we read in brief what we will experience at large in the work itself: the stately motion of a colossus in collapse. Carlyle writes not *The History of the French Revolution* but *The French Revolution: A History*. The indefinite article announces that the writing of history has become problematic. As Carlyle dramatizes in the course of the work, there were as many different French Revolutions as participants in the event, and its consequences are still unfolding (2: 214). From Gibbon's first sentence to his last, the Empire he so vividly re-creates he also firmly entombs in the past tense. That distancing past serves as his historical signature, the keystone of a syntactical structure whose majestic periods, lightened by ironies and reinforced by interlocking parallelisms, mirror the classical style of the Empire he chronicles. Where Gibbon pleases, Carlyle shocks, for he strives to render not the shaped perfection of a composed past but a rude, eye-witness encounter with a violent present.*

Even Carlyle's most sympathetic contemporaries were distressed by what they took to be his barbarous style. To John Sterling's strictures against his 'impurities', Carlyle replied:

If one has thoughts not hitherto uttered in English Books, I see nothing for it but that you must use words not found there, must *make* words. . . . [With] the whole structure of our Johnsonian English breaking up from its foundations,— revolution *there* [is] as visible as anywhere else![1]

Like Sterling, John Stuart Mill balked at Carlyle's 'abrupt, exclamatory' manner and pleaded with him privately to observe the 'ordinary grammatical mode of nominative & verb'. Carlyle's reply is the best brief statement of what he attempts and achieves stylistically in *The French Revolution*:

The common English mode of writing has to do with what I call *hearsays* of things; and the great business for me, in which alone I feel any comfort, is recording the *presence*, bodily concrete coloured presence of things;—for which the Nominative-and-verb, as I find it Here and Now, refuses to stand me in due stead.[2]

Every oddity of style, every element of structure in *The French Revolution*, works to make palpable to the reader the 'bodily concrete coloured presence of things', including the presence of Carlyle himself as he struggles to wrest order from his voluminous and conflicting sources.

Gibbon published the first volume of *The Decline and Fall* in the second year of the American Revolution, the final volume on the eve of the French Revolution. No trace of these twin upheavals ruffles the

---

* 'You do not read his books; you experience them, and what you experience in them is the storm of the world. . . . *The French Revolution* is the only work in which the past is not merely narrated, but recreated.' (A. J. P. Taylor, 'Macaulay and Carlyle', in *Essays in English History* (Harmondsworth, Middlesex: Penguin Books, 1976), pp. 60-1.)

imperturbable pages of his masterpiece. On a serene June evening in 1787, in the summer-house of his garden in Lausanne, he put a period to the last line of the last page. Rising for a stroll about the garden, he felt the joy of deliverance tempered by the melancholy of taking 'everlasting leave of an old and agreeable companion'.[3] Half a century later, on a wet January night in 1837, Carlyle left his study in Cheyne Row, handed Jane the just-finished manuscript of *The French Revolution*, and, before walking the dismal London streets, remarked that for the past hundred years the world had not seen 'any book that comes more direct and flamingly from the heart of a living man'. A few days later he called the work 'a wild savage Book, itself a kind of French Revolution. . . . it has come hot out of my own soul; born in blackness whirlwind and sorrow.'[4] History as Gibbon wrote it is unimaginable after the French Revolution; history as Carlyle conceived it would have been unthinkable before the Revolution. For the event not only overturned a whole society, but also revolutionized our modes of conceiving of society and of writing history.[5] Seen in this light, Carlyle's portrait of the Revolution is itself revolutionary, 'a kind of French Revolution' in historiography.

The view of history that Carlyle inherited from the Enlightenment and came to reject is epitomized in Viscount Bolingbroke's oft-cited aphorism: 'History is Philosophy teaching by examples.'[6] Bolingbroke takes for granted the rationality of man and the constancy of human behaviour. History, the mere handmaiden of Philosophy, can instruct us because our actions are governed by reason, events are intelligible, and all men can concur in their meaning. 'Mankind are so much the same, in all times and places,' asserts Bolingbroke's contemporary Hume, 'that history informs us of nothing new or strange.'[7] In an essay on 'Romantic Historicism', Karl Kroeber contrasts Hume's assertion of human invariability with Carlyle's counter-assertion in 'On History' that neither the outward nor the inward conditions of life are ever the same in any two ages. And in a telling observation that suggests the larger differences between neo-classic and romantic historiography, Kroeber notes that 'Carlyle seldom forgets what the neo-classic historian seldom mentions, the epitome of life's trivial incertitudes, the weather.'[8]

Scarcely a scene in *The French Revolution* is unaccompanied by its particular atmospherics, from the bone-chilling drizzle that half-freezes Jean Bailly, the Mayor of Paris, as he shivers beneath the guillotine, to the summer's deluge—'an incessant sheet or fluid-column of rain'—that drenches the hundreds of thousands crowded into the Champ-de-Mars to swear brotherhood at David's elaborately staged Festival of National Federation (4: 211; 3: 65). The arbitrary, uncontrollable power of nature threatening to drown David's neo-classic pageantry is Carlyle's emblem of the demonic forces poised to push the Revolution beyond the orbit of its rationalist and aristocratic origins. Within weeks of the fraternal oath-taking at the 'Feast of Pikes', the marquis de Bouillé led a ferocious attack on the rebellious garrison at Nancy. The 'affair' of Nancy, Carlyle writes, is 'the un-sightly *wrong-side* of that thrice-glorious Feast of Pikes, the right-side of which formed a spectacle for the very gods. Right-side and wrong lie always so near . . .' (3: 100). True to its Enlightenment origins, the Revolution enthroned Reason, but it also unleashed the Furies; it worshipped Liberty but institutionalized Terror; it proclaimed univer-sal brotherhood yet, in the words of the condemned Girondist Vergniaud, devoured its own children (4: 201). In so doing, the Revolution, as Carlyle understood it, was neither inconsistent nor hypocritical. He found much irony but no contradiction in celebrat-ing the Festival of Reason—the Goddess was enthroned with great fanfare in the high-altar of the Cathedral of Notre-Dame, renamed the Temple of Reason—on the eve of the worst atrocities of the Revolution, the fusillades at Lyons and the mass drownings at Nantes.

For Carlyle, as for the Romantics before him, the rationalism of the Enlightenment was a prime symptom of its deluded view of human nature and its denial of history. In the eyes of the *philosophes*, once the new Trinity of Reason, Nature, and Progress had replaced the old, an indefinitely perfectible mankind could flourish in a just society governed by reason and the laws of science.[9] For Carlyle, however, the darkness in man persists alongside the growth of light, the primitive alongside the civilized and 'scientific'. Throughout history only a small portion of our lives has been governed by the 'Voluntary and Conscious [compared to] the Involuntary and Un-conscious' (28: 10). Carlyle shared the contempt of the *philosophes* for the hypocrisy and privilege of the *ancien régime*, but not their convic-tion that the secular millennium was at hand or their belief, as John Morley wrote of Voltaire, that 'reason and humanity were but a single word'.[10]

Carlyle explores the dark underside of the Enlightenment in 'Count Cagliostro' (1833), which he wrote in the productive pause between

Sartor Resartus and *The French Revolution*. In the rise and fall of the notorious imposter, Carlyle saw a kind of negative apotheosis of the Enlightenment and a prelude to the Revolution. Born Giuseppe Balsamo of Palermo, renamed by himself Count Alessandro Cagliostro, this virtuoso-adventurer moved in the highest circles of the Court of Louis XVI, was implicated in the scandal of the Diamond Necklace, and condemned by the Roman Inquisition as a heretic and sorcerer in 1789. 'Count Cagliostro' radiates an extravagant gaiety of negativity that recalls Carlyle's remark to Mill that beneath all his gloom lay 'a genuine feeling of the ludicrous', and that if he had not been the sickest and saddest of men he 'could have been the merriest'.[11] The Miltonic quality of imagination that energizes *The French Revolution* here shows itself in the celebration, on a colossal scale and in a mock-heroic idiom, of Cagliostro's impostures. This 'Quack of Quacks' is an 'Incarnate Lie', a comic Satan who, issuing 'out of Chaos and Old Night', thrives in the mephitic intellectual climate of the pre-Revolution and is finally consumed 'in that same French Revolution . . . which burnt-up . . . unmeasured masses of Quackism' (28: 255, 263, 274).

Carlyle was especially sensitive to the irrational and anti-rational currents that surfaced alongside rationalism, like the winged monsters that arise in Goya's 'Sleep of Reason'. He belongs to what Isaiah Berlin calls the 'Counter-Enlightenment', that dissident movement which achieved fullest expression in the German Romantics— among them Schiller, Fichte, Jean Paul, and Novalis—who profoundly influenced Carlyle's early thought. The Age of Reason was, for Carlyle, also the Age of Unreason, of mesmerism and vampirism as well as the *Encyclopédie*, of Sade's *Justine* as well as Condorcet's *Progress of the Human Mind*. In 'Count Cagliostro' he compiles a Homeric catalogue of all the 'Quackeries' that befell Europe on the eve of the Revolution: Impostors and Enthusiasts, 'Cabalists, Swedenborgians, Illuminati, Crucified Nuns, and Devils of Loudun! . . . Rosicrucians, Freemasons, . . . Cagliostros, Casanovas, Saint-Germains, Dr. Grahams; the Chevalier d'Eon, Psalmanazar, Abbé Paris and the Ghost of Cock-Lane!' (28: 271).

Carlyle's picture of the European cultural climate in the late eighteenth century is remarkable for its inclusion of the popular and local movements that existed alongside or in opposition to the dominant intellectual culture of the Enlightenment. That such mass popular currents are worthy of the historian's concern was itself a revolu-

tionary idea born of the two revolutions—French and Romantic—
that coloured all of Carlyle's thought. In 'On History' he insists that
history is made not only by Kings and parliaments but by the whole
complex of interactions—public and private, written and unwritten,
ecological and social—that shape our collective lives in time. The
historian must strive to span this wider spectrum and make vivid
what was once indeed alive, a process that both Carlyle and
Macaulay praised Scott for having pioneered in his historical
fiction.[12] Scott's novels, Carlyle writes, have 'taught all men this
truth, which . . . was as good as unknown to writers of history and
others, till so taught: that the bygone ages of the world were actually
filled by living men, not by protocols, state-papers, controversies and
abstractions of men.'*

The French Revolution everywhere stresses the movement of history
from palaces and parliaments down onto the streets and into the consciousness of the people. However sharply Carlyle individualizes the
phlegmatic Louis XVI or the fastidious Robespierre, the protagonist
of his historical drama is clearly the people; the central lines are
always spoken in Carlyle's collective voice—'the voice of all France'
(2: 117)—as he presides over the narrative in his composite role of
biblical prophet and Greek chorus. Seen in this light, The French
Revolution is the chronicle of the new national consciousness created
by the Revolution itself.

Within Revolutionary France, history became self-consciously
'participatory' on an unprecedented scale. Vast public spectacles at
which the people constituted both actors and audience, the rise of
huge volunteer armies, the power of the populace to influence national
events—all this made history, in Georg Lukács's phrase, into a 'mass
experience'. In The Historical Novel Lukács argues that the Revolution
afforded concrete possibilities for the people 'to comprehend their

---

* 'Sir Walter Scott', 29: 77. That Carlyle credits a novelist with a major innovation in
historiography suggests how fluid are the boundaries separating history from fiction.
Scott's life provides a curious illustration of the closeness of the two genres. In 1797
Scott married the daughter of a royalist family that had fled from Lyons to Paris to
England early in the Revolution. The first-hand accounts Scott heard of the
movements of the revolutionary mobs in Paris he used to brilliant effect in his historical
dramatization, early in The Heart of Midlothian, of the Porteous Riots in the streets of
Edinburgh. A keen student of Scott, Carlyle in turn found hints in Scott's novel for his
own account of the storming of the Bastille in The French Revolution. This fertile inter-
fusion of history and fiction bore further fruit when Dickens drew heavily upon the
crowd scenes in The French Revolution for the most powerful passages in A Tale of Two
Cities.

own existence as something historically conditioned. . . . For the first time they experienced France as their own country, as their self-created motherland.'[13] Lukács links the rise of the historical novel to this growing historical self-consciousness during the Revolutionary and Napoleonic wars. Like Carlyle, and for reasons similar to Carlyle's, he credits Scott with a major role in the evolution of the new genre: 'What is lacking in the so-called historical novel before Sir Walter Scott is precisely the specifically historical, that is, derivation of the individuality of characters from the historical peculiarity of their age.'[14]

In his early, seminal essays on 'Signs of the Times' and 'Characteristics', Carlyle portrays the 'historical peculiarity' not of individuals but of a whole society caught in tumultuous transition between the destruction of an old order and the emergence of a new. The depth and imaginative force of Carlyle's early social criticism parallels and, in important ways, fosters the development of the Victorian novel, in which a living past is seen as generative of the present, and the destiny of the individual is enmeshed in the history and destiny of his culture. Scott's role in this enriching of the historical and social texture of the novel has long been acknowledged; Carlyle's role, more indirect yet more profound, is less widely understood, although it was recognized by Carlyle's great contemporaries, among them Dickens and George Eliot.[15] The Victorian novel is unimaginable without Carlyle's early essays, without the great chapters on language and on symbolism in *Sartor Resartus*, without the radical innovations in narrative in *The French Revolution* and *Past and Present*.

*

One measure of Carlyle's impact on the literature and culture of his age and ours is that we must use words of his own inventing—*industrialism*, *genetic*, and *environment* are notable examples[16]—in order to describe his achievement. Before the late 1820s, when Carlyle gave *environment* its modern meaning, the word meant the action of encircling or the state of being surrounded. The word was abstract, two-dimensional, atemporal. In Carlyle's early writings *environment* acquires a local habitation. The word becomes concrete, now signifying, as in the two earliest examples of this new sense cited in *The Oxford English Dictionary* (both examples are taken from the works of Carlyle), 'the region surrounding something'. More to our purpose, in the fullest of the *OED*'s definitions, the environment becomes historical and takes on a life and depth in time. Again the *OED* goes

to Carlyle for the earliest example in English of what is now the common meaning of the term:

Environment
   b. *esp*. The conditions under which any person or thing lives or is
developed; the sum-total of influences which modify and determine the
development of life or character.
   1827 Carlyle *Misc.* [*Essays*], *Goethe* (1869) 192. In such an element with such
an environment of circumstances.[17]

The holistic habit of thought underlying this definition was not
original with Carlyle, but he was of great importance in widening its
currency in England in the second quarter of the nineteenth century.
Beginning in his early essays and then in *Sartor Resartus*, *The French
Revolution*, and *Past and Present*, he portrays man as an evolving organism within the larger organism of nature, rooted in time and place,
shaped by culture. He rejects the mechanical model of society as an
aggregate of autonomous bodies in motion, and instead pictures
society as a living tissue held together by the 'Organic Filaments' of
language and custom, of common landscape, dress, climate, past. In
an essay comparing *Bleak House* to *The French Revolution*, Jonathan
Arac notes how many of the nineteenth-century terms of historical
perception relate parts and wholes: '"milieu," "circumstance(s),"
"influence," "air," "element," "atmosphere," "medium," "conjec-
ture," "mentality," and "background."'[18] If to this list we add *environment*, we can appreciate how much of Carlyle's writing focuses on the
fluidity of interconnection between background and foreground, past
and present, material and psychological, local and cosmic. In the
chapter on 'Organic Filaments' in *Sartor Resartus* Carlyle draws on the
language of Newtonian science to make a moral point: 'It is a mathematical fact that the casting of this pebble from my hand alters the
centre of gravity of the Universe.' The moral correlative of this
'mathematical fact' is that no man is an island unto himself, that
despite the socially fragmenting 'laws' of *laissez-faire*, we remain our
brother's keeper. The cast pebble of *Sartor Resartus* finds its counterpart in the starving Irish Widow of *Past and Present* who drags her
infected body from door to door in search of food for herself and her
children; she finally 'proves her sisterhood' in the only way she can in
a society whose sole nexus is 'cash'—by killing seventeen of her
neighbours with typhoid (10: 149). In dying she unwittingly reasserts
the indissolubility of human community that her neighbours sought

to deny, but the community she creates is a community of disease and death. She is the mortal emblem of a society that in denying connection endangers its own survival.

Physical contagion as a metaphor for the moral sickness of society at large also figures powerfully in *Bleak House*, which Dickens began after re-reading Carlyle. The festering slum of Tom-all-Alone's carries fever and sows evil through all social strata, from the illiterate outcast Jo to the icily aristocratic Lady Dedlock. *Bleak House* anatomizes in fiction the same 'universal Social Gangrene' (10: 137) afflicting industrialized England that Carlyle had diagnosed in *Past and Present*. From opposite ends of the social spectrum, Carlyle's nameless Irish Widow and Dickens's Lady Dedlock 'prove their sisterhood'. Dickens's growth as artist is in part the response of his idiosyncratic genius to the moral imagination of Carlyle. 'I am always reading you faithfully', Dickens the disciple wrote to Carlyle in 1863, 'and trying to go your way.'[19] That 'way' involved abandoning the individual villains, the particular institutions and their isolated victims, of the early novels for the later, all-encompassing vision of a mammonite society blinded by moral fog and burying itself under mounds of its own garbage and greed.

Like *Bleak House*, *Hard Times* carries over into the novel Carlyle's attack on Victorian capitalism. Dedicated to Carlyle, *Hard Times* shares not only a common message with *Past and Present* but a moral symbolism that indicts the machinery—ideological and industrial— that in the name of efficiency cripples and enslaves human beings. In much the same way, *A Tale of Two Cities* bears unmistakable witness to the influence of Carlyle.[20] In addition to hundreds of verbal borrowings, Dickens derives directly from Carlyle his sense of the Revolution as a moral drama with all the fatality of a Greek tragedy. The strength of Dickens's uneven novel lies in its demonic crowd scenes, with their insistent Carlylean symbolism of fire and flood, emblems of the elemental, annihilating force of the Revolution. Both works reflect the tumultuous ambivalence of their authors towards public and private violence. This shared fascination and loathing enabled *The French Revolution*—'Mr. Carlyle's wonderful book', as Dickens called it—to exercise a virtually hypnotic hold on Dickens's imagination.[21] *The French Revolution* also suggested to Dickens ways of shaping the anarchic fury of the Revolution into forms capable of literary representation. *A Tale of Two Cities* is never better than in its scenes of synoptic social overview, highly allegorical in tone, in which we glimpse the fate of all France in the face of its ineffectual King, or in the boy who is dismembered alive for failing to bow down before a procession of monks. The best-known passage of the novel is its Carlylean opening, with its contrasts and capitalized personifications, its bird's-eye view of a whole nation about to fall prey to 'the Wood-man, Fate', and 'the Farmer, Death'. In these opening paragraphs, Dickens borrows Carlyle's all-seeing 'Eye of History' (2: 15) and reproduces a brilliantly scaled-down epitome of *The French Revolution*. At the end of the great opening chapter, Dickens leaves the very signature of Carlyle's influence on the page, the word 'environed', used in the rich new sense Carlyle had coined.

Kathleen Tillotson in her *Novels of the Eighteen-Forties* credits Carlyle with awakening 'the poetic, prophetic, and visionary possibilities of the novel'. The reader of Dickens, Thackeray, and the Brontës, she writes, 'becomes aware of an aura of symbolism' previously absent from the English novel.[22] George Eliot belongs in this company of the awakened, but her genius, so much more normative in its concerns and expression that Dickens's, bears the marks of Carlyle's influence more subtly and they have gone largely unnoticed. Yet she pays tribute not only to Carlyle's influence on herself but on the leading thinkers and writers of her generation, for whom, she contends, the reading of Carlyle 'was an epoch in the history of their minds'. Reviewing a volume of Carlyle *Selections* in 1855, she remarks that 'there has hardly been an English book written for the last ten or twelve years that would not have been different if Carlyle had not lived.' Surprisingly for the modern reader, she reserves her highest praise not for Carlyle the 'philosopher' but for Carlyle the literary artist:

. . . to our thinking, he is yet more of an artist than a philosopher. . . . his greatest power lies in concrete presentation. No novelist has made his crea-tions live for us more thoroughly than Carlyle has made Mirabeau and the men of the French Revolution, Cromwell and the Puritans.[23]

This tribute to Carlyle's imaginative powers was paid when George Eliot was about to embark on a new career as a novelist. Her success in integrating individual characters into their larger social and historical context is central to her achievement as a novelist, an achievement that rests in part on Carlylean insights and narrative techniques. 'It is the habit of my imagination', she wrote to R. H. Hutton, 'to strive after as full a vision of the medium in which a character moves as of the character itself.'[24] George Eliot is here describing her 'main artistic' purpose in *Romola* of portraying character within the social and historical context that shapes it, but the same purpose manifests itself throughout *Middlemarch*. The symbolism of the web, woven so deftly through her 'study of provincial life', linking character to character and determining their several fates in the larger social fabric in which all are enmeshed, bears unmistakable witness to Carlyle's 'organic filaments' that shape our lives. Like the monks of *Past and Present* who live within the narrow circuit of St Edmund's Abbey and are bound by ties both invisible and compelling, the characters of *Middlemarch* act out their little provincial destinies under the all-seeing eye of a narrator who is both sympathetically involved in the action and omniscient, inside the minds of the characters yet also high above them, like 'Uriel watching the progress of planetary history from the Sun' (ch. 41).

In both *The French Revolution* and *Middlemarch* the perspective continually shifts from the limited point of view of an observer within the work to the larger overview of the author-narrator, an omniscience personified as the Eye of Uriel or the Eye of History. This movement from the minute to the panoramic, and back again, accounts for the reader's sense that even though he is reading modern prose, he is not far from the ancient world of epic, with its busy trafficking back and forth between the mundane and the cosmic. Viewed in this light Carlyle is the pivotal figure between what Gerald L. Bruns has called the older 'transcendental imagination' of the Romantics and the 'historical imagination' of the Victorians. The Victorians, Bruns argues, thought of themselves as possessing 'not a cosmos but a history', and believed that the locus of reality was no longer in timelessness but in process and change.[25] Carlyle straddles both worlds. He meditates between the older, transcendental order and the newer world of process. In *Sartor Resartus* he relocates the eternal within the temporal; in *The French Revolution* he relocates the disappearing God of the Bible within the new scripture of History, which he calls 'imprisoned Epic' (12: 17).

Heir to Carlyle's historical sense but sceptical of the 'Immensities and Eternities' that overarch his world, George Eliot cultivates in her fiction the more familiar middle-distance of moral action. The cosmic clash of Everlasting No and Yea in *Sartor Resartus*, the world-historic drama enacted in *The French Revolution*, become secularized and naturalized in her novels, which represent the domestication of the epic impulse that earlier in the century had begun to look homeward in the works of Wordsworth, Scott, and Carlyle. There is something faintly comic as well as tragic in Lydgate's quest for the 'primitive tissue' in a provincial clinic, or in the Reverend Casaubon's sepulchral search for the 'Key to all Mythologies' in his dismal library at Lowick; but these quests for the source of all life and for the symbol that will open all doors—these variations on the novel's central symbol of the all-connecting web—remain curiously Carlylean in their heroic impulse to put the fragmented world together again, an impulse that George Eliot knows must fail. Compassionate irony is her response to this shrunken world of what she calls 'home epic'.[26] In such a world no Diogenes Teufelsdröckh will again aspire—at least not until his reincarnation as Stephen Dedalus—to be 'the Poet and inspired Maker; who, Prometheus-like, can shape new Symbols, and bring new Fire from Heaven . . .'.[27]

Much of the power of *Middlemarch* resides in its unembittered burial of the heroic, its renunciation of the transcendent in favour of the quiet celebration of the secular and mundane. The fiction strikes us as moving beyond mere verisimilitude into the world of the actual; we read *Middlemarch* as fiction but remember it as history. Yet a decade before writing *Middlemarch*, when George Eliot attempted in *Romola* (1862–3) to endow fiction with the authenticity of history, she brought forth not a living novel but embalmed history. The failure of *Romola* is especially instructive,[28] for George Eliot tried to achieve in her historical novel the immediacy and credibility she had praised in Carlyle's novelistic histories. The unequal impact of the two works stems from their authors' different attitudes towards what is mythic and what is real in their narratives. *Romola* opens with a sweeping panorama—from the Levant across the Pillars of Hercules and thence to Florence—presided over by an 'angel of the dawn'. The scene recalls Carlyle's panorama of the dawn rising over the Nile and moving westward to strike the streets of Versailles as they fill to overflowing for the Procession of the States-General (2: 132). But George Eliot's 'angel of the dawn' has been stripped of his Carlylean Capitals and his credibility. Throughout *Romola* angels and demons are quite frankly figures of speech, stage directions in a historical drama whose significance is insistently terrestrial. When Carlyle describes 'the Great Fear' that spread suddenly and mysteriously throughout France in the summer of 1789 and 'like a kind of Supernatural Machinery, wondrously move[d] the Epos of the Revolution' (2: 126), he writes as both historian and mythographer. 'The Great Fear' was triggered by isolated local incidents but had the escalating effects of a chain reaction; bands of roving brigands seemed to grow in numbers with each successive report of their movements. What men believe or fear, Carlyle held, is as much a part of history as what they see and do; indeed, what they *imagine* to have happened is very much part of what *did* happen.* Hence in describing the paranoic climate of the Revolution, especially during the Great Fear and again during the Reign of Terror, with its Orwellian 'Law of Suspects',[29] Carlyle gives more and more prominence to a phenomenon he personifies as Preternatural Suspicion and likens to Apollo's spreading of panic and pestilence through the ranks of the terrified Greeks. Preternatural Suspicion looms large in *The French Revolution* not because Carlyle wishes to be 'literary', but because he understood that revolutions spawn fears and rumours and are driven as much by psycho-social as politico-

---

* As in the case of the sinking of the *Vengeur du Peuple*, with the loss of her heroic crew, off the coast of Brest in 1794. In the first edition of *The French Revolution* Carlyle faithfully reconstructs the battle from contemporary reports, including the cries in unison of *Vive la République* as the crew went down with their gallant ship. But in 1838, one year after the publication of *The French Revolution*, Carlyle and the rest of the wrold learned that the celebrated victory-in-defeat of the *Vengeur* was largely the patriotic fabrication of Bertrand Barère, a journalist and one of the twelve who ruled France through the Committee of Public Safety. In later editions of *The French Revolution* Carlyle did not alter a word of his original account. Instead, he added directly to the main text a new concluding paragraph correcting Barère's story, which he terms a 'masterpiece; the largest, most inspiring piece of *blague* manufactured, for some centuries, by any man or nation. As such, and not otherwise, be it henceforth memorable' (4: 242).

As Carlyle saw it, simply to expunge the saga of the *Vengeur* because it had later been proven false would itself have been a form of falseness, for the patriotic lie had been believed for years on both sides of the channel and was 'henceforth memorable'—but memorable only as a brilliant, pioneering example of government-manipulated 'news'. In recounting the venerable lie in one paragraph and exposing it in the next, Carlyle preserves, as if in successive archaeological layers, his own—and history's—changed awareness of the fabled *Vengeur*. In 1839 he published in *Fraser's Magazine* a detailed account of his own research into the affair, including his correspondence with the rear-admiral who, years earlier as a junior officer, had dined with the Captain of the *Vengeur* immediately after M. Renaudin had willingly surrendered his ship and several hundred of its crew to the English. Carlyle's essay traces with great vivacity the natural history of a lie. (See 'On the Sinking of the Vengeur' (29: 208–25).)

As an ironic sequel to this unmasking of error, G. P. Gooch, in a widely influential essay, accuses Carlyle of naïvely believing Barère's fabrication, although Carlyle was instrumental in exposing it. For Gooch's intelligent, often hostile, and not always reliable critique of Carlyle as a historian, see *History and Historians in the Nineteenth Century*, 2nd edn. (Boston: Beacon Press, 1959), pp. 301–9. See also fns. on pp. 103 and 138, below.

economic forces. He uses myth not as the antithesis of history but as its inevitable accompaniment, as the necessary modality by which the human imagination figures and interprets its past. He had no need to seek out mythical or literary analogues to events in the Revolution when the actual participants saw themselves as actors in a universal historical drama with antecedents they traced back to the ancient Greeks and Romans and, beyond them, to the primal wars of Titans and Olympians. At the height of the Terror, Carlyle's history virtually writes itself: as the Jacobins take to beheading their fellow revolutionaries, the doomed Girondist orator Vergniaud provides Carlyle with the cannibalistic image that dominates the closing books of *The French Revolution*: ' "The Revolution, like Saturn, is devouring its own children" ' (4: 201, 254).

Carlyle's gods and demons, like George Eliot's, are, of course, figures of speech; but whereas George Eliot's scrupulous realism compelled her to point out that they are 'mere' figures of speech, Carlyle maintained that they are real precisely *because* they are figurative. The creatures of our minds acquire an actuality in consciousness that makes them, not logically real, but real in their effects. Thus, the 'subterranean' Furies are 'fabulous and yet so true'; at any moment they may appear before us, brandishing their torches and 'shaking their serpent-hair' (2: 177). George Eliot disbelieves in her own demons and angels, with the paradoxical result that in *Romola* her fiction is not more realistic but her history is less credible. On the night of Savonarola's last sermon, a 'Masque of the Furies, called Riot', breaks out in the streets of Florence (ch. 66). The street riot is convincing but George Eliot's Furies are not. Their Masque is more decorous than demonic, no serpents writhe in their hair, no hint of burning human flesh quickens their dance.[30]

*

That *Romola* is not wholly persuasive is not surprising in view of the limited role George Eliot granted to the imagination in the writing of historical fiction. In *Leaves from a Note-Book* she describes her attempt to avoid 'the abstract treatment which belongs to grave history' on the one hand—history as it had been written by Hume and Gibbon—and the 'schemed picturesqueness' of popular historical fiction on the other. As her own ideal she posits the 'veracious imagination' that painstakingly reconstructs the past, using all the extant evidence and supplying deficiencies by 'careful analogical creation. . .'.[31] This cautious formulation of aims contrasts with the historical ideal that Carlyle puts in the mouth of Professor Sauerteig: ' "Stern Accuracy in inquiring, bold Imagination in expounding and filling-up; these," says friend Sauerteig, "are the two pinions on which History soars" ' (28: 259–60). George Eliot's ideal is more appropriate to a professional historian and Carlyle's to a historical novelist, yet both writers agree on the absolute importance in historical narrative of the circumstantial and concrete.

At issue here is not the self-evident desirability of vivid prose; rather, Carlyle is concerned with how such vivacity can best be realized, how things and thoughts in all their roundedness and interconnectedness can be embodied in rows of words on a printed page. The problem admits of no perfect solution, for much the same reason that a spherical surface cannot without distortion be mapped on a flat plane. Carlyle's attempted solution began with his outlining the problem in his Notebook and then ruminating on it in public two years later in his essay 'On History'. He first states the problem within a pregnant parenthesis in his Notebook for 8 January 1828:

(An Historian must write [so to speak] in *lines*; but every event is a *superficies*; nay if we search out its *causes*, a *solid*: hence a primary and almost incurable defect in the art of Narration; which only the very best can so much as approximately remedy. . . . I have known it for years; and written it *now*, with the purpose perhaps of writing it at large elsewhere.)[32]

That no event occurs in isolation but is part of all other events over time and space poses informational, syntactic, and stylistic problems so formidable that in theory history cannot be written, or can be written and understood only by God—conclusions Carlyle later reached in 'On History'. But in practice the historian, like the writer of fiction, circumvents this 'almost incurable defect' in narration by striving to re-create the whole nexus of circumstances—physical, psychological, temporal—of which a given 'event' is only the topical manifestation. Hence Carlyle describes an event as a '*superficies*', the outermost surface or facet of a vastly larger configuration.

The historian is thus more an interpreter of signs than a recorder of facts, which pose a multitude of epistemological dilemmas. In 'On History' Carlyle cites the old story of Sir Walter Raleigh's watching a street brawl from his prison window and giving an account that differed from those of three other witnesses on the ground, each of which differed from the other. Carlyle's analysis includes but goes deeper than issues consequent upon relativity of point of view. As he sees it, the essential problem for the historian results from the nature of historical reality itself—from the inadequacy of consciousness to conceive that reality and of language to express it. No matter how great our insight into passing things, there is a 'fatal discrepancy' between their manner of occurrence and our manner of observing them: 'The most gifted man can observe, still more can record, only the *series* of his own impressions: his observation, therefore, to say nothing of its other imperfections, must be *successive*, while the things done were often *simultaneous*; . . .' (27: 88).

This discrepancy leads Carlyle to distinguish between history as it is actually 'acted' and as it is subsequently 'written'; 'acted' history is at bottom unfathomable yet latent with prefiguration, just as life in all its later forms is implicit in the primordial chemical soup. In written history events are related to each other as parent is to offspring; in acted history, he asserts,

every single event is the offspring not of one, but of all other events, prior or contemporaneous, and will in its turn combine with all others to give birth to new: it is an ever-living, ever-working Chaos of Being, wherein shape after shape bodies itself forth from innumerable elements. And this Chaos, boundless as the habitation and duration of man . . . is what the historian will depict, and scientifically gauge, we may say, by threading it with single lines of a few ells in length! For as all Action is, by its nature, to be figured as extended in breadth and in depth, as well as in length . . . so all Narrative is, by its nature, of only one dimension; only travels forward towards one, or towards successive points: Narrative is *linear*, Action is *solid*.

(27: 88-9)

'Narrative is *linear*, Action is *solid*': Carlyle's aphorism neatly poses the dilemma facing the writer of all narrative, whether historical or fictional: how to depict beginnings and endings, or even coherent middles, when discrete beginnings and endings are chimeras of the mind and continuity itself is inherently resistant to verbal representation. *The French Revolution* marks an epoch in the development of nineteenth-century narrative if only because it articulates these limitations so sharply, both in its reflective passages on the nature of historical narrative and in the shifting, 'polycentric perspective' Carlyle uses in depicting the Revolution itself.[33] Like *War and Peace*, which begins in the middle of a sentence and ends in a fragment,[34] *The French Revolution* has no proper beginning or ending. The book opens with a parenthetical remark by a speaker almost certainly unknown to the reader about a matter seemingly without bearing on the Revolution. The abruptness of the opening, like Tolstoy's, is in fact traditional—classical epic begins *in medias res*—but *The French Revolution* starts with so deliberately muddled a middle that for an instant the reader fears he may have picked up the wrong volume. It ends with a last chapter headed 'Finis', as if Carlyle were ringing down the final curtain of a well-made play. Only a few pages earlier he had described the impending fall of Robespierre as the 'fifth-act of this natural Greek Drama' (4: 283). Yet *The French Revolution* is closer in spirit to epic than to tragedy. The chapter entitled 'Finis' begins with Carlyle's suggestion that his book, 'Homer's Epos' and 'Universal History' itself, 'does not conclude, but merely ceases' (4: 321). The *Iliad* ceases with an uneasy pause in the bloodshed, a pause that is heavy with bloodshed to come; *The French Revolution* ends with Napoleon's 'whiff of grape-shot' portending revolutions still to come. 'The Beginning holds in it the End'. Carlyle had written much earlier in the book, and every end marks a new beginning (3: 103).

No two philosophies of history could be more antagonistic than Carlyle's and Tolstoy's,[35] yet the English historian and the Russian novelist agree that, as Carlyle puts it, 'At bottom, there is no perfect History; there is none such conceivable' (*Cromwell*, 6: 7). Carlyle's 'Narrative is *linear*, Action is *solid*' finds its complement in this passage from *War and Peace*:

Absolute continuity of motion is not comprehensible to the human mind. Laws of motion of any kind become comprehensible to man only when he examines arbitrarily selected elements of that motion; . . . [The] method of history is to take an arbitrarily selected series of continuous events and examine it apart from others, though there is and can be no *beginning* to any event, for one event always flows uninterruptedly from another. . . . to assume a *beginning* of any phenomenon . . . is in itself false.[36]

Some years ago a book club brought out a condensed version of *War and Peace*, although it would have been truer to the original to print in full the first seven hundred pages and condense the second seven hundred by omitting them altogether. For the continuity of motion Tolstoy sought to express in narrative, like Carlyle's solidity of action, requires a certain irreducible scale and energy that can only be truncated, not abridged. Magnitude of design combined with minuteness of detail account for the unmistakably epic quality that energizes *The French Revolution* and *War and Peace*. For epic is not confined to a particular form, such as heroic narrative in verse, though the best-known epics have traditionally assumed this form. Rather epic embodies the dominant impulse of the literary imagination in any age—from *Gilgamesh* to *Ulysses*—by which the panoramic and the particular, the cosmic and the local, the mythic and the historic, are held in the most fruitful tension. In his *Descent from Heaven: A Study in Epic Continuity* Thomas Greene singles out as the ultimate epic quality a 'heroic energy' or 'expansiveness' that refuses enclosure in time or space and seeks to raid the unknown, if possible even to annex heaven and hell.[37] Building on Greene's theory of epic expansiveness, I would argue that epic is not only the dominant genre at any time but the colonizer of other genres, appropriating the forms most suited to its expansive energies, even if those forms had previously appeared inimical to traditional epic. A prime sign of the burst of literary creativity in the nineteenth century is that the epic impulse mani- fested itself in so many new ways—primarily in the novel, but also in autobiography (*The Prelude*), in history (*The French Revolution*; *The Stones of Venice*), in Henry Mayhew's teeming sociological panorama (*London Labour and the London Poor*), to say nothing of the great American and Continental epics, historical and fictional, of Prescott and Michelet, of Melville, Tolstoy, and Balzac.[38] Inevitably a con- ventional analysis such as E. M. W. Tillyard's *The English Epic* is in- sensitive to the invasive and transforming capacity of epic. Hence Tillyard concludes that the 'animating idea' of epic perished after Gibbon's *Decline and Fall*,[39] and he ignores three of the greatest English epics since 1800: *The Prelude*, *The French Revolution*, and *Ulysses*.

Although epic is the most ancient and traditional of literary forms, its special genius lies in its capacity to achieve perpetuity through radical innovation. Like gifted sons driven to surpass gifted fathers, the great writers of epic perpetuate their heritage by seeming to repudiate it. Virgil pays Homer the loving tribute of imitation yet everywhere subverts Homer's heroism into the privacy of his own nocturnal lyricism. Dante allows Virgil to lead him like a father to the gates of Paradise, yet he effectively destroys pagan epic, abandoning his guide and consigning Homer's Odysseus to the lowest circles of hell. Milton is never more firmly within the tradition of epic than when boasting that he will surpass it, that the 'great Argument' of *Paradise Lost* will prove 'Not less but more Heroic than the wrath / Of stern *Achilles* . . .'.[40] Wordsworth shifts the scene of his own 'high argument' from Milton's heaven and hell to 'the Mind of Man— / My haunt, and the main region of my song'.[41] 'What passed within me', Wordsworth asserts in *The Prelude*, as if scaling heights unattempted by his revered predecessors, 'This is, in truth, heroic argument.'[42] Coming late to this ancient arena of emulation and repudiation, Carlyle rejects the cosmology of the older epics as 'Superannuated lumber' (28: 51). Yet through innumerable allusions, either reverential or parodic, he makes Homer and Milton as vital to *The French Revolution* as Virgil is to *The Divine Comedy*. Like *Ulysses* a century later, *The French Revolution* manages to be radically innovative and traditional; both works illustrate Brian Wilkie's contention that to read the great epics in succession is 'like walking through a hall of mirrors'.[43]

'Are there epics in prose?' Robert Lowell wondered in a gnomic essay on Homer and Virgil, Dante and Milton, that he drafted just before his death: 'I know one, Carlyle's *French Revolution.*' Lowell is the latest in a long line of American poet-critics, reaching back to Emerson, who saw in Carlyle a great poet whose chosen medium was prose. In an admiring essay of 1847, Thoreau characterized *The French Revolution* as 'a poem, at length got translated into prose; an Iliad'. And a decade earlier, in a letter of ebullient affection thanking Carlyle for a presentation copy of *The French Revolution*, Emerson hailed Carlyle as 'my bard' and praised his having 'broken away from all books, & written a mind'.[44]

Carlyle prepared himself to write 'an Epic Poem of the Revolution'[45] with all the awesome deliberateness and self-consecration that Milton brought to the writing of *Paradise Lost* and Wordsworth to *The Prelude*. By the autumn of 1833, he was certain that he had found 'the subject of subjects',[46] and in a letter to John Stuart Mill he portrayed himself as an evangel to the English of 'the truth' of the French Revolution:

in the right understanding of [the Revolution], is involved all possible knowledge important for us; . . . the depths of Eternity look thro' the *chinks* of that so *convulsed* section of Time. . . . To me, it often seems, as if the right *History* (that impossible thing I mean by History) of the French Revolution were the grand Poem of our Time; as if the man who *could* write the *truth* of that, were worth all other writers and singers. If I were spared alive myself, and had means, why might not I too prepare the way for such a thing?[47]

In the spring of 1834, after a crisis of confidence in which he considered abandoning literature altogether, he finally committed himself to the project, and by the late summer he could write to Emerson that he was giving his 'whole might' to a book on the French

Revolution. 'It is part of my creed that the only Poetry is History, could we tell it right.'[48]

History is the only poetry possible in the modern world because the beliefs that sustained the older poets have for us collapsed into fictions. '"All Mythologies were once Philosophies; were *believed*"', Carlyle–Sauerteig proclaims in the early essay on 'Biography' (28: 49). The poet of modernity must abandon fictions and master the new poetics of fact. That Carlyle himself might be—or soon become—that poet is the covert message of 'Biography',[49] which he wrote when he was an obscure journalist in quest of a subject and style that would establish his fame. In his early essays Carlyle creates a cultural climate and an audience responsive to the radically new imaginative prose that was soon to appear in *Sartor Resartus* and *The French Revolution*. Allusive, ironic, colloquial, abrupt, steeped in both history and the actualities of the moment, this new prose embodies the fragmented realities of modern experience yet is haunted by vestiges of a once-transcendent world. Emerson characterized Carlyle's prose as 'the first domestication of the modern system with its infinity of details, into style. . . .'.[50] More than any other writer of the age, Carlyle has seen

how inexhaustible a mine is the language of Conversation. He does not use the *written* dialect of the time, in which scholars, pamphleteers and the clergy write, nor the Parliamentary dialect, in which the lawyer, the statesman, and the better newspapers write, but draws strength and mother-wit out of a poetic use of the spoken vocabulary, so that his paragraphs are all a sort of splendid conversation.[51]

It may surprise us that Emerson found Carlyle colloquial despite his frequent allusions to the Bible, to Homer, Dante, Milton, Goethe, indeed to much of Western literature. But Emerson is right. His stress on Carlyle's use of 'the spoken vocabulary' reminds us of the sovereign influence upon Carlyle's style of the dialect of his stone-mason father. Both Emerson and Carlyle strove for a spoken style; both were first trained for the pulpit and served their early literary apprenticeships as vocal exegetes of the Word of God. In the same letter in which Carlyle tells Emerson that he is working mightily on *The French Revolution*, he also says that 'there is *nothing sacred*, then, but the *Speech of Man* to believing Men!' History, for Carlyle, is the living record of that speech—'the only Poetry . . . could we tell it right'.

Carlyle compresses a whole philosophy of history into the little word *tell*, which he uses with a deliberate oddity that signals its importance: storytellers tell tales, but we expect historians to write history. In part Carlyle is stressing an idea already familiar to us—how difficult it is to write historical narrative, which is 'linear', when the stuff of history is 'solid'. To 'tell' history properly in this sense requires a technical genius in structuring narrative akin to Homer's—or Carlyle's. But that one should *tell* history at all implies a conception of history that the twentieth century has virtually lost, but that lies at the heart of Carlyle's vocation—history as *utterance* or *revelation*—ancient meanings that still cling to *tell*, as in telling a secret, or as in the joyous proclamation, 'Go, Tell it on the Mountain!' History in this ancient sense is not narration but oracle.

The threadbare image of Carlyle as a 'Victorian Prophet' turns out to contain a startling and quite literal truth. History as Carlyle understood and practised it is prophecy; whether as historian of twelfth-century England or of the present, as in the bitter journalism of the *Latter-Day Pamphlets*, he writes as a direct and self-conscious descendant of the Old Testament Prophets. Contrary to the common misunderstanding, the Prophets were not primarily predictive, not soothsayers. Rather, as in the biblical title of Carlyle's first major essay, they were inspired readers of the 'Signs of the Times'. By seeing more clearly into the life of the past and the present, they were understood to have a privileged view of the future. But their essential work was as interpreters of God's Word and proclaimers of His Will as revealed in time.[52] Brought up to believe in God's Word as the centre of his world, Carlyle reached maturity as that Word was coming under the strenuous challenges of science and the higher criticism. His first book, *Sartor Resartus*, traces his crisis of faith over God's 'disappearance' and his rhapsodic rediscovery of Him in Nature, a spiritual journey that was to prove paradigmatic for a whole generation of God-bereft Victorians. But Carlyle's Calvinism was at war with his Romanticism, and his grimly Calvinist view of Nature as an eternal battleground of 'primeval Light with the everlasting Dark' (4: 43) would not let him rest in the Wordsworthian solution to the crisis of faith he describes in *Sartor Resartus*. The literal truth of the Bible had been cast into irrevocable doubt; and Nature, God's 'second book', had begun to read like a horror story. There remained for Carlyle the saving discovery of a third Scripture, History—' "the true Epic Poem, and universal Divine Scripture" ', an inspired text of which he proclaimed himself the prophet (28: 176).

Underlying Carlyle's many metaphors for history—'an inarticulate Bible', a 'real Prophetic Manuscript', 'an imprisoned Epic', 'that divine BOOK OF REVELATIONS'[53]—is the image of an Unseen Author speaking through the cryptic tongue of time, unfolding a design at once mysterious and purposeful. The 'Prophetic Manuscript' of history presupposes such an Author and the need for a prophet-historian skilled in deciphering His message. 'Imprisoned Epic' suggests an underlying story as well as the historian's sesame-key to unlock it. Events in such a world do not simply occur and cease but also foreshadow and recapitulate all other events; they lead double lives, as it were, both in time and beyond time. Hence history is 'a looking both before and after'; time past is pregnant with the life of time to come, and only in the conjunction of both can the meaning of either be completed (27: 83). We must read such history typologically, as we read the Bible: events in the Old Testament serve as 'types' of the New, Abraham's sacrifice of Isaac, for example, foreshadowing God the Father's redemptive sacrifice of His Son. Through this underlying typological structure Carlyle relocates in history the God who had been displaced from the Divine Authorship of the Bible. Just as he supernaturalizes Nature in *Sartor Resartus*, redeeming it from the 'mechanism' of the century he despised, so in *The French Revolution* he divinizes history, redeeming it from the secularism and rationalism of the eighteenth century. The myth of progress underlying Enlightenment history yields in his pages to the older, providential myth of history in which a divinity 'shapes our ends, / Rough-hew them how we will'.[54] But in the modern world the providential design has grown obscure, the ending of the 'Prophetic Manuscript' of history is indecipherable. With the skill of a modern documentary journalist, Carlyle writes of the French Revolution as if he were a witness-survivor of the Apocalypse. But the Apocalypse has been relocated in historical time. Much of the power of *The French Revolution* lies in the shock of the transposition, the explosive interpenetration of modern fact and ancient myth, of journalism and Scripture. Hence the mixed style of *The French Revolution*, a unique 'ludicro-terrific' idiom (2: 253) that is by turns prophetic and ironic, and interlaces the language of the Bible and Homer with the abrupt argot of the barricades.

Shaping this Babel of words and events into a coherent picture is the 'Eye of History' which, like the synoptic eye of the biblical typologist, superimposes in a single picture images and actions widely separated in space and time. Carlyle is most modern in his mastery of this ancient art of temporal montage, his use of this time annihilating, space-warping Eye to transcend the limitations of linear narrative. But he is an eclectic or universal typologist whose repertory of types ranges beyond the Judaeo-Christian Scriptures to include, in Emerson's phrase, an 'encyclopaediacal allusion to all knowables'.[55] When the Bastille falls to the tumultuous roar of the crowd, Carlyle also evokes the falls of Troy and Jericho, for the modern event echoes its ancient prototypes, classical and biblical (2: 210). Through prospect or retrospect, events in *The French Revolution* echo all other events within the work, and they in turn echo their historical and mythical counterparts across time and space.[56] Three times Carlyle depicts Louis XVI in procession through the streets of Paris, the first two processions grimly proleptic of the last—to the Guillotine at the Place de la Révolution, which, Carlyle reminds us, once bore the name of Louis's grandfather, with whose death *The French Revolution* opened. 'Sovereigns die and Sovereignties', Carlyle remarked in these opening pages. In a paragraph heavy with foreboding, he paves the streets of Paris with history, in preparation for the coming processions of the doomed Louis XVI:

. . . how all dies, and is for a Time only. . . . The Merovingian Kings, slowly wending on their bullock-carts through the streets of Paris, with their long hair flowing, have all wended slowly on,—into Eternity. Charlemagne sleeps at Salzburg, with truncheon grounded; . . . Rollo and his shaggy Northmen cover not the Seine with ships; but have sailed off on a longer voyage. . . . They are all gone; sunk,—down, down, with the tumult they made; and the rolling and the trampling of ever new generations passes over them; and they hear it not any more for ever.

(2: 7–8)

Those long-haired Merovingian Kings never quite leave Carlyle's narrative or the reader's imagination. Though sunk 'down, down' into death, they are not wholly silenced but, like the sleeping Charlemagne, remain ambiguously present in the triple negative of Carlyle's close—the '*not . . . more . . . for ever*' that leaves them eternally hearing and not hearing, for ever absent yet for ever attentive, ghostly presences-to-be at King Louis's death and, in due time, at our own. In this passage, as throughout *The French Revolution*, past and present, historical and mythical, temporal and eternal, co-exist in 'wondrous new contiguity' (5: 160). Spiralling back upon itself in an ever-widening range of reference, the narrative achieves both solidity and a haunting impalpability.

All these allusive elements converge in a passage that Carlyle wrote near the end of his career as a historian—the 'Proem' to *Frederick the Great*. ' "All History" ', says Sauerteig,

"is an imprisoned Epic, nay an imprisoned Psalm and Prophecy. . . . I think all real *Poets*, to this hour, are Psalmists and Iliadists after their sort; and have in them a divine impatience of lies. . . . the highest Shakespeare producible is properly the fittest Historian producible."

(12: 17–18)

With the advent of this poet-prophet, history as Carlyle ideally understood it could at last be written—' "the inspired gift of God employing itself to illuminate the dark ways of God" ' (12: 19). The Miltonic allusion reminds us that, for Carlyle, history is theodicy as well as prophecy.[57] Milton had risen to the height of his 'great Argument' that he might 'assert Eternal Providence, / And justify the ways of God to men' (1: 24–6). Carlyle takes up the 'Argument' where his great Protestant predecessor left off, after the revolution in Heaven and the disobedience in Eden have receded into myth and the long march of history is far advanced. Underlying Milton's retelling of the biblical story is the shadow of recent history, the failed promise of the Puritan Revolution he had served.[58] Underlying Carlyle's historical portrait of the French Revolution is the omnipresent shadow of myth—the Reign of Terror as a descent into Hell, the struggle of the Sansculottes against their oppressors a re-enactment of the cannibalizing warfare of Titans and Olympians. It is as if Milton's angels and demons, along with the gods of the ancient Greeks, had resurfaced as the Personifications and Capitalizations that stalk Carlyle's pages. 'Dark is the way of the Eternal as mirrored in this world of Time', Carlyle writes as Louis XVI moves ever closer to his doom (3: 5). For Carlyle we come too late in the march of history to justify God's ways directly from Scripture, but they still can be discerned in the dark glass of history. With this shift in perspective from Scripture to history, Carlyle abandons the 'advent'rous Song' of Milton and his epic predecessors for the less elevated idiom of prose. He writes a modern epic whose hero, fittingly, is the demonic Sansculottes: 'The "destructive wrath" of Sansculottism: this is what we speak, having unhappily no voice for singing' (2: 212). Carlyle here confesses—and it is a true confession—his inaptitude for writing verse. But tucked within the modest disclaimer is the traditional boast of the epic poet—Carlyle's implied comparison of himself to Homer—and the further suggestion that, in the modern world, speech is more useful than song. And so in *The French Revolution* he writes, or rather *speaks*—for history is at bottom a 'telling'—a kind of inspired vernacular poetry that is far closer to Homer and Milton than to the prose of Gibbon and Macaulay. The scrupulously unpoetic John Stuart Mill saw and said as much at the start of his review of *The French Revolution*:

This is not so much a history, as an epic poem; and notwithstanding, or even in consequence of this, the truest of histories. It is the history of the French Revolution, and the poetry of it, both in one; and on the whole no work of greater genius, either historical or poetical, has been produced in this country for many years.[59]

The French Revolution

4

The Grocer and the King of Kings

In the tortured opening of *The French Revolution*, the reader senses something of Carlyle's anxiety as he set out, 'alone: without models, without *limits*', to write a new kind of history. To his brother John he confided that he had at last begun 'quite an Epic Poem of the Revolution . . . but the task of shaping and uttering it will be frightful',[1] a task made more frightful still by the accidental burning of the entire first volume. But the confusions of the opening, in addition to reflecting Carlyle's anxieties, serve important ends of their own:

President Hénault, remarking on royal Surnames of Honour how difficult it often is to ascertain not only why, but even when, they were conferred, takes occasion, in his sleek official way, to make a philosophical reflection. "The Surname of *Bien-aimé* (Well-beloved)," says he, "which Louis XV bears, will not leave posterity in the same doubt. This Prince, in the year 1744, . . . was arrested at Metz by a malady which threatened to cut short his days. At the news of this, Paris, all in terror, seemed a city taken by storm: the churches resounded with supplications and groans; the prayers of priests and people were every moment interrupted by their sobs: and it was from an interest so dear and tender that this Surname of *Bien-aimé* fashioned itself,—a title higher still than all the rest which this great Prince has earned."

(2: 1)

The awkward syntax of the first sentence, the uncertain anchoring of the reader in time or place, the un-Gibbonian abruptness of beginning upon a casual remark that seems to lead nowhere and is spoken by someone about whom we are told virtually nothing (who is Hénault? of what is he President?)—this muddled start underscores Carlyle's conviction that in our 'vague shoreless Universe' (2: 9), where 'every single event is the offspring not of one, but of all other events, prior or contemporaneous' (27: 88), all beginnings must be arbitrary, necessary fictions by which the historian shapes into a coherent narrative the 'ever-fluctuating chaos of the Actual' (2: 10).

The book opens with a transient illness that occurred almost a half-century before the Revolution; yet the long-deceased Louis XV and his eulogist-historian Hénault live in the continuous present that constitutes the ground of action in *The French Revolution*. That Hénault 'remarks' and 'says' rather than 'writes' (or 'wrote'—he died in 1770) reminds us that, for Carlyle, history and the human voice are inseparable, the past a mere 'slumberous mumblement' (6: 3) until shaped into articulate life by the historian. Hence this most vocal of histories opens, as it closes, with the *spoken* word.

Carlyle's avoidance of the past tense removes the distancing frame from the historical picture and thrusts both narrator and reader into the field of action. He thereby furthers his great aim as a stylist to portray not the '*hearsays* of things' but their 'bodily concrete coloured presence'.[2] But primarily he writes in the historical present because no prior act, physical or moral, is ever without consequences for the present and future. 'A most lying thing that same Past Tense always', he writes, for it denies the 'wondrous . . . contiguity' of 'all times and places with this our actual Here and Now'; and it mutes 'the haggard element of Fear' that dwells constantly and only in the present, 'haunting us, tracking us; running like an accursed ground-discord through our lives (4: 81; 5: 160-1). Yet the historian's subject is the past, and by insisting that the past exists only in the 'ever-fluctuating chaos' of the present, Carlyle subverts the whole historical enterprise. This is precisely what he does throughout *The French Revolution*, which is about the impossibility of depicting the event ('tongue of man cannot' possibly describe it (3: 112)) and is also the most powerful account of the event in English.

Carlyle casts doubt not only on the pastness of the past, but also on the solidity of the present: 'For ours is a most fictile world; and man the most fingent plastic of creatures. A world not fixable; not fathomable!' (2: 6). The result is a strange interchange whereby the past, displaced into a continuous present, is charged with hyperreality, and the present, by contrast, appears phantasmagoric. Thus Carlyle portrays Louis XV as a mere '*Solecism Incarnate*' during his ineffectual reign; but at the moment of his death, when he steps outside time altogether, Carlyle endows him with a humanity far greater than he ever possessed in life.* Rooted in time, the narrative works to annihilate time.

This displacement of past and present, with its associated inversions of the illusory and the real, is especially striking in a narrative

---

* 'Poor Louis, Death has found thee. . . . Thou, whose whole existence hitherto was a chimera and scenic show, at length becomest a reality. . . .' See above, p. 24.

filled with eye-witness reports and marked by an obsessive concern with the authenticity of observed detail. The sequence of events from the death of Louis XV through the beheading of Robespierre moves with ever-accelerating speed, but Carlyle counterpoints the linear march of calendar time with intimations of a world beyond time. The two opening paragraphs illustrate this counterpointing. In the first, set in 1744, Louis is ill and all Paris grieves; in the second Louis is dying but Paris is indifferent:

". . . and it was from an interest so dear and tender that this Surname of *Bien-aimé* fashioned itself,—a title higher still than all the rest which this great Prince has earned."

So stands it written; in lasting memorial of that year 1744. Thirty other years have come and gone; and "this great Prince" again lies sick; but in how altered circumstances now! Churches resound not with excessive groanings; Paris is stoically calm: sobs interrupt no prayers. . . . The shepherd of the people has been carried home from Little Trianon, heavy of heart, and been put to bed in his own Château of Versailles: the flock knows it, and heeds it not. At most, in the immeasurable tide of French Speech (which ceases not day after day, and only ebbs towards the short hours of night), may this of the royal sickness emerge from time to time as an article of news. Bets are doubtless depending; nay, some people "express themselves loudly in the streets." But for the rest, on green field and steepled city, the May sun shines out, the May evening fades; and men ply their useful or useless business as if no Louis lay in danger.

On first reading, the two paragraphs appear to follow the dictates of chronology, moving sequentially from a half-century before the Revolution to its eve in 1774. The thirty-year interval separating the paragraphs, however, has not been 'passed' but abruptly elided. We have no sense of moving through the dense flow of years but seem instead suddenly transported from one part of the century to another. Take a minor instance with major repercussions: the verbally quirky *other* in 'Thirty other years have come and gone; and "this great Prince" again lies sick . . .'. The word would be superfluous in any history except this one. Here it suggests that the narrator has witnessed not only these thirty pre-Revolutionary years but all other years and times, in the long perspective of which these few have passed in a twinkling.

Although the narrator avoids the first person, the reader everywhere senses his controlling presence, the covert 'I' directing our attention to times and places far removed from the field of action.

The organ that makes possible such privileged vision is the 'Eye of History' (2: 5, 15, 134). Through this narrative invention we penetrate the thick curtains that drape the dying Louis's bed-chamber; we rise high above the crowd gathered at Versailles for the procession of the States-General; we capture in a single glance the assembled notables of France, Xerxes weeping over his vast army, Napoleon retreating from Moscow, and 'some two centuries' of popular revolution that lie ahead (2: 132–3). As we move further into *The French Revolution*, the 'Eye of History' encompasses ever-widening vistas of time and space, but we sense the narrator's synoptic eye from the start. We are in the churches and streets of Paris in the simultaneous 'now' of 1744/1774, but we also follow Louis to his sickroom at Versailles. With the brief pastoral that closes the second paragraph, we enter a much wider field of action, the steepled towns and green fields of France, the great diurnal circuit of labour and rest in which Louis figures as a distant nullity.

The same omniscient narrative consciousness makes itself felt in 'the immeasurable tide of French Speech' (2: 2) that courses through the country night and day. First heard in the opening paragraphs, this verbal tide is personified as the Voice of France (2: 117) and sweeps away the *ancien régime*. Nothing in *The French Revolution* is more remarkable than this incessant evocation of sound. It is as if Carlyle, who was so sensitive to noise that he soundproofed his study with double walls, *heard* the Revolution in his head as he wrote.

At first the Voice of France is mute or half-forms itself into an inar-ticulate moan. In response to hunger and outrage—an ancient law allowed a lord returning from the hunt 'to kill not more than two Serfs, and refresh his feet in their warm blood and bowels' (2: 12)— the people in 1775 present a petition of grievances at Versailles; they are answered by the construction of a huge new gallows and the hang-ing of two petitioners (2: 34–5). That towering gallows and its mute freight stand like a sign at the start of Volume I, with 'Twenty-five dark savage Millions, looking up, in hunger and weariness, to that *Ecce-signum* of theirs "forty feet high" . . .' (2: 53). The twenty-five million are 'untaught, uncomforted, unfed! A dumb generation; their voice only an inarticulate cry . . .' (2: 34). If they protest at all, their voices rise feebly, 'in *Jacqueries*, meal-mobs; low-whimpering of infinite moan: unheeded of the Earth; not unheeded of Heaven' (2: 53). To this barely audible ground-note of discontent, Carlyle contrasts the confused whisperings and tittering intrigues of the Court at Versailles. But the 'tempest of whispers' from Versailles is soon drowned out by the larger roar of the Revolution, 'the voice of all France, this sound that rises. Immeasurable, manifold; as the sound of outbreaking waters . . .' (2: 117).

The many separate voices of France gradually concert themselves into a single voice. 'Are not Mankind', Carlyle writes, '. . . like tuned strings . . . you smite one string, and all strings will begin sounding . . .' (3: 299). The tuning begins with the election of the States-General in the spring of 1789:

. . . this multitudinous French People, so long simmering and buzzing in eager expectancy, begins heaping and shaping itself into organic groups. . . . On all highways is a rustling and bustling. Over the wide surface of France, ever and anon, through the spring months, as the Sower casts his corn abroad upon the furrows, sounds of congregating and dispersing; of crowds in deliberation, acclamation, voting by ballot and by voice,—rise discrepant towards the ear of Heaven.

(2: 121–2)

Here, as always, Carlyle uses sound to orchestrate the mood of the Revolution at any moment. From these initial murmurings and buzzings to the shout that shatters the walls of the Bastille, the Voice of France grows in fury. Like a conjurer evoking 'the Elemental Powers', Camille Desmoulins raises the cry, ' "To arms!" ' and innumerable voices respond ' "To arms!" . . . like one great voice, as of a Demon yelling from the air . . .' (2: 175). The cry echoes across some forty pages of text and 'roars tenfold' (2: 177) as the streets become a 'Fire-Mahlstrom' filled with voices raging as at 'the Crack of Doom!' (2: 191–2). With the fall of the Bastille, Carlyle ends on a trumpeted italic that epitomizes six tumultuous chapters in a single word—*sound*:

The Siege of the Bastille, weighed with which, in the Historical balance, most other sieges, including that of Troy Town, are gossamer, cost, as we find, in killed and mortally wounded, on the part of the Besiegers, some Eighty-three persons: on the part of the Besieged, after all that straw-burning, fire-pumping, and deluge of musketry, One poor solitary Invalid, shot stone-dead (*roide-mort*) on the battlements! The Bastille Fortress, like the City of Jericho, was overturned by miraculous *sound*.

(2: 210)

With this final flourish Carlyle emphasizes, as he does at the end of *The French Revolution*, the disparity between the great historical importance of the Revolution and its relatively low cost in lives. But he is also stressing the power of concerted human speech—the spoken, written, and shouted Voice of France—as the principal instrument of the Revolution.

From the fall of the Bastille to the Oath of National Federation sworn a year later in thunderous unison across the cities and towns of France—'Over Orléans and Blois it rolls, in cannon-recitative; Puy bellows of it amid his granite mountains . . .' (3: 64)—the Voice of France rises in pitch and volume. Accompanied by wild pealings of the tocsin, it reaches a 'deafening screech of madness' (3: 299) during the Terror. It then grows feebler as the last Girondists are beheaded one by one while singing the Marseillaise in dwindling chorus at the foot of the guillotine, and expires altogether in the shriek of Robespierre, 'hideous to hear and see', as Samson the Executioner tears the bandages from his shattered jaw (4: 199, 285).

This vocal 'imagery' is especially prominent in scenes of mass action—the storming of the Bastille, the crowds buzzing and radiating over the highways of France. The prose is rapid and cinematic, now sweeping over 'the wide surface of France', now closing in on a single figure, like 'the Sower [who] casts his corn abroad upon the furrows' as sounds of congregating and dispersing 'rise discrepant towards the ear of Heaven'. In a text so charged with biblical allusions, the solitary Sower seems more a figure in a parable than a peasant working the spring fields. He prepares the way for a phrase like 'the ear of Heaven', and he reminds us that this circumstantial account of a quite recent event (the Revolution was as close to Carlyle's audience as the Second World War is to us) is often written in the idiom of Old Testament prophecy. Of the many voices of the narrator of *The French Revolution*, the most distinctive is that of the biblical prophet who 'reads' secular history as a continuation of ancient Scripture and portrays the Revolution as a modern Apocalypse. The Sower of 1789 plants the seeds of revolution that will be reaped in the Reign of Terror.[3]

This portrayal of modern history as the unfolding of an ancient providential design pervades the narrative from beginning to end. 'Ye and your fathers have sown the wind', Carlyle writes of a glittering royal procession that rides past faces haggard with hunger: 'ye shall reap the whirlwind' (2: 48; cf. Hosea 8: 7). Here the idiom is insistently biblical; elsewhere Carlyle invests the narrative with the fatality of Greek tragedy: the impending fall of Robespierre is the

'fifth-act of this natural Greek Drama . . .' (4: 283). In the eyes of the
narrator-prophet, history is a moral drama of collective crimes and
punishments; but history is also the realization in the life of nations of
the natural cycles that govern the seasons and regulate the growth and
decay of our own bodies. The Sower casting his seeds in the spring of
the Revolution is a biological as well as biblical metaphor, and it is in
his former guise that he reappears in the invocation to growth and
change that opens Volume 2, book 3. All of nature, Carlyle writes,
manifests process and change as it moves

towards prescribed issues. . . . The seed that is sown, it will spring! Given the
summer's blossoming, then there is also given the autumnal withering: so is it
ordered . . . philosophies, societies, French Revolutions, whatsoever man
works with in this lower world. The Beginning holds in it the End,[4] and all
that leads thereto. . . . All grows, and seeks and endures its destinies . . .

(3: 103)

Almost a third of *The French Revolution* consists of these reflective
passages in which the narrative pauses and history broadens into
philosophy.* Action and meditation on the action alternate in a kind of
systole-diastole, just as geographical and temporal perspectives
periodically rise above the barricaded streets of Paris to encompass all
of France and all of time. Set against this wider, cosmic background,
events and actors within the story take on a second significance; what is
'ordered' for man and his works 'in this lower world' implies the
governing presence of a world above this one. In so charged a setting
nothing occurs at random, events and characters cast long symbolic
shadows, living double lives as realities and as emblems. The result is
a narrative rich in allusion in which the forebodings of prophecy and
the inevitabilities of history replace the surprises of fiction. Through
anticipation, repetition, and retrospect the narrative becomes virtually self-validating: the beginning contains the seeds of the end, the
text reflecting in its own intricate design the larger design Carlyle saw
working through history. Thus the Revolution unfolds under the
watchful 'Eye of History', and the agonized Voice of France, although
ignored on earth, rises 'discrepant towards the ear of Heaven, where it
is heeded:

* Charles F. Harrold points out that of the roughly 1,700 paragraphs comprising the
work, 'more than 500 contain no historical material whatever' but express Carlyle's
response to the ideas and events of the Revolution. 'Carlyle's General Method in *The
French Revolution*', *PMLA*, 43 (1928), 1150.

O ye poor naked wretches! and this, then, is your inarticulate cry to Heaven, as of a dumb tortured animal, crying from uttermost depths of pain and debasement? . . . Ye are heard in Heaven. And the answer too will come,— in a horror of great darkness, and shakings of the world, and a cup of trembling which all the nations shall drink.

(2: 13-14)

*

Yet to read *The French Revolution* as a prophetic epic in prose, as it assuredly is in these lines that end in a paraphrase of Isaiah, is to ignore contrary aspects of the work that defy generic labelling and contribute equally to its power. For example, the reader is struck by an abundance of Homeric epithets that in fact deflect the narrative into un-Homeric or anti-Homeric directions. So frequent as to amount to a stylistic tic, the epithets, like all forms of allusion in *The French Revolution*, manifest Carlyle's will to incorporate the whole of the historical and mythical past into the modern moment of which he writes. The epithets also point to Carlyle's preoccupation with history as a species of naming, of the fitting or misfitting of certain appellations to people and events, as with the royal misnomer *Bien-aimé* in the opening lines. All these intentions converge in a dizzying profusion of epithets: Danton, brawny Titan of the Revolution (4: 256); Hercules-Mirabeau, the Cloud-Compeller (3: 137-8); Camille Desmoulins, the bright-fallen Lucifer (2: 236); Scipio-Americanus Lafayette, Hero of two Worlds, but after the hero falters, Lafayette the Gossamer-Colossus (2: 233; 3:266); resolute-tremulous, incorruptible sea-green Robespierre (3: 202);* and finally, 'Sorrowful, incurable Philoctetes Marat; without whom Troy cannot be taken'

---

* Carlyle rings changes on this arpeggio of epithets for several hundred pages. That he allows the humanity of the man to be displaced by his epithets is wholly apt, for he portrays Robespierre as a creature of Formulas. Yet if Carlyle hoists Robespierre on his own rhetorical petard, he does so with finesse and with considerable respect for his historical sources. Robespierre's indubitable devotion to virtue earned from his contemporaries the title 'The Incorruptible', the third element in the double set of oxymorons that make up his epithet: *resolute/tremulous*; *incorruptible/sea-green*. Sea-green Carlyle derives from Mme de Staël's description of Robespierre's prominent forehead veins as *verdâtre*. *Sea-green* suggests something unnatural, almost repugnant about Robespierre's incorruptibility, an effect heightened by the earlier *tremulous*. The first oxymoron, *resolute/tremulous*, nicely captures Robespierre's fanatical fixity of purpose together with a certain fastidiousness and timidity of action. The appearance of so inventively epic an epithet in a work of English prose suggests that Stately, plump Buck Mulligan cannot be far behind.

(4: 8), an epithet that evokes Sophocles and Homer while satirizing David's great icon of the diseased, tubbed martyr of the Revolution.[5]

In this last instance, as with gossamer Lafayette and sea-green Robespierre, Carlyle converts the epithet of heroic poetry into an instrument of mock-epic. This up-ending of genres nicely complements his reversal of the myth of the Titans and Olympians in *The French Revolution*. He takes as the type of all political and generational revolutions the overthrow of the elder Titans by the new Olympian gods. But in the inverted myth of *The French Revolution*, Versailles is a defeated, parodic Olympus. The Court and its defenders are impotent imposters; the uprisen Sansculottes are the Titans, half-infant, half-giant, who emerge from the volcanic, primordial underworld and overturn, in one swoop, the repressive *ancien régime* and the old mythology: 'It was the Titans warring with Olympus,' Carlyle writes of the masses storming the Bastille and beheading its commander; 'and they, scarcely crediting it, have conquered: prodigy of prodigies . . .' (2: 197).

The radical political upheaval, Carlyle suggests, calls for a radical rewriting of the old dynastic myths and a redefinition of the hero. Sea-green Robespierre and Philoctetes Marat are part of that redefinition. They are the anti-heroes of Carlyle's modern epic, as the Brobdingnagian Sansculottes are his equivocal heroes. His comic heroines are the drenched procession of hungry women—'Judiths', 'Menads', 'Amazons', Carlyle calls them—who march from Paris to Versailles like 'a wild unwinged, stork-flight, through the astonished country' and, dripping wet and demanding bread, burst into the National Assembly. Wine, loaves, and sausages circulate 'along the benches; *nor*, according to the Father of Epics, *did any soul lack a fair share of victual*. . . . Thus they, chewing tough sausages, discussing the Penal Code, make night hideous' (2: 256, 272–3).

Like everything else in *The French Revolution*, the Homeric idiom is double-edged. Here the effect is purely parodic; in the earlier panorama of the States-General, as Carlyle introduces the chief actors in his historical drama, each passing before us with his full panoply of epithets, the effect is uncannily like the procession of ships and heroes in Book 2 of the *Iliad*. This mixed use of Homer accords with Carlyle's sense of the incongruities of history and of the human condition. For if history is remembered heroism and the tagging of heroes and heroines with appropriate epithets, it is also absurdity and accident and horror. In this real-life 'Pickleherring Tragedy' (3: 187), as Carlyle calls it, eighty-three theatres and dance halls open their doors every night during the worst of the Terror (4: 206), and doomed prisoners on the eve of their beheading 'act the Guillotine' in fantastic mummery before a satanic Judge dressed in black-face (4: 272).

Although scenes of mock-heroism abound in *The French Revolution*, the mock-heroic was at bottom too tame a game for Carlyle, too constrained by what it parodies, for his imagination needed the freedom to pause and apostrophize a ghastly Hand protruding from a tumbril 'through the heaped embrace of brother corpses, in its yellow paleness, in its cold rigour; the palm opened towards Heaven, as if in dumb prayer . . .' (4: 42). Carlyle tightens the generic screws, as it were, composing his epic on 'the "destructive wrath" of Sansculottism' (2: 212) in a 'ludicro-terrific' (2: 253) idiom poised midway between the Bible and yesterday's newspaper, Homer and Theatre of the Absurd.

Within this improbable world incongruity is the norm and the everyday appears surreal. The narrative gives flesh and sinew to this reversal, making bedfellows of the actual and the spectral. During the long debate in the National Convention over the fate of Louis XVI, the deputies mount the tribune-steps 'like Phantoms in the hour of midnight; most spectral, pandemonial!' (4: 102). The vast hall takes on Miltonic dimensions, yet out of the mythic shadows living men rise to cast mortally real votes: 'see the figure of shrill Sieyes ascend; hardly pausing, passing merely, this figure says, "*La Mort sans phrase*, Death without phrases"; and fares onward and downward.' High in the galleries Carlyle focuses on a contrary reality—boredom, gossip, drinking, while on the floor below, dozing deputies are prodded into wakefulness by passing ushers. 'Figures rise, like phantoms, pale in the dusky lamp-light; utter from this Tribune, only one word: Death. "*Tout est optique*", says Mercier, "The world is all an optical shadow"', (4: 103). The phrase might serve as epigraph for *The French Revolution*.

*

In a world where '*tout est optique*', daily life may be a mere veil between us and a transcendent reality, or there may be nothing but the passing show, an 'ever-working Chaos of Being, wherein shape after shape bodies itself forth . . .' (27: 88). The narrative plays on this ambiguity with inexhaustible virtuosity, now painting in vivid detail, now dissolving into shadow, the day-to-day life of Revolutionary

France. The beginning may contain the seeds of the end, but those seeds bear extraordinary fruit in our 'most fictile world' (2: 6). Carlyle's imagination feeds on those moments when historical fact behaves more strangely than fiction, and characters caught up in great events mimic, consciously or unconsciously, their counterparts in literature and myth. A master of history as documented improbability, he is drawn to the story of the real-life King and Queen who, imprisoned in their own palace, disguise themselves like fairy-tale characters—he as a valet, she as a waiting-maid—and flee for their lives in a huge lumbering coach. Late at night the royal 'Berline' passes under the archway at Varennes, where it is stopped by the astonished M. Sausse, procurator of the sleeping town and owner of a local grocery:

[The King] steps out; all step out. Procureur Sausse gives his grocer-arms to the Queen and Sister Elizabeth; Majesty taking the two children by the hand. And thus they walk, coolly back, over the Market-place to Procureur Sausse's; mount into his small upper story; where straightway his Majesty "demands refreshments." Demands refreshments, as is written; gets bread-and-cheese with a bottle of Burgundy; and remarks, that it is the best Burgundy he ever drank!

Meanwhile the Varennes Notables, and all men, official and non-official, are hastily drawing-on their breeches; getting their fighting gear. Mortals half-dressed tumble out barrels, lay felled trees; scouts dart off to all the four winds,—the tocsin begins clanging, "the Village illuminates itself." Very singular: how these little Villages do manage, so adroit are they, when startled in midnight alarm of war. Like little adroit municipal rattle-snakes suddenly awakened: for their storm-bell rattles and rings; their eyes glisten luminous (with tallow-light), as in rattle-snake ire; and the Village will *sting*.

(3: 181)

The bizarre unreality of the scene is as striking as its indubitable historicity. The bits of local colour, the brief excerpts from contemporary accounts, ground the event in actuality, but in so momentous a setting even the most prosaic details lose their innocence and take on a significance beyond the literal. The dormant metaphor contained within ' "the Village illuminates itself" ' awakens into a glittering, venomous municipal rattlesnake that 'rings' (the tocsin bells) and 'stings' (the aroused National Guard) a King into immobility. The metaphor is itself a sort of snake-in-the-grass, coiled around the bilingual pun on *tocsin/toxin*.

Equally hidden and far more important to Carlyle's design is the scene enacted in the reader's mind alongside the supper in Procureur Sausse's room. In this second scene another King, also in the guise of a servant, orders refreshments in an 'upper room', breaks bread, drinks wine, eats his last supper, is taken captive, tried, and publicly executed at the urging of his own people. Behind the grocer and the king looms the shadow of the King of Kings. Parody is too blunt an instrument for Carlyle's purpose here, Louis too pathetically human a figure to play the role of mock-Christ. Yet irony abounds in the juxtaposition of the Incarnate God and this 'Solecism Incarnate' of the French monarchy, on whom only a few lines earlier Carlyle hung the limp epithet, 'semi-animate phlegm' (2: 22; 3: 180). The full import of the supper at M. Sausse's awaits disclosure in the scene of Louis's execution, with the dipping of handkerchiefs in his blood, the dividing of his puce coat, the murmurs of the municipal councillors, 'It is done, It is done.'[6] Here, as befits Carlyle's typological retelling of modern history, we have only hints and glimmerings: '. . . straightway his Majesty "demands refreshments." Demands refreshments, as is written . . .'. Louis breaks bread and blesses the wine after his fashion ('remarks that it is the best Burgundy he ever drank!'), but he feeds only himself; in this he recalls his namesake at the start of *The French Revolution*, Louis 'the Well-beloved', the shearer and not 'the shepherd of the people'. The archaic, biblical ring of 'straightway' is reinforced by the gratuitous 'as is written', the key that unlocks the passage. 'As is written' of course refers to the printed sources Carlyle is citing, but the quotation marks around ' "demands refreshments" ' have already made it perfectly clear that Carlyle is quoting contemporary accounts of the flight. The redundant phrase points to the scriptural supper that the modern one mirrors, however darkly. The familiar tag, 'as is written', is one half of the biblical formula; the other half, 'so that it might be fulfilled', Carlyle everywhere builds into the narrative of the King's flight, trial, and death.

In so shaping the narrative Carlyle is not distorting or inventing history but getting as close as he can to the events themselves as they were felt and recorded by contemporary witnesses. He knew that the *mémoires* and *pièces officielles* on which he drew were often contradictory and self-serving, especially in assigning responsibility for the King's capture and death. He knew, too, that in an age in which kings were still hedged about with divinity, it was impossible to witness the regicide in the Place de la Révolution without recalling the deicide on Calvary. But the highlighting of such patterns is very different from the fabricating of facts. Here we do well to recall Carlyle's insistence in *Past and Present* on the immeasurable gulf separating 'the poorest historical Fact from all Fiction whatsoever' (10: 46). Nothing could be further from the temper of Carlyle's historical writings than the modern vogue of the quasi-documentary. To blur the boundaries between fact and fiction is, in Carlyle's heightened idiom, to mistake death for life.[7] The king's flight to Varennes reads like a suspense story, his capture and execution like a modern re-enactment of the betrayal and passion of Christ, because that is precisely how they appeared to many who witnessed them.

The room in which the King ' "demands refreshments" ' was in fact located in the 'upper story' of M. Sausse's house, just as Carlyle describes it; but such a detail would not have figured in so many contemporary accounts of the King's arrest, nor would Carlyle have been likely to retain it, were it not for the typological tug exerted on the narrative by the 'upper room' of the Lord's Supper. Almost a century after the royal family spent the night at M. Sausse's, in the autumn of 1885, the Cambridge historian Oscar Browning painstakingly retraced the route of the King's flight, performing the critical last leg of his research—from Châlons to Clermont and thence to Varennes—on a tricycle.* Browning entered what had been M. Sausse's shop, mounted the narrow spiral staircase the King had climbed, and found intact the very room in which Carlyle depicts the captive King holding diminished court. Virtually all else in Carlyle's narrative Browning dismisses as 'inaccurate and untrustworthy from beginning to end'.[8]

Most damaging to Carlyle's claim on us as a serious historian is Browning's assertion that the climax of the narrative—the scene in which his Majesty ' "demands refreshments," *as is written*'—is 'apocryphal . . . a fable', a charge repeated verbatim in the two annotated editions of *The French Revolution* printed in our own century.[9] Since Carlyle's account of the King's capture and 'last supper'

---

* *The Flight to Varennes and Other Historical Essays* (London: Swan Sonnenschein, 1892), p. 53. Browning reconstructs the flight according to his own lights in the first of two essays, and in the second, originally read before the Royal Historical Society in 1886, minutely details his 'Criticism on Carlyle's Account'. The building in which M. Sausse detained the King survived until 1914, when it was demolished by German artillery. See Charles Aimond's *L'Énigme de Varennes* (Paris: J. de Gigord, 1936), pp. 134–5.

is so circumstantial, and since Browning gives no contemporary source, however unreliable, the clear implication is that Carlyle concocted the story in whole or in part. Yet if Carlyle invented it, if he is wilfully false in the least detail, let alone 'from beginning to end', he would be of no interest to us whatsoever. 'As is written' means nothing unless it means, first, 'as actually appears in contemporary records', and second, 'as is written in Scripture'.

Carlyle's authority for the scene, unnoticed by his critics and unacknowledged by himself in the footnotes he usually provides when following a single source so exactly, is the *Mémoires* of the Marquis de Ferrières (1741–1804). Ferrières clearly underlies Carlyle's account of the royal family's descent from the carriage and their touchingly decorous procession to M. Sausse's house, a scene for which Browning asserts 'there is no authority':*

[Le roi] descend le premier; la reine et madame Élisabeth acceptent le bras de Saulse. Le roi prend ses enfans par la main: ils s'acheminent vers la maison du procureur de la commune . . .	He steps out; all step out. Procureur Sausse gives his grocer-arms to the Queen and Sister Elizabeth; Majesty taking the two children by the hand. And thus they walk, coolly back, over the Market-place to Procureur Sausse's . . .

Carlyle preserves the dramatic immediacy of the present-tense original as the royal family mounts the narrow staircase ('un mauvais escalier') and enters the upper room; and he scrupulously refrains from putting into direct quotation what Ferrières—*as is written*—reports indirectly:

Le roi, d'un air content, et affectant une tranquillité qu'il était loin de ressentir, demande un coup à	. . . straightway his Majesty "demands refreshments," as is written; gets bread-and-cheese with a bottle of

---

* Browning, p. 74; Ferrières, 2: 352; Carlyle, 3: 181. Carlyle read Ferrières's *Mémoires* in the three-volume second edition, edited by Berville and Barrière (Paris: Baudouin Frères, 1821–22) and published as part of the larger *Collection des mémoires relatifs à la révolution française*, one of Carlyle's chief sources. At the time of the flight, Ferrières was in Paris serving as deputy of the nobility in the States-General. His letters to his wife describing the King's arrest are quite circumstantial but contain nothing of the scene inside M. Sausse's house that later appears in the *Mémoires*. (See *Correspondance inédite*, edited by Henri Carré (Paris: Armand Colin, 1932), pp. 363–7.) Carlyle's source for this scene is almost certainly Ferrières's *Mémoires*; Ferrières's source, however, remains something of a mystery. That Carlyle does not follow Ferrières's spelling of *Sausse* is not surprising, since there are almost as many variants of the name as accounts of the flight.

boire. Saulse apporte une bouteille de vin de Bourgogne et un morceau de fromage: le roi assure qu'il n'a jamais bu d'aussi bon vin . . .

(2: 352–3)

Burgundy; and remarks, that it is the best Burgundy he ever drank!

(3: 181)

The King's call for 'un coup à boire', suggestive of Jesus's cry of 'I thirst' on the Cross, Carlyle picks up and repeats as ' "demands refreshments" '. The phrases in Ferrières that evoke Jesus's thanksgiving over the passover bread and wine Carlyle translates word-for-word, taking only two minor liberties. Ferrières's 'morceau de fromage' becomes 'bread-and-cheese', a useful clarification for an English audience. The bread also points up the parallel with the Lord's Supper and has the added virtue of having in fact been served to the King, if we can trust the eye-witness account of the Duc de Choiseul, whose *Relation du départ de Louis XVI le 20 juin 1791*, written in prison immediately after the flight, was one of Carlyle's principal sources. Choiseul arrived in Varennes ninety minutes after the King's arrest, climbed the narrow staircase, and forced his way into the upper room. There he found the King and Queen standing near 'une table sur laquelle il y avait du pain, quelques verres . . .'[10] Carlyle's only other liberty is the exclamation mark added at the end of Louis's thanksgiving for the wine, an emphasis justified by the King's hyperbolical praise of M. Sausse's burgundy. But the exclamation mark serves as more than a stage direction to the reader indicative of how Louis proclaims his lines. Like the reiterated 'demands refreshments' and the redundant 'as is written', the exclamation expresses Carlyle's own astonishment that so improbable a scene veritably occurred.*

* The episode at M. Sausse's, like the circumstances surrounding the entire flight, is inherently improbable, as Carlyle repeatedly suggests. Yet Carlyle's narrative is accurate in its essential outlines, and in its details displays considerable sophistication in the handling of conflicting or dubious sources. For a fine assessment of Carlyle as a professional historian, see Hedva Ben-Israel's *English Historians on the French Revolution* (Cambridge: Cambridge University Press, 1968), pp. 136–44. Of Browning's attack on Carlyle, Professor Ben-Israel writes that it 'is, on the whole, trifling' (p. 142). The mitigating 'on the whole' is doubtless due to the one substantive error of fact to which Browning calls attention: Carlyle mis-states the distance between Paris and Varennes as 69 miles instead of the actual 150. By miscalculating the distance but not the duration of the flight ('Sixty-nine miles in Twenty-two incessant hours' [3: 169]), he underestimates the speed of the coach, reducing a respectable pace of 6 or 7 miles an hour to an excruciating crawl, and making of the Berline a more cumbersome vehicle than it in fact was. For further discussion of Carlyle's accuracy, see above, p. 41, and below, p. 103.

*

Early in the King's aborted flight to the Marquis de Bouillé and safety the Berline enters the woods of Bondy. As always Carlyle makes the reader aware of the larger natural environment in which human events take place, from the local weather to the seasons and greater circuits of the stars. On this shortest night of the year—21 June 1791—the cover of darkness is at its thinnest when the coach enters the forest on its flight to the east. An emaciated herb-merchant is the only human figure visible from the carriage. The reader, like the royal party inside the Berline, pays him little notice, but he figures importantly a few pages later, for he recognizes the occupants and alerts the authorities to their flight. This living scarecrow of an herb-merchant, real enough to have secured a footnote in history, also serves Carlyle as a spectral amphibian in a paragraph that links the living and the dead, the local and the cosmic:

. . . And so they rush there, not too impetuously, through the Wood of Bondy:—over a Rubicon in their own and France's History.
   Great; though the future is all vague! If we reach Bouillé? If we do not reach him? O Louis! and this all round thee is the great slumbering Earth (and overhead, the great watchful Heaven); the slumbering Wood of Bondy,—where Longhaired Childeric Donothing was struck through with iron; not unreasonably, in a world like ours. These peaked stone-towers are Raincy; towers of wicked D'Orléans. All slumbers save the multiplex rustle of our new Berline. Loose-skirted scarecrow of an Herb-merchant, with his ass and early greens, toilsomely plodding, seems the only creature we meet. But right ahead the great Northeast sends up evermore his grey brindled dawn: from dewy branch, birds here and there, with short deep warble, salute the coming Sun.

(3: 163-4)

The journey eastward through the Wood of Bondy is also a journey backward through time, to Caesar's Rome and to Longhaired Childeric, father of the conqueror of ancient Gaul. Of the many ghosts who accompany Louis XVI through Carlyle's pages, perhaps the most haunting are the long-haired Merovingian Kings who first appear in the opening pages and twice reappear with Louis on his ill-fated flight to Montmédy. *The French Revolution* is plotted around a series of royal processions, including Louis's forced return to Paris after his capture at Varennes. But the first of these processions is, fittingly, a procession of ghosts occasioned by the death of Louis

XVI's grandfather, Louis the Well-beloved. 'Sovereigns die and Sovereignties', Carlyle comments: 'The Merovingian Kings, slowly wending on their bullock-carts through the streets of Paris, with their long hair flowing, have all wended slowly on,—into Eternity. . . . Charles the Hammer, Pepin Bow-legged, where now is their eye of menace, their voice of command?' (2: 7). Along with the skeletal gatherer of herbs, the Merovingian Kings, each trailing his epithet, silently track Louis XVI as the Berline winds through the Wood of Bondy.

The long temporal vistas prepare us for the leap in perspective in which the narrator takes a god's-eye view of the scene below. The King dwindles to his mere Christian name ('O Louis!'), and in a single sweeping glance the narrator gazes on the slumbering Earth and the 'great watchful Heaven', brooding like an anxious parent over its charge. The herb-merchant plodding along the road keeps the scene half-anchored to earth, as does the 'multiplex rustle' of the Berline and the pre-dawn singing of the birds. However heightened the prose, it is grounded in observed fact: the orientation of the coach to the first streakings of the brindled dawn—'right ahead [out of] the great Northeast'—is exactly accurate for the summer solstice on the Paris–Châlons road.

In a scene so precisely observed yet so spectral the warbling of the birds from 'dewy branch' has a touch of triteness that undercuts even as it proclaims itself 'poetic'. Carlyle is importing the idiom of eighteenth-century pastoral into a passage that mixes styles and genres as boldly as it mixes worlds. The phrase 'grey brindled dawn' looks back half-fondly, half-ironically, to the rosy-fingered dawns of Homer. The Homeric epithet also anticipates the great lines that conclude the paragraph. Like the pre-dawn lines that end Book Eight of the *Iliad*, as the poet glances above the thousand campfires to the high cold light of the stars, Carlyle looks beyond all terrestrial boundaries to hail the Great High King, the Sun:

Stars fade out, and Galaxies; Street-lamps of the City of God. The Universe, O my brothers, is flinging wide its portals for the Levee of the GREAT HIGH KING. Thou, poor King Louis, farest nevertheless, as mortals do, towards Orient lands of Hope; and the Tuileries with *its* Levees, and France and the Earth itself, is but a larger kind of doghutch,—occasionally going rabid.

(3: 164)

Miraculously poised between mockery and sublimity, the lines belong to a genre of Carlyle's inventing—cosmic pastoral. The great English nature-poets of the nineteenth century—Wordsworth and Ruskin, for example—are poets of the earth, of 'the living inhabitation of the world—the grazing and nesting in it,—the spiritual power of the air, the rocks, the waters. . .'.[11] Carlyle's imagination, however, is rarely engaged by the features of natural landscape.* The genius that his contemporaries expended on the depiction of nature Carlyle displaces upon the cosmos, as in the metaphor, dazzling as the new gaslights of London,[12] of the stars as 'Street-lamps of the City of God' (3: 164). Here, or in the passage from *Sartor Resartus* that describes, seemingly from outer space, the living skin of our planet as a 'habitable flowery Earth-rind' spinning on its dark foundations (1: 207), Carlyle creates a macrocosmic poetry in which he naturalizes the sublime, a kind of 'natural supernaturalism' in reverse. In such a world, Heaven flinging open its portals for the rising of the Sun-King is only a phrase away from 'poor King Louis', descended from the great 'Roi-Soleil' and now fleeing his rabid doghutch of a palace for 'Orient lands of Hope' (3: 164), a Solecism Incarnate rushing eastward towards the birthplace of the King of Kings. Mock-heroism and lyric exaltation combine as Carlyle satirizes the elaborate court rituals of the bedding

---

* One thinks of the birds warbling from 'dewy branch', or of this description of sunset as the Berline passes the Mill of Valmy:

> The great Sun hangs flaming on the utmost Northwest; for it is his longest day this year. The hill-tops rejoicing will ere long be at their ruddiest, and blush Good-night. The thrush, in green dells, on long-shadowed leafy spray, pours gushing his glad serenade, to the babble of brooks grown audibler; silence is stealing over the Earth. Your dusty Mill of Valmy, as all other mills and drudgeries, may furl its canvas, and cease swashing and circling. The swenkt grinders in this Treadmill of an Earth have ground out another Day; and lounge there, as we say, in village-groups; movable, or ranked on social stone-seats. . . .
>
> (3: 173)

Hilltops blush, brooks babble, silence steals over the earth —and Carlyle nods, or seems to; yet at bottom the passage is no more trite than those weathered stone medallions of the seasons carved on church porches with bent figures planting and harvesting. Even the conventional painting of the foreground has its keenly perceived details, like the leaves 'long-shadowed' by the setting sun, the brooks grown louder as human labour grows quieter, the 'social stone-seats'. But what most redeems the passage is Carlyle's genius for enveloping the familiar in an atmosphere of the unfamiliar, his sudden transit from the natural to the preternatural and back again. The village mill at Valmy enlarges before our eyes into the vast Treadmill of Earth; the 'glad serenade' of the thrush appears intentionally alien in the face of the daily grind of human labour. Beneath the lilting pastoral Carlyle wants us to sense the much fiercer reality soon to fracture the old diurnal rhythms. And so the mellifluous gush of the thrush ends in the harsh Anglo-Saxon reality of the 'swenkt' ('tormented') villagers as the Berline rushes obliviously by.

and rising of the Bourbon Kings, whose sun is soon to set for ever, and celebrates the eternally-recurrent *levée* of the Great High King of Heaven.

5

Narrative Voices

Otto Jespersen once suggested that the so-called historical present be termed the 'dramatic present', a suggestion that any reader of *The French Revolution* would readily endorse.[1] The action seems to take place before our eyes, yet despite our recollection of hosts of contending persons and voices, there is little dialogue in *The French Revolution*. And despite our awareness of Carlyle's controlling presence, he almost never speaks in the first-person singular. He often adopts the editorial 'we' ('may we not say . . . as we often repeat . . .'), but this bland plural is the least distinctive of the many voices that contend for our attention. Just how the narrator manages to place himself both above and within the action, to depict and at the same time to impersonate his own characters, is the great rhetorical puzzle of *The French Revolution*, but such narrative sleights of hand could not occur without the 'dramatic present'.

At the start of the King's trial, the narrator stations himself among the expectant crowd of deputies, but as Louis enters and 'looks round', both narrator and reader begin to see out of the King's eyes and to think his thoughts. Disarmed by the dramatic present, we slip effortlessly into the royal 'we', feel the shock of having our past-tense reverie broken into by Barrère's abrupt, ' "Louis, you may sit down" ', the abbreviated title portending our abbreviated life:

The singular Procession fares on . . . Santerre holding Louis's arm with his hand. Louis looks round him, with composed air, to see what kind of Convention and Parliament it is. Much changed indeed:—since February gone two years, when our Constituent [Assembly], then busy, spread fleur-de-lys velvet for us; and we came over to say a kind word here, and they all started up swearing Fidelity; and all France started up swearing, and made it a Feast of Pikes; which has ended in this! Barrère, who once "wept" looking up from his Editor's-Desk, looks down now from his President's-Chair, with a list of Fifty-seven Questions; and says, dry-eyed: "Louis, you may sit down." Louis sits down. . . .

(4: 92–3)

Nothing is more characteristic of *The French Revolution* than these narrative glides from third person to first and back again. With the enhanced mobility of the dramatic present, the narrator crosses the barriers of time, place, and person that separate *then* from *now*, *there* from *here*, *they* from *we*, thought from speech. The result of these crossings is not confusion but greatly heightened realization. Vernon Lee [Violet Paget] makes just this point by transcribing all the verbs in a passage from *The French Revolution* from the present to the past.[2] The effect of her 'travesty', as she calls it, is devastating. Immediacy and narrative suspense are greatly diminished, as we would expect; but in addition the voice of the prophet-historian disappears from the page, along with the coherence of the narrative itself. The language is slack and uninflected, like a dramatic monologue of Browning's spoiled by retelling in the third person, past tense. Perhaps the subtlest effect of the travesty is the loss of dialogue, or what might better be called *implied speech*. Although not a word of actual dialogue is spoken in the original passage, implied dialogue figures most importantly, and it is this reader-generated shadow speech that vanishes in the travesty. The date is 13 July, 1793, and Charlotte Corday is stalking Marat. For the moment we let Carlyle's tenses stand untouched:

> About eight on the Saturday morning, she purchases a large sheath-knife in the Palais Royal; then straightway, in the Place des Victoires, takes a hackney-coach: "To the Rue de l'Ecole de Médecine, No. 44." It is the residence of the Citoyen Marat!—The Citoyen Marat is ill, and cannot be seen; which seems to disappoint her much. Her business is with Marat, then? Hapless beautiful Charlotte; hapless squalid Marat! From Caen in the utmost West, from Neuchâtel in the utmost East, they two are drawing nigh each other; they two have, very strangely, business together.—Charlotte, returning to her Inn, despatches a short Note to Marat; signifying that she is from Caen, the seat of rebellion; that she desires earnestly to see him, and "will put it in his power to do France a great service." No answer. Charlotte writes another Note, still more pressing; sets out with it by coach, about seven in the evening, herself. Tired day-labourers have again finished their Week; huge Paris is circling and simmering, manifold, according to its vague wont: this one fair Figure has decision in it; drives straight,—towards a purpose.
>
> (4: 168)

We rush through the paragraph to reach the foreknown climax, but Carlyle has in fact co-opted us into performing the passage as we read it. He supplies the script and stage directions, as it were, and we enact the scene in our heads. This illusion of enactment is wholly lost in Vernon Lee's transcription:

> About eight on the Saturday morning she purchased a large sheath knife in the Palais Royal; then straightways, in the Place des Victoires, took a hackney coach: "To the Rue de l'Ecole de Medicine [*sic*], No. 44." It was the residence of the Citoyen Marat! The Citoyen Marat was ill, and could not be seen; which seemed to disappoint her much. Her business was with Marat, then? Hapless beautiful Charlotte; hapless squalid Marat!

In this altered version the quotation marks around ' "To the Rue de l'Ecole de Medicine, No. 44" ' make no sense: the words are spoken by no one and heard by no one. But in the dramatic present of the original, the quoted phrase can only be Charlotte's impatient command to the coachman, uttered 'straightway' as she enters the carriage. The inertness of the travesty is also evident in the past-tense announcement, addressed to nobody, that 'The Citoyen Marat was ill, and could not be seen'. In the original we hear the implied exchange, complete with an authenticating touch of French ('The *Citoyen* Marat is ill, and cannot be seen'), between Charlotte and an unidentified speaker—Marat's friend and housekeeper, as we learn in the next paragraph. Without benefit of conventional signs of dialogue, the unaltered narrative takes us into the midst of an altercation outside Marat's apartment, where we overhear the determined Charlotte exclaim, 'It is the residence of the Citoyen Marat!' as if her initial demand to see him had been refused seconds before our own arrival on the scene. The friend's jealously protective reply ('The Citoyen Marat is ill, and cannot be seen') makes sense only in response to a prior request of Charlotte's, just as the question in search of an asker—'Her business is with Marat, then?'—makes sense only as the friend's unspoken foreboding as Charlotte turns away from Marat's door.*

---

* 'Her business is with Marat, then?' is an interrogative in declarative form, a kind of colloquial and anglicized 'n'est-ce pas?' We have no difficulty intoning such implied speech exactly as Carlyle intends, although our clue to the rising intonation comes only with the mark at the end. Carlyle often moves from narration into impersonation via these declarative questions. My own favourite example occurs in 'The Insurrection of Women', just after a deputation returns from an audience with the King at Versailles:

> Behold, however, the Twelve She-deputies return from the Château. Without President Mounier, indeed; but radiant with joy, shouting "*Life to the King and his House.*" Apparently the news are good, Mesdames? News of the best! Five of us

With that departure the narrator's glance shifts to the distant perspective of Charlotte's return across Paris at dusk. Transposing this part of the paragraph into the past and pluperfect is as damaging as the earlier transposition; here, however, it is not the illusion of dialogue that vanishes but the controlling voice of the narrator, which now sounds halting and disjointed:

Charlotte wrote another note, still more pressing; set out with it by coach, about seven in the evening, herself. Tired day labourers had again finished their work [*sic*]; Paris was circling and simmering, manifold, according to its wont: this one fair Figure had decision in it; drove straight, towards a purpose. . . .

The power of the original lies in its simultaneous depiction of two worlds in two distinctly different narrative voices, the reportorial and the prophetic. The first voice is abrupt, documentary, mimetic of the rush and confusion of daily life ('"To the Rue de l'Ecole de Médecine, No. 44"'). The second voice rises above events, transcends history, sees the larger design that binds 'utmost West' to 'utmost East', looks down upon huge Paris 'circling' below, and foretells infallibly the swift accomplishment of Charlotte's purpose. The dramatic present is Carlyle's bridge between these two voices and two worlds; alter it, and the narrative collapses. The Carlylean yoking of the phenomenal and noumenal, of history as accident and history as providential design, pulls apart. The transposed narrative also ceases to express Carlyle's conviction that all of history is *now*,

---

were admitted to the internal splendours, to the Royal Presence. This slim damsel, "Louison Chabray, worker in sculpture, aged only seventeen," as being of the best looks and address, her we appointed speaker. On whom, and indeed on all of us, his Majesty looked nothing but graciousness. Nay when Louison, addressing him, was like to faint, he took her in his royal arms, and said gallantly, "It was well worth while (*Elle en valût bien la peine*)." Consider, O Women, what a King!

(2: 265)

Only the first sentence bears any resemblance to straight narration. The jubilation of the deputies in the second sentence is followed by the declarative question of the third—'Apparently the news are good, Mesdames?'—an unanchored interrogative asked either of the characters by the narrator or of the twelve deputies by their compatriots. The question hovers ambiguously between the two possible speakers, but *Mesdames* suggests a French interlocutor, and with the answer of the deputies—'News of the best! Five of *us* were admitted . . .'—it becomes clear we are witnessing a scene consisting almost entirely of dialogue, including the question from the crowd of eager women, the answer of their deputies, and the speech-within-a-speech of the King, complete with retranslation back into the French. To the English ear the dialogue sounds heavily accented, so ingeniously has Carlyle insinuated French idioms and intonations into the gallicized English of the passage.

that every event is contiguous with 'all other events, prior or contemporaneous' (27: 88).

A final word about tenses: because the past occurs so rarely in *The French Revolution*, it conveys a deadly finality. Except for the very last sentence, the narrative of the King's execution is in the dramatic present. We watch Louis mount the scaffold; we lose his last words in the roll of the drums; we witness the strapping of the desperate King to the plank, the clanking of the axe. Then with dramatic suddenness the narrative drops into the past, and in a single sentence of liturgical simplicity Carlyle gives the King's age in years, months, and days. The shift in tense rings like a bell tolling Louis out of time and into eternity, his age forever fixed at 'Thirty-eight years four months and twenty-eight days' (4: 111). The tense-shift at the moment of Charlotte Corday's death occurs in mid-sentence and is made especially memorable by the accident of a blush she carries from life into death, red on red as the executioner lifts her severed head above the crowd. Her transit out of time occurs in the narrow space on either side of a semi-colon:

At the Place de la Révolution, the countenance of Charlotte wears the same still smile. The executioners proceed to bind her feet; she resists, thinking it meant as an insult; on a word of explanation, she submits with cheerful apology. As the last act, all being now ready, they take the neckerchief from her neck; a blush of maidenly shame overspreads that fair face and neck; the cheeks were still tinged with it when the executioner lifted the severed head, to show it to the people.

(4: 171)

*

I have described two distinct narrative styles in *The French Revolution*, the reportorial and the prophetic, but there are nearly as many different narrative voices in the work as there are historical personages. The Old Testament prophet is familiar to us, but very little has been said of his opposite number—the *blagueur* who comments ironically on the action and makes dark jokes about the sharpness of the 'national razor'. This prophet-turned-ironist achieves a kind of comic apotheosis in the closing paragraphs, in which the narrator impersonates the 'Arch-quack Cagliostro', a character from 'The Diamond Necklace', and then vanishes in a puff of rhetorical smoke.

Midway between the prophet and his *alter ego*, the quack, is the narrator as working historian, digging, seeking, sorting, very much in evidence as he struggles to wrest order from his intractable materials: 'To describe this Siege of the Bastille . . . perhaps transcends the talent of mortals. Could one but, after infinite reading, get to understand so much as the plan of the building!' (2: 191). Close kin to the working historian but more philosophical is the author of speculative passages on the causes of the Revolution and the nature of historical change. This is the voice that speaks to us in the invocations to the various books, and that John Holloway characterizes as 'the Victorian Sage'.

More distanced from the reader than the sage, and endowed with powers far beyond those of the working historian, is the 'Eye of History', the ocular impresario who presides over the great historical panoramas of *The French Revolution*. At times this personification of narrative omniscience sounds like an epic poet turned modern ironist; at times he steps outside the narrative altogether and speaks with the inhuman detachment of the Olympian gods: 'Unhappy mortals: such . . . throttling of one another, to divide . . . the joint Felicity of man in this Earth; when the whole lot to be divided is such a "feast of *shells!*"' (2: 238).[3] Passages like these turn history into story, tragedy into spectacle. The fictive quality of the flight to Varennes depends upon these sudden elongations of narrative perspective, the narrator now stationed within the fleeing carriage, now rising so high above his characters that they seem to vanish 'from the tissue of our Story' (3: 185). Carlyle's tone here anticipates Thackeray's at the end of *Vanity Fair*, where the omniscient narrator addresses his readers as unhappy children and his characters as puppets to be returned to their wooden box.

In all these many roles, the narrator keeps to his own side of the street, but he is quite capable of crossing over and impersonating a character he is in the act of portraying. These impersonations may be of individuals (Louis XVI at the start of his trial) or they may assume a choric or collective character (the Voice of France). Such narrative glides would be impossible without a kind of neutral textual ground that belongs neither to narrator nor character but can be appropriated by either. On this textual no-man's-land such normally fixed markers as person and point of view become fluid and the reader feels a kind of dizzying mobility, like that of 'poor Abbé Lefèvre', dangling high over the streets of Paris. Lefèvre had been found hiding in the topmost belfry of the Hôtel-de-Ville by a crowd of angry women and hanged there, 'in the pale morning light; over the top of all Paris, which swims in one's failing eyes . . .'. Paris swims before *one's* failing eyes—not *Lefèvre's*—because in that vertiginous instant distinctions of person are blurred, and narrator, character, and reader are drawn into the same orbit.*

The multiple perspectives of this scene converge upon a single word; in a later scene of mass confusion and terror—the murder of thirty non-jurant priests during the September massacres—the shifts in point of view cannot be so precisely pinpointed, for Carlyle places us both inside and outside the carriages that convey the priests to their death; we are both the attacking mob and the assaulted clergy:

Carriages enough stand deserted on the streets; these six move on [to the Abbaye Prison],—through angry multitudes, cursing as they move. Accursed Aristocrat Tartuffes, . . . Priests of Beelzebub and Moloch . . .!—Such reproaches have the poor Nonjurants to endure, and worse; spoken-in on them by frantic Patriots, who mount even on the carriage-steps; the very Guards hardly refraining. Pull up your carriage-blinds?—No! answers Patriotism, clapping its horny paw on the carriage-blind, and crushing it down again. Patience in oppression has limits: we are close on the Abbaye, it has lasted long: a poor Nonjurant, of quicker temper, smites the horny paw with his cane; nay, finding solacement in it, smites the unkempt head, sharply and again more sharply, twice over,—seen clearly of us and of the world. It is the last that we see clearly. Alas, next moment, the carriages are locked and blocked in endless raging tumults; in yells deaf to the cry for mercy, which answer the cry for mercy with sabre-thrusts through the heart. The thirty Priests are torn out, are massacred about the Prison-Gate, one after one. . . .

(4: 26-7)

As one of the mob mounts the carriage steps, the narrator's eye turns to the priests within and we hear, as if coming through the dropped blinds, the angry challenge of the Patriot standing on the steps—'Pull up your carriage-blinds?—No!' With the narrator's change of place comes a change in class and idiom: the frantic Patriot riding outside now appears, to the menaced eyes within, to be subhuman, a 'horny paw' to be beaten off with a cane. The locus of the narrative remains within the carriage—the beating of the horny paw is the last thing '*we* see clearly' in this world—until the forcible eviction at the prison gate, when the perspective shifts back from the dying priests to their executioners.

* 'A horrible end?' the passage concludes: 'Nay the rope broke, as French ropes often did; or else an Amazon cut it. Abbé Lefèvre falls, some twenty feet, rattling among the leads; and lives long years after, though always with "a *tremblement* in the limbs" ' (2: 254).

Carlyle's language, normally ambivalent when depicting the Sansculottes, is here clearly hostile. For it has been coloured by his impulse to impersonate the point of view of his characters, as if one of the anti-Revolutionary priests were telling the story in his own idiom. To borrow an image from Hugh Kenner, the normal language of a narrator in such passages is 'bent' by a character's proximity 'as a star defined by Einstein will bend passing light'.[4] Kenner's simile reminds us that Carlyle's characters not only bend the narrator's idiom but can capture the story itself, momentarily pulling the narrator into their own orbit. One thinks of the spirited adventuress Lamotte as she stands on the brink of exposure in 'The Diamond Necklace'. 'Methinks', the narrator warns, 'stood I in thy pattens, Dame de Lamotte, I would cut and run.—"Run!" exclaims she, with a toss of indignant astonishment: "Calumniated Innocence run?"'[5]

In a world in which characters talk back to their creator, abstractions burst into speech and personifications can kill. The mayor of Étampes, Carlyle tells us, was trampled to death by Hunger, the mayor of St Denis 'hung at the Lanterne, by Suspicion and Dyspepsia' (3: 221). Sansculottism rises like a Brobdingnagian infant from the fiery bowels of the earth and asks of the disconcerted reader, 'What think ye of *me*?'[6] Fear first walks abroad in this hypercharged atmosphere in the guise of 'Preternatural Suspicion', is then mobilized by the Terror as the infamous 'Law of Suspects', and finally breaks into speech in Carlyle's grim parodic conjugation of totalitarian paranoia: ' "I am suspect, thou art suspect, he is suspect, we are suspect, ye are suspect, they are suspect!" ' (4: 250). Actual or imagined speech is everywhere rampant in *The French Revolution*, words shouted in the streets, declaimed in the Assembly, broadcast on handbills, words drowned out in a torrent of still more words, as with the peevish squabbling of the courtiers over the causes of their fall from power:

Nay, answer the Courtiers, it was Turgot, it was Necker, with their mad innovating; it was the Queen's want of etiquette; it was he, it was she, it was that. Friends! it was every scoundrel that had lived . . . from the time of Charlemagne and earlier.

(2: 58)

It was he, it was she, it was that is dialogue scored as pure sound-effect, a kind of courtly rhubarb, rhubarb, rhubarb. The hectoring, pulpit voice of the narrator—'Friends!'—strikes like a gavel, quells the squabbling courtiers, and reaches all the way to the silent spectator who stands on the edge of the crowd: Carlyle's reader.

In 'this Whirlpool of Words' (2: 101) silence startles, as at the end of the long debate over the King's fate, when the Tribunal 'suddenly ceases droning' and the reader, like one of the dozing deputies, is prodded into wakefulness (4: 100). Revolutions are by turns tedious and apocalyptic, Carlyle suggests, and the reader needs an occasional shake. Much earlier, when D'Espréménil is haranguing the Parlement of Paris, Carlyle abruptly cuts him off at mid-sentence, at once shattering and intensifying the illusion of our actual presence in the Palais de Justice. We can read more of the same, Carlyle adds, in Toulongeon's *Histoire de France depuis la Révolution de 1789* (2: 102). Vast, intricate, vociferous as *The French Revolution* is, at such moments we feel that the events it strains to evoke are vaster, the whirlpool of words beyond our fathoming or ever fully recovering.

This implied world of lost voices and half-glimpsed faces is the sable ground against which the action is highlighted. An old letter, unearthed in the rubble of the Bastille, serves as a type of the workings of Carlyle's historical imagination. Read it, Carlyle urges, and 'long-buried Despair' will at last speak. There follows the anguished petition of a prisoner begging 'news of my dear wife; were it only her name on a card, to show that she is alive!' (2: 198). The prisoner compels Carlyle's imagination because he has no history other than these few stifled words, because he still speaks to us after he and his wife have long lain dead and apart.

The unburied letter reminds us that much of history survives for Carlyle in the artefacts of human speech and little in bones or tools or buildings. The chapter entitled 'A Trilogy' illustrates his fondness for the articulate fragment. The chapter consists of eye-witness accounts of three survivors of the September massacres in Paris, each with a very different perspective. The three harrowing accounts together comprise, as Carlyle puts it, a 'wondrous trilogy, or triple soliloquy: uttering simultaneously, through the dread night-watches, their Night-thoughts,—grown audible to us!' (4: 38). One of the three writers, Abbé Sicard, a revered teacher of mute children and sole survivor of the massacre of the thirty priests, recounts his escape from a high, cage-like cell:

"I tapped gently, trembling lest the murderers might hear, on the opposite door, where the Section Committee was sitting: they answered gruffly, that they had no key. There were three of us in this *violon*; my companions thought they perceived a kind of loft overhead. But it was very high; only one of us could reach it by mounting on the shoulders of both the others. One of them said to me, that my life was usefuller than theirs: I resisted, they insisted: no denial! I fling myself on the neck of these two deliverers; never was scene more touching. I mount on the shoulders of the first, then on those of the second, finally on the loft; and address to my two comrades the expression of a soul overwhelmed with natural emotions."

(4: 35)

The image of the three prisoners stacked like acrobats on each other's shoulders is self-reflexive, an emblem of the chapter itself, with its separate narrators performing 'in wondrous trilogy' while Carlyle oversees and co-ordinates them all. The chapter epitomizes the narrative method of *The French Revolution*: each of the myriad contending voices is partial, fragmented, locked into its own idiosyncratic moment; yet through the overriding voice of the narrator each is orchestrated into the whole.[7]

*

Of all Carlyle's many narrative voices the most moving and, to the modern ear, the strangest, is that of witness and brother. It is as a brother that he takes leave of us in the closing paragraph, and it is as witness to the darkness within history and our own hearts that he testifies so powerfully throughout the book. Like the sight of grown men weeping in public, such intimacy of address is unnerving, and *The French Revolution* is by design a heroically unnerving book.

The narrator first speaks to us as a witness from the noisome sick-room of Louis XV, where his three daughters (called *Graille, Chiffe*, and *Coche* by their father; *Rag, Snip*, and *Pig* by Carlyle) stand alone in attendance on the dying King. Within a single paragraph we see the princesses as children coldly ignored by their royal father, as adults attending his bedside after everyone else has fled his contagion, and as ancient homeless crones fleeing across the face of Europe. In the closing lines the narrator mourns the future fate of the three women:

Poor withered ancient women! in the wild tossings that yet await your fragile existence, before it be crushed and broken; as ye fly through hostile countries, over tempestuous seas, are almost taken by the Turks; and wholly, in the Sansculottic Earthquake, know not your right hand from your left, be this always an assured place in your remembrance: for the act was good and loving! To us also it is a little sunny spot, in that dismal howling waste, where we hardly find another.

(2: 17)

May this place—this passage in my book—be for ever consecrated in remembrance of you three: such is the epitaph Carlyle carves on the page for Rag, Snip, and Pig. The words give voice to what is the deepest of the many emotions in *The French Revolution*, the passion for history as a memorial, for the historian in his ancient bardic role of singer and preserver of the deeds of the noble dead.

Carlyle plays an ironic variation on this theme when he buries Marat, epithets and all, to the accompaniment of an old Homeric formula: Charlotte Corday strikes, and 'there is no Friend of the People . . . left; but his life with a groan gushes out, indignant, to the shades below' (4: 169).* For over five hundred pages Carlyle has portrayed Marat as an infernal pariah hiding in Paris cellars, living apart, a 'cruel *lusus* of Nature', unclean, croaking in voice, sooty in aspect; 'acrid, corrosive, as the spirit of sloes and copperas, is Marat, *Friend of the People*. . . .'[8] Carlyle has no need to make explicit what the reader has all along sensed—the etymological time-bomb ticking away inside the epithet: The People's *Friend* is in reality The People's *Fiend*,† the plutonic demon who presides over the final volume of *The French Revolution*. But with Marat's death comes a kind of victory: the humanity of The People's Friend momentarily triumphs over Carlyle's ferocious antipathy. Marat's brother, he tells us, came from Neuchâtel to implore the Convention to give him Marat's Musket: 'For Marat too had a brother and natural affections; and was wrapped once in swaddling-clothes. . . . Ye children of men!—A sister of his, they say, lives still to this day in Paris' (4: 170). The Convention deified Marat on learning of his murder; Carlyle for the first time bears witness to his humanity.

---

* The most purely Homeric memorial in *The French Revolution*, complete with genealogy and splattered brains, is that of 'poor Jerôme l'Héritier, an unarmed National Guard he too, "cabinet-maker, a saddler's son, of Paris," with the down of youthhood still on his chin,—he reels death-stricken; rushes to the pavement, scattering it with his blood and brains!' (2: 277-8).

† The epithet comes from the radical journal Marat founded in September 1789, *L'Ami du Peuple*. Carlyle's inversion of friend into fiend capitalizes on an etymological accident: *friend* (OE *frēond*) derives from an old form of the verb meaning *to love*; *fiend* (OE *fēond*), from an old form of the verb meaning *to hate*. Until the fifteenth century the vowel sound in both words was identical and plays on the two were common.

The narrator grows in compassion as the events he witnesses gain in ferocity. 'Pity them all, for it went hard with them all', he urges in his choric role of chief mourner: 'Not even the seagreen Incorruptible but shall have some pity, some human love, though it takes an effort' (4: 120). The plea for pity is addressed to the reader, but it is also self-addressed, for *The French Revolution* stretches the moral imagination of its author as well as of its readers. In the pause between the trial and the beheading of Louis XVI, Carlyle reminds us that, at bottom, 'it is not the King dying, but the man! Kingship is a coat: the grand loss is of the skin' (4: 107). When the blade falls a few pages later, we feel the cut all the more keenly, for Carlyle democratizes Louis's dying even as he ennobles the deaths of the less exalted:

Miserablest mortals, doomed for picking pockets, have a whole five-act Tragedy in them, in that dumb pain, as they go to the gallows, unregarded; they consume the cup of trembling down to the lees. For Kings and for Beggars, for the justly doomed and the unjustly, it is a hard thing to die. Pity them all: thy utmost pity. . . .

(4: 107)

In the *Iliad* each of the warriors dies to his own individualizing simile, redeemed however briefly from the anonymity of the general slaughter; in *The French Revolution* no death passes unremarked by the narrator, either in eulogy or, more rarely, in execration. Carlyle buries the sadistic and carbuncular Jourdan 'Coupe-tête' with a curse, but follows the curse with a requiem for all the unnamed dead:

The all-hiding Earth has received him, the bloated Tilebeard: may we never look upon his like again!—Jourdan one names; the other Hundreds are not named. Alas, they, like confused fagots, lie massed together for us; counted by the cart-load: and yet not an individual fagot-twig of them but had a Life and History; and was cut, not without pangs as when a Kaiser dies!

(4: 215–16)

I have brought together three choric passages separated in the text by over one hundred pages; but even in such exaggerated proximity the plea to 'pity them all; for it went hard with them all', is free of sentimentality. If we recall our embarrassment over similar passages of rhetorical insistence in Victorian fiction, we can appreciate the remarkable freedom Carlyle has won for the narrator in *The French Revolution*. Unconstrained by conventions of point of view or the need to create a verisimilar world (he *begins* with the 'real' world of history), the narrator can impersonate Louis XVI, curse Jourdan

Coupe-tête, or eulogize the lone Hand sticking up above the heaped embrace of its brother corpses, 'as if in dumb prayer, in expostulation *de profundis*, Take pity on the Sons of Men!' (4: 42).

Eloquent in tribute to the Hand, the narrator is uncharacteristically laconic in eulogy of Jean Bailly, a distinguished astronomer and first President of the National Assembly. Bailly had figured prominently in the first volume, and by now his long, sensitive, lugubrious face is familiar to the reader. Every detail of the narration underscores the solitary dignity of the old man, the cruelty of the crowd, and the bone-chilling cold that numbs them both:

It is the 10th of November 1793, a cold bitter drizzling rain, as poor Bailly is led through the streets; howling Populace covering him with curses, with mud; waving over his face a burning or smoking mockery of a Red Flag. Silent, unpitied, sits the innocent old man. Slow faring through the sleety drizzle, they have got to the Champ-de-Mars: Not there! vociferates the cursing Populace; such Blood ought not to stain an Altar of the Fatherland: not there; but on that dung-heap by the River-side! So vociferates the cursing Populace; Officiality gives ear to them. The Guillotine is taken down, though with hands numbed by the sleety drizzle; is carried to the River-side; is there set up again, with slow numbness; pulse after pulse still counting itself out in the old man's weary heart. For hours long; amid curses and bitter frost-rain! "Bailly, thou tremblest," said one. "Mon ami, it is for cold," said Bailly, "*c'est de froid.*" Crueler end had no mortal.

(4: 211–12)

The reader hears '*c'est de froid*' as a chattered whisper and silently adds what the narrator leaves unsaid—'*et pas de peur*'. The narrator's final comment is so brief because he too has been numbed by cold and grief; and because his tribute has already been paid in the 'loving minuteness'* of every detail of the narrative.

Seen in this light, the ghastly Hand uprisen as if in prayer is not merely grotesque: it is an emblem of the hopes of mankind awakened by the Revolution and smashed by the Terror. '*Seest* thou that cold

---

* The phrase 'loving minuteness' appears in the chapter entitled 'Mankind', where Carlyle contrasts the 'theatricalities' of the Revolution, such as David's vast outdoor pageants, with 'unpremeditated outbursts of Nature', such as the march of the Parisian women on Versailles. Factitious events are 'like small ale palled', a mere 'effervescence that has effervesced', and may be described from a distance; spontaneous movements deserve the historian's 'loving minuteness' of attention (3: 49). To appreciate the full force of the phrase we must give equal weight to adjective and noun, to the moral idea (intensity of sympathy) that illuminates the stylistic principle (exactitude of realization). The first element enables the historian imaginatively to grasp the past, the second, to portray its 'bodily concrete coloured presence'. See above, p. 30.

Hand . . .' (4: 42), the narrator says in what looks like a question but is in fact an imperative, like the *look, observe, glance,* and *conceive* that alert the reader's attention throughout *The French Revolution*. The last of these imperatives appears in the paragraph describing the execution of the Girondists on the morning of 31 October, 1793. On the previous night, after hearing the verdict of the Tribunal, the lawyer Valazé stabbed himself in the court-room, but his suicide fails to thwart the guillotine:

On the morrow morning all Paris is out; such a crowd as no man had seen. The Death-carts, Valazé's cold corpse stretched among the yet living Twenty-one, roll along. Bare-headed, hands bound; in their shirt-sleeves, coat flung loosely round the neck: so fare the eloquent of France; bemurmured, beshouted. To the shouts of *Vive la République,* some of them keep answering with counter-shouts of *Vive la République.* Others, as Brissot, sit sunk in silence. At the foot of the scaffold they again strike up, with appropriate variations, the Hymn of the Marseillese. Such an act of music; conceive it well! The yet living chant there; the chorus so rapidly wearing weak! Samson's axe is rapid; one head per minute, or little less. The chorus is wearing weak; the chorus is worn *out;*—farewell for evermore, ye Girondins. Te-Deum Fauchet has become silent; Valazé's dead head is lopped: the sickle of the Guillotine has reaped the Girondins all away. "The eloquent, the young, the beautiful and brave!" exclaims Riouffe. O Death, what feast is toward in thy ghastly Halls!

(4: 199)

This remarkable *diminuendo* is itself 'an act of music', Carlyle's requiem for the silencing of the most eloquent voices of France. The rapid run of clauses—'Samson's axe is rapid. . . . The chorus is wearing weak; the chorus is worn *out*'—mimics the tempo of Samson's axe. Into this final silence obtrudes the final horror: the beheading of the already-dead Valazé. The redundance of the act is mimed in the internal rhyme of the subject (*dead head*) and the apt passivity of the predicate (*is lopped*). In its intransitive sense *lop* means *to hang limply, too droop,* and Valazé's lifeless head offers no resistance to the blade. One lops dead limbs from a tree, a sickle lops tall grass; all flesh is as grass, Carlyle reminds us, for the blade of the guillotine makes a grim *sickle* that *reaps away* the Girondists in a harvest of Terror.

A small band of Girondists survives in hiding in the south of France, but the last two are found in a wheat field, their bodies half-eaten by dogs. The narrator's eulogy, borrowed whole from the opening lines of the *Iliad*, gives a new twist to the old Greek horror of posthumous mutilation: 'So many excellent souls of heroes sent down to Hades; they themselves given as a prey of dogs and all manner of birds!' (4: 201). We are now late in the calendar of the Revolution and at the end of the book entitled 'Terror', the mythic Underworld of *The French Revolution*. As befits such a world, the epigram that closes the book is spoken posthumously by the just-beheaded Vergniaud. The epigram now serves double-duty as epitaph: 'As Vergniaud said: "the Revolution, like Saturn, is devouring its own children."'

6

The Revolution Devours Itself

The force of Vergniaud's epigram lies not in its literary grace but its literal and monstrous truth. Throughout the narrative, metaphors become literalized as stark realities, and stark realities, like the uprisen Hand, are transformed into symbols. The placards paraded by an angry Paris mob pursuing Bertier de Sauvigny—'He devoured the substance of the People—He drank the blood of the widow and orphan'—read like pure political hyperbole. But the rhetoric quickly turns into grim retributive reality when the mob tears out Sauvigny's heart and sticks his head on a pike (2: 207–8).

This literalizing of the figurative and figuralizing of the literal has a central function in a work that anatomizes in such detail our complementary impulses to mythologize history and to historicize myth. It is a cliché of writers sympathetic to the Revolution that the *ancien régime* 'lived off the sweat' of the people; for Carlyle the cliché conceals a more pertinent and primitive reality: the *ancien régime* devoured the flesh of the people, the Revolution then devoured the *ancien régime*, and finally in Vergniaud's words, the Revolution devoured itself.[1]

The cycle begins with Carlyle's citation of the ancient privilege, fallen into desuetude, that allowed a lord returning from the hunt to warm his feet in the blood and bowels of 'not more than two Serfs' (2: 12). The middle act in this sequence is the beheading of the quasi-divine Louis XVI, a regicide which is also portrayed as deicide and patricide. The final act is the beheading of the head of the Revolution, Robespierre. But the association of the Revolution with cannibalism has been implicit from the beginning, where Carlyle describes a forty-foot gallows that towers like a 'grim Patibulary Fork' over the starving peasantry (2: 34, 58). The gallows of the old order is replaced by the insatiable guillotine of the new, its huge axe rising and falling 'in horrid systole-diastole' (4: 193).* Imagery of gorging and disgorg-

---

* The vivacity of Carlyle's descriptions of public execution has an element of the perverse, for his revulsion at pain had as its other face an equally strong fascination. At the age of 15 he watched a man ' "hanged for horse-stealing. He was a strong man,

ing, of eating and being eaten, is so prevalent as to suggest that, for Carlyle, revolution is the politics of aggression by ingestion: the 'least blessed' fact on which society rests, he contends, appears to be 'the primitive one of Cannibalism: That *I* can devour *Thee*. What if such Primitive Fact were precisely the one we had (with our improved methods) to revert to, and begin anew from!' (2: 55). This is Carlyle's version of aboriginal social sin, his 'anti-social contract'; fittingly, it appears in a chapter that satirizes the naïve optimism of Rousseau ('Contrat Social').

Fraternity may be the most desirable of social goals, but Carlyle insists that it is scarcely 'natural' and never lasting. The louder the nation 'swears Brotherhood', the sooner it will revert to Cannibalism, he says ominously of the Festival of Federation, a 'universal *Hep-hep-hurrah* [and] . . . National Lapithae-feast of Constitution-making' (3: 70). The fraternal oath-taking, followed so soon by fratricidal bloodletting, puts him in mind of the wedding-feast of Lapiths and Centaurs that degenerated into a battle of legendary ferocity. All the great *fêtes* of the Revolution—the Festival of National Federation, of Reason, of the Supreme Being—Carlyle calls *feasts*, not *festivals*, as if to underscore by his very literalism the primitive and ritual origins of David's neo-classic celebrations of popular enlightenment.

That revolution involves a 'reversion' to 'primitive Fact', an overthrow that is both renewal and regression, lies at the heart of Carlyle's understanding of the upheaval of 1789. The Revolution creates by destroying: it is a 'Fire-Mahlstrom' that annihilates established institutions and a 'world-phoenix' that rises renewed out of its own ashes. Revolution is cyclic, thus in large measure inevitable; and it is inherently generational and familial, like the archetypal revolt of the sons of Uranus against their father. 'That *I* can devour *Thee*' is Carlyle's aggressively ingestive metaphor for class warfare. It is also his Malthusian update of an old story: Cronus (in Roman mythology, Saturn) castrates his father Uranus and, with the aid of his brother Titans, seizes the throne of the world; fearing usurpation by his own

---

grimly silent. His body spun and twitched horribly."' The scene obsessed him, '"until at last I drew the horrible figure on paper exactly as I could, and thenceforth it ceased to haunt me."' (Cited in Fred Kaplan, *Thomas Carlyle: A Biography* (Ithaca: Cornell University Press, 1983) p. 31.) *The French Revolution* is filled with such 'exactly' drawn scenes, acts of exorcism in which Carlyle at once indulges and controls his lifelong fascination with cruelty and violence. Similar tensions play themselves out in his seemingly contradictory traits of compassion and contempt, sentimentality and bullying egotism, generosity and frugality, sensitivity and bigotry.

children, Cronus devours them all except Zeus, by whom he is in turn overthrown.

The association of revolution with patricide and cannibalism was made graphically clear to early nineteenth-century readers in anti-Revolutionary tracts and cartoons. For the modern reader the association is likely to come from another source, *Totem and Taboo*, where Freud advances the ur-revolution of Greek mythology into the shadowy but recognizably human time of pre-history; 'One day the brothers that had been driven out [by the father] came together, killed and devoured their father and so made an end of the patriarchal horde. . . .' In an important essay on 'Psychoanalysis and the Iconography of Revolution', Lee Sterrenburg links this passage to certain nineteenth-century revolutionary myths that depict violent group behaviour as a collective unleashing of primitive impulses latent within modern man. 'Just as primitive man survives potentially in every individual,' Freud writes, 'so the primal horde may arise once more' in any group. Carlyle's argument clearly shares a common cultural origin with Freud's: ' "every man . . . holds confined within him a *mad*-man" '; once society's ' "*fixed ways* of acting and of believing" ' are broken, once the thin ' "Earth-rind of Habit" ' is ruptured, ' "the fountains of the great deep boil forth" ', unleashing the ' "authentic Demon-Empire" ' pent up within each of us.*

To the modern, enlightened mind an authentic Demon-Empire seems a contradiction in terms. Look again, Carlyle urges. Witchcraft, spectres, demonology are now called 'Madness and Diseases of the Nerves', but 'what is Madness, what are Nerves?' Is Luther's picture of the Devil any less real because it was formed inside his head? (1: 207). In *Sartor Resartus* Carlyle explores the persistence of the irrational within the individual psyche; in *The French Revolution* he explores the psychopathology of an entire society. France during the Reign of Terror manifests 'one of the strangest temporary states Humanity was ever seen in. A nation of men, full of wants and void of habits!' (4: 206). Civilization, laboriously built upon the 'dark

---

* See Sterrenburg, 'Psychoanalysis and the Iconography of Revolution', *Victorian Studies*, 19 (1975), 263; and Carlyle, 1: 207 and 2: 38. The cluster of ideas associating revolution with repression first appears in Carlyle's *Journal* of 28 December 1832, while he was reading Thiers's *Histoire de la Révolution Française*: 'French Revolution . . . a stripping bare of the human soul: a fearful bursting out of the Infinite thro' the thin rinds of Habit (of the manufactured Finite) which constrains it and makes it effectively active (industrious) and a Life. How do men act in these surprising circumstances? This is a question well worth asking. . . .' Compare Carlyle's letter to J. S. Mill of 12 January 1833, in Sanders, *Collected Letters*, 6: 302.

foundations' of the 'Demon-Empire', is both sustained and menaced by its origins. The elegant Princess de Lamballe is dragged from her bed and cleft with an axe. Her body 'is cut in fragments; with indignities, and obscene horrors of mustachio *grands-lèvres*, which human nature would fain find incredible . . .' (4: 30). That last clause is perhaps the most despairing Carlyle ever wrote: we devoutly *wish* such acts were unnatural, but they are not, however much we would fain—or feign—otherwise. After cataloguing the myriad ways we abuse and destroy one another, Freud concludes in *Civilization and its Discontents* that '*homo homini lupus*', man is a wolf to man, a polite version of Carlyle's '*I* can devour *Thee*.'[2] Freud's great theme is the irremediable conflict between the demands of instinct and the constraints of civilization, a conflict that he, like Carlyle, couches in myth. For Freud the fate of civilization hinges on the immemorial struggle between Eros and Thanatos, between love and the authentic demon empires of aggression and self-destruction. Who can foresee the outcome, Freud asks, in a chilling final sentence added as Hitler was rising to power. At the end of *The French Revolution* Carlyle reminds us of the Human Tannery at Meudon, where breeches were made from the skins of the guillotined, and he prays that 'there be no second Sansculottism in our Earth for a thousand years' (4: 313). In this context *Sansculottes*—literally, *without knee-breeches*—suddenly stares at us as *without skin*; the term, all along a synecdoche for the revolutionary underclass, now suggests the perennial and frightening vulnerability of the human condition. Is civilization only a 'wrappage', Carlyle had asked in the chapter on Meudon, a cover only skin-deep through which our savage nature 'can still burst, infernal as ever?' (4: 247).*

---

* This most chilling of all paragraphs in *The French Revolution* comes at the end of the book entitled 'Terror the Order of the Day':

> "At Meudon," says Montgaillard with considerable calmness, "there was a Tannery of Human Skins; such of the Guillotined as seemed worth flaying: of which perfectly good wash-leather was made"; for breeches, and other uses. The skin of the men, he remarks, was superior in toughness (*consistance*) and quality to shamoy; that of the women was good for almost nothing, being so soft in texture!—History looking back over Cannibalism, through *Purchas's Pilgrims* and all early and late Records, will perhaps find no terrestrial Cannibalism of a sort, on the whole, so detestable. It is a manufactured, soft-feeling, quietly elegant sort; a sort *perfide*! Alas, then, is man's civilisation only a wrappage, through which the savage nature of him can still burst, infernal as ever? Nature still makes him: and has an Infernal in her as well as a Celestial.

(4: 247

J. Holland Rose dismisses l'Abbé Montgaillard's account as 'one of the many myths of the period', an 'absurdity'. (*The French Revolution: A History*, ed. Rose, 3 vols.

Several times he refers to the Revolution as a *holocaust*, in the Old Testament sense of a burnt offering wholly consumed by fire,[3] but the twentieth-century reader cannot ignore the newer and more terrible sense of the term. To postpone a second holocaust as long as we possibly can, Carlyle urges that we 'understand well what the first was; and let Rich and Poor of us go and do *otherwise*'.* *Let us do otherwise* is the one-line moral of *The French Revolution*. Among its many guises the book is a tract for the times, Carlyle's warning that the England of the 1830s and 1840s—the England of the Birmingham Riots and Engels's *Condition of the Working Class*—would erupt in revolution if it did not feed the hungry and clothe the naked.

*

The one-line moral of *The French Revolution*—'let us do otherwise'—suggests an underlying hostility to the Revolution, but in fact Carlyle's deepest response combined elements of admiration and fear. True, he dreaded civil disorder, and his passion for social justice was in part fuelled by his fear of anarchy. From this perspective, 'let us do otherwise' is the message of a political conservative who valued community over individual liberty and held it more important to feed men than to enfranchise them. Yet the Carlyle who detested civil disorder was also fascinated by violence in all its manifestations. Cataclysmic upheaval within the self or society is his overriding subject; more to our point, he understood revolution to be not a passing aberration but an inevitable and recurrent process, and hence beyond any categorical moral judgement. This moral ambivalence stems not from confusion on Carlyle's part but from the inherent complexity of his subject. Philip Rosenberg, in his defence of Carlyle's radical activism, points to Carlyle's audacity among contemporary English

---

(London: G. Bell, 1913), 3: 289 n.) But the myth was widely believed, however unlikely the fact. Experiments in tanning human skin were reportedly made at Meudon during the reign of Louis XV. The Convention investigated and, according to Rose, dismissed charges that the practice continued during the Revolution. But C. R. L. Fletcher calls attention to a letter in the *Archives Nationales* from the Strasbourg firm of Ziegler & Mauss, 'breeches-makers, addressed to Garnerin, an agent of the Committee in Alsace, proving that they had tanned human skin and made breeches of it, and were prepared to do it again. Garnerin laid the letter before the Committee, which prohibited it altogether.' (*The French Revolution: A History*, ed. Fletcher, 3 vols. (London: Methuen, 1902), 3: 165–6 n. 3.)

* 4: 313. For the source of this bitter allusion to England as the Bad Samaritan, see Luke 10: 37.

intellectuals in depicting the Terror as a ' "New-Birth" ', a ' "Fact of Nature . . . in an Age of Formulas" ', the organization of anarchy into that paradox of paradoxes, 'a revolutionary government'.[4] In the face of this awesome phenomenon, Carlyle transcends the partisanship of the left or of the right: 'To Marat and the Committee of Watchfulness not praise;—not even blame, such as could be meted out in these insufficient dialects of ours; expressive silence rather!'[5] Four years later, in *On Heroes*, he persists in viewing the Revolution as essentially salutary—'A true Apocalypse, though a terrible one'. And he adds an important qualification to his earlier use of madness as a metaphor for the Revolution. The metaphor wrongly implied a kind of temporary national insanity, after which France returned to the happier condition of normality. But the Paris barricades of July 1830 prove that the Revolution remains a vital fact. There follows a brave assessment of the Revolution from which Carlyle never turns renegade, despite the growing stridency of his attacks on democracy:

We will hail the French Revolution, as ship-wrecked mariners might the sternest rock, in a world otherwise all of baseless sea and waves. A true Apocalypse, though a terrible one, to this false withered artificial time; testifying once more that Nature is *preter*natural; if not divine, then diabolic; that Semblance is not Reality; that it has to become Reality, or the world will take-fire under it,—burn *it* into what it is, namely Nothing!

(5: 201–2)

The most striking feature of this dithyramb is its depiction of the Revolution as a great natural force, a manifestation of energies either divine or diabolical. This sympathy with the sheer undifferentiated dynamism of life—'There is nothing dead in this Universe. . . . "The leaf that lies rotting . . . has still force; else how could it *rot*?" ' (3: 102)—makes Carlyle the instinctive partisan of revolution, whatever the vicissitudes of his politics, his religion, or his digestion. Yet his portrait of the Revolutionary proletariat is scarcely flattering; never neutral, at times condescending, at times downright insulting,[6] his attitude towards the Sansculottes is finally one of awe, as at the power of an earthquake: 'Your mob is a genuine outburst of Nature . . . a Sincerity and Reality' (2: 251). Sansculottism will inevitably annihilate much, but it will also be the 'beginning of much . . . it too came from God . . . in the whirlwind also He speaks . . .' (2: 213).

As whirlwind, tidal wave, or volcanic upheaval exploding from the fiery bowels of the earth, the mob is the energizing force of the book. In its aristocratic and bourgeois phases the Revolution, in Carlyle's eyes, is largely talk; when the Constitution fails and power passes to the proletariat, the Revolution becomes 'a Reality'. Carlyle's own ambivalence towards that power is the hidden drama that parallels the struggle in the streets. On this level *The French Revolution* is a *psychomachia* waged between Carlyle the Jacobin and Carlyle the authoritarian, between his demand for justice and his need for order.

Carlyle invites a psycho-analytic reading of *The French Revolution* by portraying the political struggle in the streets as an externalization of an inner conflict within ourselves. In terms of this psycho-political myth, the Sansculottes are not simply a particular class at a particular time, but the surfacing and momentary usurpation of power by a repressed part of our nature—the primitive and demonic that dwells in us all, despite our particular class, dress, gender, or moment in history. Hence the psychological emphasis in Carlyle's definition of the Revolution:

For ourselves, . . . [the] French Revolution means . . . the open violent Rebellion, and Victory, of disimprisoned Anarchy against corrupt worn-out Authority: how Anarchy breaks prison; bursts-up from the infinite Deep, and rages uncontrollable, immeasurable, enveloping a world; in phasis after phasis of fever-frenzy;—till the frenzy burning itself out, and what elements of new Order it held (since all Force holds such) developing themselves, the Uncontrollable be got, if not reimprisoned, yet harnessed. . . .

(2: 211–12)

In this principal definition of the Revolution, personifications stalk the page like old gods in new dress. The 'infinite Deep' from which Rebellion bursts up recalls Milton's Satan rising from Hell, or the giant Enceladus erupting from his fiery prison under Aetna (2: 39, 207); but this eruption also suggests the bursting of unconscious energies from the prison of repression. Our lives, Carlyle writes, are a 'singular Somnambulism, of Conscious and Unconscious, of Voluntary and Involuntary' (3: 105); the Reign of Terror is the breaking into waking life of the world of nightmare—a 'black *Dream become real* . . . where Upper has met Nether . . .' (4: 70–1). Although revolutions may seem propelled by external forces, those forces are part of the 'Daemonic' within nature and, hence, within ourselves (3: 249). In its energy and capacity for renewal, our revolutionary daemon is divine; in its cruelty and nihilism it is diabolical. But these labels are too simple for the moral reality Carlyle perceives—a struggle not between opposites or strangers but between twins who leapt into the world cleaving together. That Carlyle's sympathies are in part with the Devil's party explains why his most astute contemporaries found him subversive, at times brutal. John Sterling, for example, condemned Carlyle's account of the Terror as 'wretchedly perverse', a symptom of his 'hatred for things as they are, showing itself in cool mockery at their destruction, and in joy at manifestations, however monstrous, of the will to destroy them . . . '.[7]

What Sterling condemns as Carlyle's will to destroy we see as a profound ambivalence towards chaos and pain as necessary adjuncts to the fragile enterprise of civilization. To express the mixture of heroism and horror that characterizes France during the Terror, he devises a rhetoric of Manichean contrasts: 'Whatsoever is cruel in the panic frenzy of Twenty-five million men, whatsoever is great in the simultaneous death-defiance of Twenty-five million men, stand here in abrupt contrast . . .' (4: 1–2). As Carlyle strains to express the 'hateful contraries' of the Revolution, his language becomes more Miltonic and at the same time more purely psychological: the various Revolutionary factions tear each other apart 'in utmost preternatural spasm of madness, with Principalities and Powers, with the upper and under, internal and external; with the Earth and Tophet and the very Heaven!' (3: 211). Milton's fallen angels ('Principalities and Powers') serve as a second image, along with Saturn and his sons, of the revolution in the heavens that mirrors the revolution below. The final triplet of Earth, Hell, and Heaven reminds us that all along Carlyle has portrayed the Revolution as the local arena of a cosmic power struggle, with Paris the battleground, its streets mined with explosives and dangerously poised 'midway between Heaven and the Abyss' (3: 55).

*

One casualty of the conflict is the human personality in all its vagary and diversity. The individual, as Carlyle puts it, is 'enveloped in an ambient atmosphere of Transcendentalism and Delirium. . . . instead of the man and his volition there is a piece of Fanaticism and Fatalism incarnated in the shape of him.'[8] Men and women walk about like somnambulists, their individuality volatilized in the heat of the causes they espouse, their hearts enchanted to a stone. Carlyle stresses this eclipse of the self through clusters of epithets, which displace the indi-

viduality of the characters to whom they are attached, like parasites
that consume their host. 'Seagreen Robespierre' sheds his own name
and becomes merely 'the Seagreen Incorruptible', and when he and
Danton fatally quarrel, they confront one another not as human
adversaries but as glowering epithets:

One conceives easily the deep mutual incompatibility that divided these two:
with what terror of feminine hatred the poor seagreen Formula looked at the
monstrous colossal Reality, and grew greener to behold him;—the Reality,
again, struggling to think no ill of a chief-product of the Revolution; yet feeling at bottom that such chief-product was . . . not a man, with the heart of a
man, but a poor spasmodic incorruptible pedant, with a logic-formula instead
of a heart. . . .*

Carlyle here sacrifices any pretence of verisimilitude for a rhetoric
of bizarre incongruities that convey the felt essence of the Revolution.
At the height of the Reign of Terror, dance halls and theatres did a
brisk nightly business, while the day bakers and brewers, carpenters
and washerwomen, plied their trades (4: 206). In an image which
mirrors Carlyle's own style of painting the Revolution, he describes
the Terror as

a sable ground, on which the most variegated of scenes paints itself. In startling transitions, in colours all intensated, the sublime, the ludicrous, the horrible succeed one another; or rather, in crowding tumult, accompany one
another.†

(4: 206–7)

Startling transitions, a kaleidoscopic succession of the absurd, the
sublime, and the horrible—this expressionist picture of the Terror
also suggests the workings of a dream. Earlier Carlyle had compared
the Terror to a waking nightmare, 'a black *Dream become real*' (4: 70).

---

* (4: 254). The ultimate displacement of character by epithet occurs a few pages later,
where Robespierre becomes a mere simulacrum for personified Vengeance: 'Saint-
Just is verily reading that Report of his; green Vengeance, in the shape of
Robespierre, watching nigh' (4: 279).

† Compare this description of his intended style in the final volume: 'A hundred pages
more, and this cursed Book is flung out from me. I mean to write with the force of fire
till that consummation;—above all, with the speed of fire . . . Louis is to be tried and
guillotined; then the *Gironde* &c &c: it all stands pretty fair in my head; nor do I mean
to *investigate* much more about it, but to splash down what I know, in large masses of
colours; that it may look like a smoke-and-flame conflagration in the distance,—which
it is.' (Letter to Jane of 24 July 1836, Sanders, *Collected Letters*, 9: 21–2.)

Two of his leading metaphors for the Revolution are the dream and the theatre. As befits the dualistic bent of his imagination, each image has a double face: as dream, the Revolution begins in wish-fulfilment and ends as nightmare, begins in the hope of justice and brotherhood (the 'Gospel according to Jean Jacques') and ends by cannibalizing itself. As political theatre, Carlyle's representation of the Revolution ranges from high tragedy to farce. He evokes pity and terror at the deaths of Louis XVI and Charlotte Corday; he is 'ludicro-terrific' at the half-hanging of Abbé Lefèvre; and he turns the Feast of the Supreme Being into pure farce: 'the Seagreen Pontiff', bedecked in sky-blue coat and muttering 'Mumbo-Jumbo', mistakenly scorches Wisdom while putting a torch to David's pasteboard effigy of Atheism (4: 266–7).

Despite the mockery, Carlyle saw that David's pageants were important manifestations of the essential theatricality of the Revolution. They were history enacted into spectacle, 'people's theatre' on a scale not to be seen again until Red Square and Nuremberg. For the Fête de la Fédération, the Champ-de-Mars was excavated by an army of volunteers and transformed into tiers on tiers of seats and triumphal arches. In describing Paris on the day of the festival as one vast 'peopled Amphitheatre' (3: 62), Carlyle underscores the Revolution's genius for self-dramatization. For a writer to whom all the world seemed a stage, the Revolution as spectacle exercised a compelling fascination, as indeed it did for the participants themselves. In an essay on 'The French Revolution as "Theatrum Mundi"', Joseph Butwin points out that the great hall of the National Convention never lost its original theatrical character as a *Salle de Spectacle*.[9] When the Convention first met on 21 September 1792, Robespierre and Marat were flanked by their Montagnard friends, the painter David and the playwright-actor Collot-d'Herbois, who introduced the motion to abolish the Monarchy. Collot, who had once acted on the Lyons stage, could now strut on the stage of the world: 'Shall the Mimetic become Real?' Carlyle asks in a question that anticipates the role of this actor-turned-terrorist in directing the mass murders at Lyon (3: 18; 4: 217). Robespierre and Marat saw themselves as principal actors on the stage of history, with the people as supporting cast and the whole of Europe for an audience.[10]

This hyper-consciousness of oneself as a central figure in a national drama, as incarnating in one's personal style the public destiny, Carlyle found repugnant in Robespierre but highly attractive in

Mirabeau, who comes closest to being the Carlylean hero of *The French Revolution*. Mirabeau's death, more an apotheosis than an end, is the first of a series of grand theatrical exits. Death as theatre and death as atrocity, dying as a virtuoso performance and as mass slaughter, accompany one another in macabre counterpoint in the closing chapters. The one harks back to a civilized world of well-chosen last words and gestures, the other presages faster and more frightful methods of killing, when our still savage nature will use 'all the tools and weapons of civilisation: a spectacle new in History' (2: 14; 4: 214, 247).

'I carry in my heart the death-dirge on the French Monarchy' (3: 141), the stricken Mirabeau remarks, and when he hears the muffled cannon signalling his own last moments, he compares himself to Achilles (3: 142) and asks of his friend La Marck, 'Well my dear connoisseur in beautiful deaths, are you satisfied with me?'[11] Carlyle's comment—'the man dies as he has lived; self-conscious, conscious of a world looking on' (3: 142)—suggests that heroic dying was an art-form of the Revolution, performed at leisure by Mirabeau, who died of natural causes, and as a command performance by the guillotined. At the foot of the scaffold Mme Roland called for pen and paper to record her last thoughts. Her request refused, she turned to the Statue of Liberty next to the guillotine, cried out, ' "O Liberty, what things are done in thy name!" ' and herself became an emblem of truncated Liberty (4: 210). Charlotte Corday wanted her portrait painted in prison and sent as a memorial to her native district.[12] Sentenced to death by the Revolutionary Tribunal, the Girondist Lasource cried out to his judges, ' "I die on the day when the People have lost their reason; ye will die when they recover it" ' (4: 198). Asked his name, age, and abode by Fouquier-Tinville, the Public Accuser, Danton replied that his abode would soon be ' "Annihilation" ' but that he would ' "live in the Pantheon of History" ' (4: 257). Camille Desmoulins's reply has an even sharper edge: ' "My age is that of the *bon Sansculotte Jésus*; an age fatal to Revolutionists." ' 'O Camille, Camille!' Carlyle exclaims, as if applauding a performance (4: 257). Phillippe Égalité, the former Duc d'Orléans, prepared for execution with a kind of low-comedy Last Breakfast of oysters, cutlets, and a bottle of vintage claret.[13] He arrived at the guillotine dressed like a dandy. 'On the scaffold Samson [the Executioner] was for drawing off his boots: "Tush," said Phillippe, "they will come better off *after* . . ." ' (4: 208–9).

Within very few years Girondists, Jacobins, and Royalists became as adept at dying to epigrams as the twentieth-century man in the street, once a mere stammerer, has become adept at performing before an interviewer's camera. Such skills seem to be transmitted almost unconsciously and transfer easily from one cultural medium to another. David's *Oath of the Horatii* (1785) and *Brutus [and] the Bodies of His Sons* (1789), first exhibited when the neo-classical tastes of the Revolution were emerging, reflected and formed those tastes. For the Parisians who flocked to the exhibitions began to mimic in their fashions and public demeanour the dress and heroic morality of David's paintings.[14] Mme Roland's death epitomizes that morality, Phillippe Égalité's death parodies it.

Consciousness of the Roman past pressed like a weight on the Revolutionary present, even when the present most ostentatiously sought to assert its independence. Carlyle finds much irony in this historical persistence, as did Karl Marx, who observed that just when men seem most 'engaged in revolutionizing themselves and things, in creating something that has never yet existed, precisely in such periods of revolutionary crisis they anxiously conjure up the spirits of the past to their service and borrow from them names, battle-cries and costumes. . . .' The great events in world history tend to repeat themselves, Marx observes in a famous sentence, 'the first time as tragedy, the second as farce'. For Marx the tragic or heroic stage of the French Revolution was the 'old Revolution' of Robespierre and Danton, the farcical replay, the Second Republic of 'the idiot' Louis Bonaparte.[15] For Carlyle tragedy and farce take place on the same historical stage, the heroic, the horrible, and the ludicrous all 'huddled together' (2: 282. Cf. 4: 206–7).

A chilling instance occurs nightly in the prisons, where the condemned enact mock-trials at which they subject an effigy of Fouquier-Tinville to the same torments they will suffer on the morrow (4: 272). The scene rings with ironies within ironies. For although the Bastille had disgorged its prisoners in 1789, the whole of France had become one vast prison by 1793, as Carlyle makes clear in the section entitled 'Terror the Order of the Day'. The mock-trial in the real prison, dispensing mock-justice in a society in which true justice has been mocked by the Law of 22 Prairial*—'imagination herself', as Carlyle writes 'flags[s] under the reality' (3: 47).

* Passed by the Convention on 10 June 1794, the law virtually eliminated all judicial guarantees for the accused.

The real and the surreal again conjoin in the ancient person of Catherine Théot, a lunatic prophetess who had been released from the Bastille in 1779. 'Poring over the Book of Revelation', she now proclaimed that she was the ' "mother of God" ' and that Robespierre was the true Messiah whose coming would regenerate the world. She enters the narrative immediately after Carlyle's farcical account of the new cult of the Supreme Being, with its Age of Reason liturgy intoned by the Seagreen Pontiff. But here is the one true believer in Robespierre's 'Mumbo-Jumbo', a seventy-nine-year-old serving maid whom Robespierre's enemies arrested and falsely accused of conspiring to have him declared the Son of God.[16]

Throughout Carlyle's account of the Terror, displays of madness and violence normally confined to dreams, myths, or the tragic stage erupt into daily life, which becomes a waking nightmare populated by gory fragments of half-remembered tales. The high decorum of David's *Horatii*, balletic in its gestures and symmetries, is half the story; the hacking to pieces of the Princesse de Lamballe, or the forcing of Mlle de Sombreuil to drink human blood,* is the other half: 'right-side and wrong lie always so near' (3: 100).

Imagination breaks down in the face of such atrocity, as does language. A major theme of Carlyle's chapters on the Terror is the need for language to confess its inadequacy in confronting deeds 'for which language has no name'.[17] In part Carlyle is asserting that atrocity mocks the language that attempts to depict it. In part he is asserting that any assault on our humanity is an assault on our most sacred faculty, the Word incarnate within us as human speech. Silence is truer than speech when speech can only lie, as in the macabre euphemism of Carrier, who drowned ninety priests in a scuttled river-barge and dubbed their sentence *vertical* deportation (4: 221). The Revolution, which was to have ushered in the second

* My Father is not an Aristocrat: O good gentlemen, I will swear it, and testify it, and in all ways prove it; we are not; we hate Aristocrats! "Wilt thou drink Aristocrats' blood?" The man lifts blood (if universal Rumour can be credited); the poor maiden does drink. "This Sombreuil is innocent, then!" Yes, indeed,—and the tiger-yells become bursts of jubilee over a brother saved. . . . (4: 30-1)

G. P. Gooch cites this passage, along with the sinking of the *Vengeur*, as an instance of Carlyle's credulity in accepting 'legends' as facts (*History and the Historians in the Nineteenth Century*, 2nd edn. (Boston: Beacon Press, 1959), p. 303). But Carlyle's parenthesis—'(if universal Rumour can be credited)'—is qualification conspicuous enough for all but those who run as they read. For a letter attesting to the truth of the incident, see Fletcher, 2: 306 n. 2. Spared in 1792, M de Sombreuil was guillotined two years later.

Golden Age, resulted instead in a second Fall—a Fall not from God but from our own humanity. Hence Carlyle portrays the Reign of Terror as a *man-made* Hell over whose gate is inscribed the motto, 'Terror the Order of the Day.' This decree of the National Convention on 5 September 1793 is for Carlyle the ultimate oxymoron of the Revolution, a uniquely modern fusion of the rational and the monstrous, the horrific and the mundane. How could the sons of the Englightenment have fathered such a state? *Because* they were sons of the Englightenment, Carlyle grimly replies. In his *Pursuit of the Millennium* Norman Cohn traces the long association in European history between periods of revolutionary messianism and popular outbursts of anarchic terror and persecution, an irregular continuum of hope and horror reaching from the Middle Ages to modern totalitarianism. Carlyle places the French Revolution within this tradition, although his historical perspective perforce falls short of our own. With his keen sense of the irrational underside of the Enlightenment, he makes of Catherine Théot a parodic Robespierre, a figure out of the old Apocalypse who rose again in Paris in the month of Prairial, Year II.

*

Robespierre succeeded in sparing Catherine Théot from going to trial, but only after quarrelling with the Committee on Public Safety, from which he withdrew for several weeks. His self-imposed withdrawal from the Committee and his infrequent appearances at the Convention strengthened his enemies at a time when his own position was visibly weakening. Carlyle describes this period of withdrawal as Robespierre's ' "forty-days" ' during which he 'sits apart' and meditates in solitary places (4: 274). These glancing allusions to Jesus's forty days in the wilderness and to the agony in Gesthemane[18] mark a new dimension in Carlyle's portrait of Robespierre and prepare us for the extraordinary scene to come, which he aptly calls 'our fifth-act of this natural Greek Drama' (4: 283). The stress falls on *natural*, for Carlyle wants to contrast the genuine pity and terror of Robespierre's death with the contrived theatricality that precedes it, including the Seagreen Pontiff's performance at the Feast of the Supreme Being.

The scene opens in a tumult of shouting from the Convention floor that drowns out Saint-Just and Robespierre and ends in their arrest. Besieged within the Hôtel de Ville, Robespierre's brother Augustin and the Jacobin commander Henriot leap from a window, only to land alive in a mess of masonry and sewage. This Dantesque 'fall' is prelude to the discovery of Robespierre, who for the first time in one thousand pages is depicted as utterly speechless:

Saint-Just, they say, called on Lebas to kill him; who would not. Couthon crept under a table; attempting to kill himself; not doing it.—On entering that Sanhedrim of Insurrection, we find all as good as extinct; undone, ready for seizure. Robespierre was sitting on a chair, with pistol-shot blown through not his head but his under-jaw; the suicidal hand had failed. With prompt zeal, not without trouble, we gather these wrecked Conspirators; fish up even Henriot and Augustin, bleeding and foul; pack them all, rudely enough, into carts; and shall, before sunrise, have them safe under lock and key. Amid shoutings and embracings.

Robespierre lay in an anteroom of the Convention Hall, while his Prison-escort was getting ready; the mangled jaw bound up rudely with bloody linen: a spectacle to men. He lies stretched on a table, a deal-box his pillow; the sheath of the pistol is still clenched convulsively in his hand. Men bully him, insult him: his eyes still indicate intelligence; he speaks no word. "He had on the sky-blue coat he had got made for the Feast of the *Être Suprême*"—O Reader, can thy hard heart hold out against that? His trousers were nankeen; the stockings had fallen down over the ankles. He spake no word more in this world.

(4: 284–5)

That the eloquent Robespierre should have shattered his own jaw is a bit of natural symbolism Carlyle neither overlooks nor needs to underscore.[19] A few pages earlier he cited a phrase Camille Desmoulins quoted in the last number of the *Vieux Cordelier*, just before his beheading: ' "Les dieux ont soif." ' Camille attributed the phrase to Montezuma, with the seditious implication that the Revolution was exacting too heavy a toll in human sacrifice. The blood-thirst of the gods harks back to Vergniaud's epigram on Saturn and anticipates the execution of Robespierre.[20] Given the hostility of Carlyle's earlier portrait of Robespierre, it is remarkable that he can now portray Robespierre's execution as a moving sacrifice; it is virtually miraculous that, without an iota of comedy or blasphemy, he can persuade us that Robespierre's death, like that of Louis XVI, partakes of elements of the sacrifice of Christ. Only Carlyle could create a death-scene of high tragedy out of a self-mutilated pedant in silk trousers and a sky-blue coat. Just when the reader might be moved to mockery, he is asked, instead, if his 'hard heart' can keep back its tears: tears rather than derision because of the 'loving minuteness' that focuses on the blood-stained linen, that detects Robespierre's keen intelligence still animating the eyes that look out from the shattered head and register every instant of the protracted agony. But most of all we are moved because we are made to witness two martyrdoms enacted simultaneously, the one before our eyes, in 'an anteroom of the Convention Hall', the other, in the wings of our recollection, where 'the soldiers led him away into the hall, called Praetorium. . . . And they clothed him with purple. . . . And they smote him on the head. . . . And when they had mocked him, they . . . led him out to crucify him.'[21] Robespierre's silence before his accusers—a reiterated silence, for Carlyle twice says that Robespierre spoke 'no word more' in this world—echoes Jesus's refusal to answer the chief priests and Pilate—'he answered to him never a word.'[22] The emphasis on Robespierre's silence is especially significant because so gratuitous: he could scarcely be expected to speak. The silence heightens the horror to come, when, instead of 'My God, my God, why hast thou forsaken me?' we hear a shriek of pain.

After a night and day of public display and humiliation, Robespierre, along with some twenty others, is led to the Place de la Révolution. It is late in the afternoon of 28 July 1794. This is the last of the great processions of *The French Revolution*, 'the very roofs and ridge-tiles budding forth human Curiosity', and it evokes all previous processions—Louis XVI to the same spot only eighteen months earlier, the grand convocation of the Estates-General on 4 May 1789, and a millennium before that, the ghostly procession of the Merovingian Kings, 'slowly wending on their bullock-carts through the streets of Paris' (2: 7). Along the route an unidentified woman leaps onto Robespierre's tumbril to curse him, a latter-day Fury who serves to remind us that this is the last act of Carlyle's 'natural Greek Drama':

All eyes are on Robespierre's Tumbril, where he, his jaw bound in dirty linen, with his half-dead Brother and half-dead Henriot, lie shattered; their "seventeen hours" of agony about to end. The Gendarmes point their swords at him, to show the people which is he. A woman springs on the Tumbril; clutching the side of it with one hand, waving the other Sibyl-like; and exclaims: "The death of thee gladdens my very heart, *m'enivre de joie*"; Robespierre opened his eyes; "*Scélérat*, go down to Hell, with the curses of all wives and mothers!"—At the foot of the scaffold, they stretched him on the ground till his turn came. Lifted aloft, his eyes again opened; caught the bloody axe. Samson wrenched the coat off him; wrenched the dirty linen from his jaw: the jaw fell powerless, there burst from him a cry;—hideous to hear and see. Samson, thou canst not be too quick!

(4: 285)

The whole gathered power of *The French Revolution* compresses to a single point in that shriek of Robespierre. The Revolution had begun in words: first the words of the *philosophes*, then a buzzing in the streets that rose to a roar and shattered the walls of the Bastille. Robespierre had mastered those words and for a time became the articulate intelligence of the Voice of France, 'the Chief Priest and Speaker' of the Revolution, as Carlyle calls him (3: 246). Speech had been fine-tuned into slogan and decree and epigram; even the phlegmatic Louis XVI arrived at the scaffold prepared to speak his final piece, until the drummers and Samson cut him off. But in this last act of Carlyle's drama, death lapses into pure savagery, the Revolution cannibalizes itself, and, fittingly, speech degenerates into an aboriginal scream. The cries of the self-blinded Oedipus, the howls of Lear, are not more chilling than the shriek of Robespierre.

One wants to put this painful scene aside, but meanings unfold within meanings, like wounds hidden within wounds. Samson's wrenching off the sky-blue coat and the bandage is an act of pure malice: neither coat nor bandage could resist the axe, which Robespierre's still-sentient eyes see poised above him. In Matthew, when Jesus is mocked, the soldiers bedeck him in a scarlet cloak; in Luke, with a robe of royal purple, which is taken from Him before the Crucifixion.[23] We now see why Carlyle pauses over the nankeen trousers, the sky-blue coat, the brutal stripping on the scaffold, just as he had paused over the dividing of the King's puce coat and the dipping of handkerchiefs in his blood. The very unlikeness of Robespierre to Louis and of both to Christ enables Carlyle to pile resemblance upon resemblance without the parallel rising to consciousness or collapsing into parody. The gruesomeness of the narrative further impedes such recognition, but on the deeper level where dream meets reality and symbols take on flesh, the full power of the scene discloses itself. Robespierre's execution–crucifixion is a narrative enactment of the question posed at the Human Tannery: is civilization 'only a wrappage', a clothing that conceals our savage nature? The central symbol of *Sartor Resartus* and the central question of *The French Revolution* return in the guise of a soiled coat and a bloody bandage, 'wrappages' both, emblems of desecrated humanity. At the end of *The*

French Revolution, in the farewell to the reader, Carlyle speaks of man as ' "an incarnated Word" ' and of human speech as a living, sacred fountain. He was perhaps recalling his first letter to Emerson, in which he announced his intention to write a book on the French Revolution and remarked that at bottom 'there is *nothing sacred*, then, but the *Speech of Man* to believing Men!'[24] Seen in this light, Samson's act is the ultimate blasphemy, a mutilation of the 'incarnated Word' within man. Robespierre's scream of animal terror is also the cry of the stricken God: 'Jesus, when he had cried again with a loud voice, yielded up the ghost.'[25]

Once Samson's work is accomplished,* there burst from the crowd shouts of applause that reverberate over Paris, 'over Europe, and down to this generation' (4: 285). The Voice of France has changed its tune, as has Carlyle, who in the face of public jubilation over Robespierre's fall seems to heed his own injunction to pity them all, for it went hard with them all. Much earlier Carlyle had portrayed the death of Mirabeau as an apotheosis, the return of a wounded Titan to his immortal home. Robespierre's death, like Marat's, elicits from Carlyle a belated and moving recognition of humanity. Until his humiliation and death, Robespierre was a Seagreen Formula for whom words had displaced realities. But now Carlyle's compassion for the shattered human being overcomes his contempt for the revolutionary ideologue. Robespierre's epithets fall from him like cast clothing. Only 'Advocate of Arras' and 'incorruptible' remain, but the first is an innocuous reminder of Robespierre's earlier career, and the second has lost its sting, along with its initial capital. The eulogy, if it may be called that, begins in grudging admiration and then rises to something much greater:

O unhappiest Advocate of Arras, wert thou worse than other Advocates? Stricter man, according to his Formula, to his Credo and his Cant, of probities, benevolences, pleasures-of-virtue, and suchlike, lived not in that age. A man fitted, in some luckier settled age, to have become one of those incorruptible barren Pattern-figures and have had marble-tablets and funeral-

---

* Samson appears only rarely in *The French Revolution* but always to dramatic effect. A figure of towering strength, he is a sinister version of his biblical namesake, who is also a kind of executioner. Charles Henri Sanson (Carlyle's misspelling of the name is surely significant) was the public executioner of Paris from 1788 to 1795. He inherited the office from his father and in turn bequeathed it to his son. Carlyle's Samson is the Executioner standing at the gates of a mythic Hell; Fouquier-Tinville, signing his batches of indictments, is the Judge. The hoarse-voiced, sooty Marat, a fugitive who hides in cellars and calls for 260,000 aristocratic heads, is Cerberus—Pluto.

sermons. His poor landlord, the Cabinet-maker in the Rue Saint-Honoré, loved him; his Brother died for him. May God be merciful to him and to us!
(4: 285–6)

The cadences of the liturgy—'Lord, have mercy upon us; Christ, have mercy upon us'—first heard faintly at the King's death, now ring clearly through the final sentence, as if Carlyle were conducting the service for the burial of the dead in the presence of the insulted body. That *we* are present among the mourners and beside Carlyle follows from the wording of the closing prayer: 'May God be merciful to him and to *us*!' In our long journey through *The French Revolution* ('O Reader!—Courage, I see land!' (4: 288)), we are close to that final moment when Carlyle will move still closer and call us Brother.

*

'Vendémiaire', the brief last book of *The French Revolution*, is the satyr play Carlyle appends to his natural Greek tragedy. In place of the frenzy of the Carmagnole, we have the soirées of the fair Cabarus and costume balls graced by young Minervas, Junos, Nymphs in sheer tunics that scarcely conceal their ' "flesh-coloured drawers" ' (4: 293–5, 310). Instead of Furies, we have Dandies, *Jeunesse Dorée* in superfine dress (4: 295); Sansculottism in all its guises has become hateful. 'Is not the Dandy *culottic*, habilatory, by law of existence; "a cloth animal; one that lives, moves, and has his being in cloth"?' (4: 295). All Carlyle's old metaphors return, but now stood on their heads or otherwise distorted. Those flesh-coloured drawers elicit a shock of delayed recognition: the new decadence of feigned nudity has supplanted the old Sansculottism of naked power, but through the flesh-coloured drawers peep the human skins of Meudon and the 'mustachio *grands-lèvres*' of the Princesse de Lamballe.

In the interval between the fall of Robespierre and the establishment of the Directory, Sansculottism lies writhing, a mortally-wounded lion with ' "fractured . . . under-jaw" ' (4: 288). Street bands of gilded youth attack Jacobin ' "Blood-drinkers, *Buveurs de Sang*" ', pale replicas of earlier blood-baths in the streets (4: 309). Wit now plays over motifs that earlier evoked spectres of paranoia and cannibalism: 'The Revolutionary Committees, without Suspects to prey upon, perish fast; as it were, of famine' (4: 290). One incident signals the movement from high drama to farce. A band of *Jeunesse Dorée* 'in plaited hair-tresses' smashes to pieces busts of Marat and scatters the fragments in the cesspool of Montmartre. His remains are dragged from the Pantheon and thrown into the same pit: 'Shorter godhood had no divine man. Some four months in this Pantheon, Temple of All the Immortals; then to the Cesspool, grand *Cloaca* of Paris and the World!' (4: 300.) The Revolution exalted Marat into a god; Carlyle portrayed him as a demon; here he becomes food for a scatalogical joke.

This apotheosis-in-reverse nicely illustrates Carlyle's demythifying of the Revolution throughout the closing book. Marx's aphorism on history repeating itself as farce again comes to mind, but the comic replay is not complete and the Old Terror once or twice obtrudes into the New Farce. On 20 May 1795, ten months after Robespierre's beheading, a hungry army of Sansculottes from the district of St-Antoine marches across Paris and beats down the doors of the Convention. In this final uprising of 'disimprisoned Anarchy' against authority, 'plaster-work crackles, wood-work booms and jingles', the mob rushes into the Convention and seizes Jean Féraud, a veteran of the wars in Spain. Féraud is trampled to death, his head stuck onto a long pike and thrust in the face of the President, Boissy D'Anglas. For two days more the insurrection rages. Féraud's assassin 'flings himself from a high roof', the Army subdues St-Antoine, and the writhing lion at last lies sprawled on the ground, dead in body if not in spirit (4: 307–10).[26] Into this power-void Napoleon steps cautiously at first, then boldly. Appointed by the Convention to command its troops, he suppresses with a 'Whiff of Grapeshot' the Royalist insurrection of 5 October 1795. From this point on, the Revolution becomes the instrument of Napoleon's ambitions and, in Carlyle's eyes, loses all interest.

The short closing chapter presents Carlyle with a special problem beyond that of any narrator bringing a story to its end. For in Carlyle's view the Revolution is by nature unending and its history continues to be written in the events of the present. And so he begins his conclusion by reminding us that 'Universal History', like Homer's epic, 'does not conclude, but merely ceases' (4: 321). Endings are lies or at best partial truths. Yet Carlyle provides a provisional ending that manages to be both truth and lie—the mock-apocalyptic prophecy he puts into the mouth of the arch-quack Cagliostro. Fittingly for a quack, Cagliostro's prophecy is '*ex postfacto*' and foretells, in wildly inflated rhetoric, the universal conflagration to come, in which the 'EMPIRE OF IMPOSTURE' will be annihilated along with Kings, Queens, and prisons (4: 322–3). In a parody of Carlylese, Cagliostro prophesies the millennium that never arrived, the burning up of the old order that failed to bring in its stead a new earth and a new heaven.

Another name for an '*ex postfacto*' prophet is *historian*, and in momentarily playing the part of Cagliostro, Carlyle combines the roles of prophet, historian, and quack. He had tried in 'The Diamond Necklace' to write an 'attempted *True Fiction*', a new kind of historical narrative which, if successful, would embolden him to undertake *The French Revolution*.[27] The experiment succeeded, and now the last 'document' to be quoted in *The French Revolution* is this self-quotation from an earlier work about one of the celebrated impostures of modern history. Carlyle's lifelong fascination with hoaxers, quacks, and liars is the other side of his exaltation of sincerity and truth. It is highly characteristic that he should put into the mouth of a detested charlatan his own most deeply-held suspicions of the proximity of truth to illusion and of reality to dream. In 'The Diamond Necklace' Cagliostro exclaims:

. . . Sham is indispensable to Reality, as Lying to Living. . . . Wondrously, indeed, do Truth and Delusion play into one another; Reality rests on Dream. Truth is but the *skin* of the bottomless Untrue: and ever, from time to time, the Untrue *sheds* it; is clear again; and the superannuated True itself becomes a Fable.

(28: 394)

These words are spoken by a prince of liars, but on a level which Cagliostro cannot perceive they are also Carlyle's words and may be taken as canonical. The fantastical end of *The French Revolution* recalls the beginning, with its evocation of our 'most fictile' and phantasmagoric world (2: 6). By the end, Carlyle has taught us that fiction is not the opposite of history but its luminous shadow; that illusion is not the antithesis of reality but a precondition of our knowing reality.

The simplicity, clarity, and beauty of Carlyle's closing sentences have the ring of the spoken word, as befits an utterance about the sacredness of human speech:

And so here, O Reader, has the time come for us two to part. Toilsome was our journeying together; not without offence; but it is done. To me thou wert as a beloved shade, the disembodied or not yet embodied spirit of a Brother. To thee I was but as a Voice. Yet was our relation a kind of sacred one; doubt not that! For whatsoever once sacred things become hollow jargons, yet while the Voice of Man speaks with Man, hast thou not there the living fountain out of which all sacrednesses sprang, and will yet spring? Man, by the nature of him, is definable as "an incarnated Word." Ill stands it with me if I have spoken falsely: thine also it was to hear truly. Farewell.

The book that opened in the dramatic present here for the first and only time slips into the past. The shift is startlingly right. So long as Carlyle's words were about the Revolution, whose consequences are still unfolding, they belong in the present. Hedva Ben-Israel, a distinguished historian of historians of the French Revolution, points out that 'the greatest effects of the Revolution' have been wrought after the fact through the power of words on paper, including Carlyle's words.[28] Like the event which it mirrors and of which it is now itself a part, *The French Revolution: A History* is open-ended and awaits completion in the minds of generations of Carlyle's readers. But in this moment when Carlyle puts down his pen, he steps back into the stream of time, three years older than when he began. His past-tense parting from the 'beloved shade' of the Reader is charged with a sense of mortality and of the transcendence of mortality, the special gift of words touched by 'once sacred things'.

The Later Writings

7

Past and Present: Miracles and Metamorphoses

Carlyle was in his forty-second year when he published *The French Revolution*; with the publication of *Past and Present* five years later, in 1843, he completed the great sequence of critical and historical works he had begun a decade earlier with *Sartor Resartus*. He continued to publish over the next three decades, but his creative life as a writer wanes in *Cromwell* (1845) and *Frederick the Great* (1858–65) and ends with his guilt-haunted 'reminiscence' of his wife Jane, who died in 1866. His last public pronouncement of note is 'Shooting Niagara: and After?'—a strident, frightened, ferociously anti-democratic invective occasioned by the passage of the Second Reform Bill in 1867.

Between *The French Revolution* and 'Shooting Niagara' lies an immense, uneven body of work that, with the exception of *On Heroes* (1841) and *Past and Present*, is terra incognita for the modern reader. *On Heroes* has achieved a certain notoriety because of its purported role in fostering twentieth-century totalitarianism.* The fault with *On Heroes*, however, is not that it idolizes dictators but that it is intellectually thin, as Carlyle himself realized.[1] Most of his heroes are writers (Dante, Shakespeare, Dr Johnson, Rousseau, and Burns) or revolutionary religious leaders. The finest scene in *On Heroes* portrays not the worship of authority but its defiance: 'one man, the poor miner Hans Luther's Son', defending 'God's Truth' against the combined powers, temporal and papal, of Europe (5: 134). Of Carlyle's odd lot of heroes (Jesus and Goethe are curious absences), only Napoleon gives the modern reader pause, as he does Carlyle, who finds him flawed by selfish ambition and a 'charlatan-element' that preyed on the '*Dupeability* of men' (5: 238, 241). The book that Carlyle actually wrote is not the proto-Nazi tract he is popularly supposed to have written.

* For an example of this kind of guilt by a-historical association, see Joseph E. Baker's 'Carlyle Rules the Reich', *Saturday Review of Literature* (25 Nov. 1933). In the same year H. C. Grierson published *Carlyle and Hitler*, a lecture given three years earlier under the title, 'Carlyle and the Hero'.

Yet *On Heroes* is, I believe, at bottom pernicious; its attempt to substitute a new 'Hero-archy' for a vanishing secular and religious hierarchy is simplistic and alarming. *Sartor Resartus* is rich in ideas, chief of which is 'natural supernaturalism'. *The French Revolution* teems with ideas on history, myth, primitivism, language, authority, typology, repression, revolution, and anarchy. 'Hero-worship', however, is not an idea but an emotion in search of an object. No one living in the twentieth century can doubt that it is a dangerous emotion. *Sartor Resartus* was written in the hope of remaking the world; *On Heroes* was written out of fear that the post-Revolutionary world was drifting into anarchy, for Carlyle 'the hatefulest' of all conditions (5: 124). The gospel of 'Hero-worship' is a gospel of desperation: 'For myself in these days,' Carlyle writes, 'I seem to see in this indestructibility of Hero-worship the everlasting adamant lower than which the confused wreck of revolutionary things cannot fall' (5: 15). Perhaps *The French Revolution* is Carlyle's central work because it was written in the period of equilibrium between the manic aspiration of *Sartor* and the desperation of *On Heroes* and all that followed.

Carlyle's quest for heroes begins in the mythological past with Odin ('The Hero as Divinity') and ends on the eve of the French Revolution with his tribute to the enlightened despot Frederick the Great. His long search for heroes suggests how inexhaustible was his fund of reverence and his need to express it, a need correlative with his compulsion to rage against the 'howling doggeries' of the human animal.[2] Reverence and rage, compassion and contempt, radicalism and reaction consort in strange fellowship throughout Carlyle's writings. Always and unabashedly himself, he combines attitudes generally held to be antithetical; the result is that those who admire certain of his works but detest others appear to be writing about two different authors. Critics on the left take *Past and Present* to mark the great Carlylean divide: up to and including *Past and Present* lies all that is original, humane, and lasting; after *Past and Present* lies all that is reactionary or worse. Critics on the right find Carlyle conservative from the start but truest to himself in the later works. The reality is more perplexing. 'Early Carlyle' *is* essentially of a piece with 'late Carlyle', yet one cannot deny a certain loss of energy and centrality in the later writings. The biological metaphor of growth, flowering, and decay exercises an almost coercive power over our sense of a writer's career, especially a career as long as Carlyle's, and doubtless the metaphor helps account for what is undeniable—the greater vitality of his earlier works. But the common belief that the young Carlyle is a great writer who espouses radical ideas and the old Carlyle a bad writer who espouses reactionary ideas reflects the prejudices of Carlyle's critics rather than the substance of his writings. In some gross measure the quality of the writing declines, just as, in equally gross measure, one notes a coarsening in the quality of Carlyle's moral awareness. But anomalies abound. For example, in an essay-review of *Past and Present* Friedrich Engels pays fervent tribute to Carlyle's humanity and radical social vision; yet in the same year in which *Past and Present* exerted so historically decisive an influence on the author of *The Condition of the Working Class in England in 1844*,[3] Carlyle also published his perversely brilliant 'Dr. Francia', an apologia for the Supreme Dictator and virtual owner of Paraguay from 1814 until his death in 1840. The bigotry, misanthropy, and anti-egalitarianism of the *Latter-Day Pamphlets* is almost exactly contemporary with Carlyle's tribute to *John Sterling* (1851), which Froude thought 'perhaps the most beautiful biography in the English language'.[4] This genial celebration of Carlyle's closest friendship is radiant with the quiet play of his own powers of affection and recall.

In assessing Carlyle's vast and uneven output from the 1840s into the 1870s, I am variously struck by continuities and discontinuities, by persistence and decline. At the outset there is Engels's praise of *Past and Present* and Emerson's tribute in the *Dial* to Carlyle's great 'Iliad of English woes'.[5] At the end there is *Frederick the Great*, the 'grandest' of all Carlyle's works, according to Froude;[6] but according to Macaulay, 'the philosophy [is] nonsense and the style gibberish.'[7] The most revealing modern response to *Frederick* comes from a German reader a century after Engels reviewed *Past and Present*. In April 1945, deep within the Berlin bunker, Goebbels tried to dispel Hitler's forebodings of doom by reading aloud from *Frederick*, the Fuehrer's favourite book. When Goebbels reached the passage late in the Seven Years War in which Frederick was saved from disaster by a seeming miracle, he looked up and saw that 'tears stood in the Fuehrer's eyes'.[8] That Carlyle, a recipient of the Order of Merit from Bismarck's Prussia and an incessant prophet of apocalypse, should have figured in Hitler's fiery last days, has an appalling aptness, Yet the Carlyle who kindled the enthusiasm of Emerson and Engels and Whitman ('Never had political progressivism a foe it could more heartily respect')[9] is not another creature from the Carlyle who brought tears of hope to the eyes of Hitler.

*

In the late summer of 1842, outward accident and inner necessity led Carlyle on a journey that resulted in the publication of *Past and Present* the following spring. He had been struggling unsuccessfully to get on with his history of Cromwell, and in search of inspiration he set out on horseback for the Cromwell country of East Anglia. With cloak, knapsack, and broad-brimmed hat he rode into St Ives, where he saw Cromwell's first farm and, though not on his itinerary, the local Workhouse. The 'picturesque Tourist' who stares incredulously at the pauper-inmates of St Ives at the start of *Past and Present* is Carlyle himself, transposed from the back of his heavy-footed horse into the opening pages of his book, an astonished witness to the human wreckage in the midst of England's bounty. ' "There was something that reminded me of Dante's Hell in the look of all this," ' the picturesque Tourist remarks, ' "and I rode swiftly away" ' (10: 2).

Carlyle's tour of East Anglia also included Bury St Edmunds, where he encountered ruins of another kind and from another age:[10] the charred stones of the once-great Abbey that grew up around the shrine of the martyred St Edmund. In 1840, two years before Carlyle stood gazing at the massive Norman ruins that jut out from the ground 'like an old osseous fragment, a broken blackened shinbone of the old dead Ages' (10: 49), the Camden Society published Jocelin of Brakelond's *Chronicle* of daily life in the Abbey under the rule of Abbot Samson. Carlyle read Jocelin on his return to London, and the two walled communities, the twelfth-century Abbey of St Edmund and the 'Poor-Law Bastille' of St Ives (10: 1–2), became fixed in his mind as contrasting emblems of ancient community and modern alienation, of hope and hell.

Into a few months of intensive writing, Carlyle compressed a decade of growing anxiety over what was known as 'the condition of England question'. The Reform Bill of 1832 had done nothing to alleviate the plight of the urban and agricultural poor, and with the severe economic depression in 1836–7, their condition became desperate. On the eve of the Hungry Forties, Carlyle was moved to write *Chartism* (1839), a radical assault on the intolerable human costs of *laissez-faire*. The modern European revolutions on which he had been lecturing in London in 1839 seemed daily more likely to cross the Channel and erupt in the streets and factories of England. A week before setting out for East Anglia in September 1842, he complained to Emerson, 'I cannot write *two Books at once*; cannot be in the seven-teenth century and in the nineteenth at one and the same moment. . . . For my heart is sick and sore in behalf of my own poor generation. . . .'[11] At the time Carlyle sat down to write *Past and Present*, nearly one person in ten was classified as a pauper. The Corn Laws and bad harvests kept the price of bread high at a time of falling wages and widespread unemployment. According to the report Carlyle cites on the opening page, 1,207,000 paupers were on relief and another 221,000 were incarcerated in Workhouses, under a punitive regimen mandated by the Poor Law Amendment Act of 1834. This grimly Malthusian piece of legislation treated poverty as a crime. Within the Workhouses labour was hard, diet was intentionally inadequate, and families were forcibly separated, for continued breeding would only compound their problems and raise the cost of maintaining them.[12]

The bare statistics of the Hungry Forties are well known; what is harder for a non-Marxian reader to comprehend is the fact of such intense and widespread human suffering in a professedly Christian society. Children of 8 or 9 years of age, occasionally of only 5, worked fourteen to sixteen hours a day, exclusive of meals. Factory workers were flogged by overseers and mutilated by unsafe machines; hungry infants left at home by working mothers were drugged with massive doses of 'quietness' (tincture of opium); women and children in the posture of animals were harnessed to the coal-carts they pulled on hands and knees through narrow mineshafts. The air of the great industrial centres was acrid with coal smoke; rivers were clogged with noxious effluents and, in at least one instance, at Bradford, 'took fire'. In 1842 the streets of Manchester were tense with hungry, strik-ing workers. Within a few months of each other, Carlyle, in transit from Scotland, and Engels, a newly-arrived immigrant, saw the rebellious workers gathered on street-corners, milling about under skies unaccustomedly clear because of the idled factories. The strikers' demands for 'a fair day's-wages for a fair day's work' resound through the third chapter of *Past and Present*, 'Manchester Insurrection'.[13]

That such demands were judged seditious, such misery held to be inevitable, attests to the power of the ideology Carlyle attacks in the opening chapters of *Past and Present*. *Laissez-faire*, so the political economists argued, was rational, natural, ultimately productive of the greatest riches for the greatest number. Government regulation of working conditions would be ruinous to the economy and exacerbate unemployment. Thus Lord Brougham, the Liberal leader, could argue in the House of Commons that the sponsors of factory legislation were 'victims of a misguided and perverted humanity'.[14] The same logic led to the abolition of outdoor relief and the institution of the dreaded Workhouse. The old system, in effect since Elizabethan times, had merely increased the 'surplus population' by protecting 'the idle, the improvident, and the vicious'.[15] Yet in 1841–2 bread cost a shilling a loaf while the 'improvident' fieldhand who planted and harvested the grain earned only ten shillings a week. In the face of widespread hunger and unrest, *The Economist*, the leading organ of *laissez-faire*, had

no hesitation in pronouncing, because the masses are suffering, and have long been suffering, without much amending their condition, that they are greatly to blame. . . . Nature makes them responsible for their conduct—why should not we? We find them suffering, and we pronounce them in fault.[16]

If to our ears this sounds more like parody than serious argument, we owe our enlightenment at least in part to Carlyle.

*

A book of metamorphoses and miracles, *Past and Present* opens with a chapter entitled 'Midas' and has at its centre the miraculous exhumation of a martyred King. Ovid's myth of the gold-hungry King symbolizes for Carlyle the deathly paradox at the heart of Victorian industrialism—starvation in the midst of increasing abundance:

England is full of wealth, of multifarious produce, supply for human want in every kind; yet England is dying of inanition. With unabated bounty the land of England blooms and grows; waving with yellow harvests, thick-studded with workshops, industrial implements, with fifteen millions of workers, understood to be the strongest, the cunningest and the willingest our Earth ever had; these men are here; the work they have done, the fruit they have realised is here, abundant, exuberant on every hand of us: and behold, some baleful fiat as of Enchantment has gone forth, saying, "Touch it not, ye workers, ye master-workers, ye master-idlers; none of you can touch it, no man of you shall be the better for it; this is enchanted fruit!"

(10: 1)

The word *enchantment* runs like a motif through the chapter and points the reader back to Midas, an ancient type of modern English mammonism. As the picturesque Tourist stares at the men confined

within the ring-walls and railings of the workhouse, *laissez-faire* looks
neither rational nor natural but inhuman and absurd, like the ass-
eared King.

"They sat there, near by one another; but in a kind of torpor, especially in a
silence, which was very striking. In silence: for, alas, what word was to be
said? An Earth all lying round, crying, Come and till me, come and reap
me;—yet we here sit enchanted! In the eyes and brows of these men hung the
gloomiest expression, not of anger, but of grief and shame and manifold inarticulate distress. . . . There was something that reminded me of Dante's Hell
in the look of all this; and I rode swiftly away."

(10: 2)

All of *Past and Present* radiates outward from this opening scene of
sunlight and darkest despair. It leads 'in a circuitous way'* to
Jocelin's account in Book II of the unveiling in the dead of night of St
Edmund's uncorrupted body, emblem of victory over death. The
scene of able-bodied men frozen into Midas-like living death symbolizes modern England's miracle-in-reverse, whereby poverty
abounds despite increasing productivity, horses are better fed than
human beings, and Hell has come to mean 'not making money' (10: 22,
169).

Myth and fact, the timeless and the topical, go hand in hand in *Past
and Present*. Carlyle depicts the crisis of the moment as it explodes in
the streets and *sub specie aeternitatis*. In Emerson's phrase, *Past and Present* is an 'immortal newspaper'.[17] Life within the walls of the St Ives
Workhouse seems in calendar time aeons apart from life within St
Edmund's Abbey, yet in Carlyle's 'immortal newspaper' they appear
on facing pages. From the St Ives Workhouse Carlyle turns to a
report in *The Times* of a child-murder at Stockport that he compares
to Dante's 'Ugolino Hunger-tower', where, six centuries earlier, a
starving father fed off the corpses of his sons (10: 4). At the inquest at
Stockport a father and mother were found guilty of poisoning three of
their children and defrauding a burial society of the sum due on the
death of each child; the parents' motive, it was hinted at the inquest,
was to avert their own starvation and that of their remaining

* The phrase 'circuitous way' recurs several times, as in the last paragraph of Book I
and the first paragraph of Book II. Its recurrence mirrors Carlyle's structuring of *Past
and Present* around a series of juxtaposed symbols. The 'circuitous way' also suggests
the familiar trope of a book as a journey and its author as guide. Hence Carlyle poses
as a 'picturesque Tourist' at the entrance of his book. But *picturesque* alerts us to the
inadequacy of the pose, and we quickly realize that our tourist-guide, like Dante, is
taking us on a voyage to Hell.

children. 'And now Tom being killed, and all spent and eaten'
Carlyle asks in the mock-psychotic idiom of a society that consumes
rather than nurtures its children, 'Is it poor little starveling Jack that
must go, or poor little starveling Will?' (10: 4).

Enchantment, paralysis, disease—these are the metaphors that
organize Carlyle's diagnosis of England's 'condition'. Underlying
them all is the metaphor of the body-politic, with its ancient and
powerful assumption of the interdependence of limbs, heart, and
head joined in a common enterprise. 'We have more riches than any
Nation ever had before; we have less good of them than any Nation
ever had before' (10: 6). Carlyle's whole argument rests on the distinction between 'riches' and 'good', between wealth and common-
wealth. 'To whom, then, is this wealth of England wealth? Who is it
that it blesses; makes happier, wiser, beautifuler, in any way better?'
(10: 6).

The answer Carlyle seeks from his reader is assumed by the very
asking, just as the answer to the question, 'Am I my brother's
keeper?' is assumed by its wording. Carlyle asserts our interdependence in countless ways, not least effectively by addressing his
reader as *brother*. The reality of the social nexus, he argues, is indisput-
able; the only question confronting England is whether the connection will be for good or ill. 'Supply-and-demand is not the one Law of
Nature; Cash-payment is not the sole nexus of man with man . . .'
(10: 186). In the opening chapter Carlyle alludes to the Duke of
Newcastle, who evicted all the families on his estate that did not vote
as he wished: 'Cannot I do what I like with my own?' he demanded
of his critics in the House of Lords (10: 6, 180). Carlyle's answer
comes, 'circuitously' but inexorably, one hundred and fifty pages
later, in the form of the begging Irish Widow who, repulsed by her
neighbours, 'proves her sisterhood' by infecting them with typhoid
(10: 149). A late-breaking 'item' in Carlyle's immortal newspaper,
the Widow's avenging presence is felt from the beginning. She is
proleptically present in the mention in Chapter I of the 'brave and
human Dr. Alison' (10: 3), in whose book on poverty Carlyle first
read her story. And she seems to flit through the opening paragraphs
with their imagery of 'fever-fits' and 'fatal paralysis spreading
inwards, from the extremities, in St Ives workhouses, in Stockport
cellars, through all limbs, as if towards the heart itself' (10: 6). Early
in Book III Carlyle writes of the 'frightful nosology of diseases' afflicting modern England, chief among them 'the universal Social

Gangrene' (10: 137) of disbelief and alienation. A few pages later the metaphors of disease come home to roost in Dr Alison's account of the unregarded Widow dying and spreading death in the streets (10: 149). At the end of Book II Carlyle had cited Jocelin's account of Abbot Samson's touching the miraculously-preserved body of St Edmund. English Saint and Irish Widow: around the body of the one a thriving community grows up; around the other, a trail of contagion and death. Carlyle never explicitly links the two, but they are the embodied symbols of his belief that we are indissolubly bound together for good or ill, like 'living nerves in the same body' (10: 286).

*

'The Ancient Monk' is the most joyous of Carlyle's historical writings. In all his other histories, he is contemptuous of his sources; he groans, vituperates, complains of being buried alive under the combined weight of their purported stupidity. But for Jocelin, Carlyle feels and communicates a lived affection. 'The Ancient Monk' radiates a power of pure delight akin to a child's in finding buried treasure or in witnessing magic. The book that opens with the myth of the death-in-life of a Phrygian king, we recall, has at its luminous centre the victory over death of an early Christian king. 'The Ancient Monk' not only describes but in itself is a kind of miraculous exhumation, an 'unwrapping', as Carlyle puts it, of Jocelin's *Chronicle* 'from its thick cerements' of time (10: 43). Through the medium of the *Chronicle*, Carlyle writes in the first sentence of Book II, we will 'look face to face' upon an ancient century. The phrase *face to face* points back to the promised time in 1 Corinthians 13 when we shall no longer see through a glass darkly, and it points forward to the end of 'The Ancient Monk', where Carlyle's promise that his readers will look face to face upon the once-buried time is fulfilled in the dead of night. In the year 1198, filled with awe and trepidation, Abbot Samson opened the sacred loculus containing the body of King Edmund, who had been tortured to death by the Danes three hundred years earlier.* Samson strips away layer upon layer of outer cerements, unveils the innermost covering of linen, then pauses,

"saying he durst not proceed farther, or look at the sacred flesh naked. Taking the head between his hands, he thus spake, groaning: 'Glorious Martyr, holy Edmund, blessed be the hour when thou wert born. Glorious Martyr, turn it

---

* 'Cannot we kill you? cried they.—Cannot I die? answered he' (10: 54). Edmund's life is sketched in the chapter entitled 'Landlord Edmund'.

not to my perdition that I have so dared to touch thee, I miserable and sinful; thou knowest my devout love, and the intention of my mind.' And proceeding, he touched the eyes; and the nose, which was very massive and prominent (*valde grossum et valde eminentem*); and then he touched the breast and arms; and raising the left arm he touched the fingers, and placed his own fingers between the sacred fingers. And proceeding he found the feet standing stiff up, like the feet of a man dead yesterday; and he touched the toes and counted them (*tangendo numeravit*)."

(10: 122)

'What a scene,' Carlyle comments, 'shining luminous effulgent . . . through the dark Night' (10: 123). He has faithfully translated some hundred lines of Jocelin without a syllable's interpolation, and all the while the reader senses the presence of the double miracle, the one palpable to Abbot Samson's touch, the other performed by Carlyle, through the medium of Jocelin, of bringing 'that deep-buried Time' (10: 49) back to effulgent life. A 'laying on of hands' takes place on the page, Samson touching the long-buried Edmund, Carlyle touching us through the freshly unearthed words of Jocelin.

We do not actually see or touch Edmund, but neither does Jocelin; as he ruefully remarks, he was not one of the favoured twelve chosen by his Abbot to witness the unveiling of the body. But that there might be ' "abundance of witnesses, one of our Brethren, John of Dice, sitting on the roof of the Church, with the servants of the Vestry, and looking through, clearly saw all these things" ' (10: 122). Carlyle's eye is caught by John of Dice, high among the roof beams, while most of his fellow monks were 'all asleep, and the Earth all asleep,—and since then, Seven Centuries of Time mostly gone to sleep!' (10: 123). At the climactic moment of Book II, the clear eyes of Jocelin no longer serve us. But the shift in perspective from Jocelin to the surveillant John mirrors the circuitous ways of the narrative: through a chink in a twelfth-century roof the nineteenth-century historian glimpses the features of a ninth-century martyr whose sacrifice, in turn, mirrors a martyrdom already eight centuries old.

Like mirrors facing mirrors or magical boxes inside boxes, *Past and Present* often reflects itself. The 'thick cerements' of time wound around Jocelin's *Chronicle* are peeled, layer by layer, from Edmund's body after its removal from a coffin so tightly filled ' "you could scarcely put a needle between the head and the wood" ' (10: 122). Recovering Jocelin's long-buried world requires digging down through archaeological and linguistic strata, through the 'ninefold

Stygian Marshes' of 'Monk-Latin' (10: 40) to a language and way of life 'covered deeper than Pompeii with the lava-ashes and inarticulate wreck of seven hundred years!' (10: 40).

The unburying begins with Jocelin himself, who first appears all caked in Monk-Latin as 'a certain Jocelinus de Brakelonda' (10: 40). Within a very few lines he is Anglicized as 'Jocelin of Brakelond', then familiarized as 'our Jocelin, . . . a kind of born *Boswell*' (10: 41). With his distinctive personality Jocelin serves as a fixed vantage-point in a shadowy world in which 'all fluctuates chameleon-like' (10: 54), including the forms and meanings of words. Before Jocelin entered the Abbey as a novice, Carlyle tells us, 'some three centuries or so had elapsed since *Beodric's-worth* became St Edmund's *Stow*, St Edmund's *Town* and Monastery . . .' (10: 50). Often at the start of chapters Carlyle rings changes on placenames, as if tolling in their successive forms the passage of lives and epochs: 'The *Burg*, Bury, or "Berry" as they call it, of St Edmund is still a prosperous brisk Town . . . with its clear brick houses, ancient clean streets . . .' (10: 46). In 'Twelfth Century' he compresses into the triplet '*Mancunium*, Manceaster . . . Manchester' (10: 66) the two thousand years separating ancient Roman from modern industrial Britain. The writing strains under the burden of latency and change, of ancient wildernesses that will later roar with machinery, 'James Watt still slumbering', like an animate stratum of coal, 'in the deep of Time'. Both landscape and language seem in flux, as this paragraph about change ends on a passage about change in Ovid's *Metamorphoses*.

How much [from the twelfth century] is still alive in England; how much has not yet come into life! . . . How silent . . . lie all Cotton-trades and suchlike; not a steeple-chimney yet got on end from sea to sea! North of the Humber, a stern Willelmus Conquaestor burnt the Country, finding it unruly, into very stern repose. Wild-fowl scream in those ancient silences, wild cattle roam in those ancient solitudes; . . . The Ribble and the Aire roll down, as yet unpolluted by dyers' chemistry; tenanted by merry trouts and piscatory otters; the sunbeam and the vacant wind's-blast alone traversing those moors. Side by side sleep the coal-strata and the iron-strata for so many ages; no Steam-Demon has yet risen smoking into being. Saint Mungo rules in Glasgow; James Watt still slumbering in the deep of Time. *Mancunium*, Manceaster, what we now call Manchester, spins no cotton,—if it be not *wool* "cottons," clipped from the backs of mountain sheep. The Creek of the Mersey gurgles, twice in the four-and-twenty hours, with eddying brine, clangorous with sea-fowl; and is a *Lither*-Pool, a *lazy* or sullen Pool, no

monstrous pitchy City, and Seahaven of the world! The Centuries are big;
and the birth-hour is coming, not yet come. *Tempus ferax, tempus edax rerum.* *
                                                                    (10: 65–6)

Carlyle's immortal newspaper is written in many dialects, and sometimes the movement from past to present reverses itself; we fall back-
ward in time and stumble upon linguistic bedrock. The interpolated
Latin excerpts from Jocelin have this archaizing effect. They bypass
the 'Editor', as Carlyle calls himself in 'The Ancient Monk', and,
like the chink in the Abbey roof, provide a direct opening into
Jocelin's world. We are not privileged to touch or number St
Edmund's toes, but in Carlyle's italicized interpolation from
Jocelin— *'tangendo numeravit'*—we press as close to the miracle as
language permits.

Abbot Samson's 'face to face' sight of St Edmund at the end of
'The Ancient Monk' has a remarkable counterpart at the beginning,
when Carlyle sees his own image reflected in the eyes of a nameless
stranger I take to be Jocelin. He prepares us for the encounter by
comparing Jocelin's *Chronicle* to a 'magical speculum, much gone to
rust' (10: 43), which fitfully mirrors the past. This is the same 'intermittent magic-mirror' (10: 46) in which King John Lackland
appeared a few pages earlier with his raucous retinue, leaving his
miserly gift of *tredecim sterlingii* and vanishing like an apparition, 'at
once inscrutable and certain; so dim, yet so indubitable' (10: 46). In
the passage at hand, the mirror returns Carlyle's own gaze in an
equivocal epiphany. He tells us that in the gossip of Jocelin we can
discern a whole peopled world 'face to face' (10: 49). That resonant
phrase leads directly to the ghostly encounter of Carlyle and Jocelin:

> Readers who please to go along with us into this poor *Jocelini Chronica* shall
> wander inconveniently enough, as in wintry twilight, through some poor
> stript hazel-grove, rustling with foolish noises, and perpetually hindering the
> eyesight; but across which, here and there, some real human figure is seen
> moving: very strange; whom we could hail if we would answer;—and we look
> into a pair of eyes deep as our own, *imaging* our own, but all unconscious of
> us; to whom we, for the time, are become as spirits and invisible!
>
>   (10: 50)

This imaginary winterscape with its 'real human figure' wandering
within it, returning our stare yet not seeing us, made in our image yet

---

* 'Time the bearer, time the devourer of [all] things.' The last three words are from
Book XV, line 234 of the *Metamorphoses*.

deaf to our call, this haunting evocation of distance and likeness is Carlyle's vision of the past seen through a dark glass at twilight and yet also face to face. In the heat of Carlyle's 'earnest loving glance', the 'void black Night' of the past becomes luminous (10: 49–50). But it is a fitful luminousness, hedged about by the hazel-thicket of time, hence both dim and indubitable. 'What a historical picture, glowing visible', Carlyle exclaims of a vivid moment in Jocelin when a crowd of angry old women, their houses invaded by the tax-collector, rush out into the street shouting and brandishing their distaffs (10: 64). The picture glows all the more brightly for its arrested evanescence, like the miraculous effulgence around St Edmund's shrine, still visible in Jocelin's words after seven centuries of darkness.

The historian's art for Carlyle consists in making the vanished past visibly present by evoking its very absence. Not one stone of the Winchester manor house of King Henry II still stands, Carlyle tells us, yet one Sunday in February 1182 a delegation from St Edmundsbury verily appeared before the King to choose a new Abbot. King Henry was 'visibly there', surrounded by earls and bishops, 'a vivid, noble-looking man, with grizzled beard, in glittering uncertain costume . . .' (10: 79). The vivid but vanished King dressed in brilliant but uncertain costume—the portrait suggests much and delineates little. Carlyle will not add an iota of detail he cannot authenticate, and hence can only guess at 'what gilt seats' or carved tables once adorned the Great Hall that centuries ago 'fled bodily, like a Dream of the Old Night' (10: 79–80). The incongruous image of a dream in *bodily* flight conveys Carlyle's sense of the past as a tangible presence, like the royal feet which the newly-elected Abbot Samson stoops to kiss.

To see the past in such fullness the historian must 'read . . . with ancient yet with modern eyes' (10: 107). The writing of history as Carlyle practised it is essentially an act of exegesis, and hence he most often appears in his works as an exegete or 'Editor', whether of the fictional papers of Teufelsdröckh, the *Chronicle* of Jocelin, or the writings of Cromwell. With the same 'earnest loving glance' that he had directed at Jocelin, Carlyle teaches himself to '*read*' through the maze of Cromwell's letters and speeches until they become 'completely luminous again', and glow with their 'old veracity and sacred zeal and fire . . .' (7: 111).

That light wavers in *Cromwell*; it burns brilliantly through the hundred pages of 'The Ancient Monk'. Carlyle creates a peopled world within the walls of the Abbey, and in the tight, hierarchical cohesion of Samson's rule he sees mirrored the cohesion of the feudal society beyond St Edmundsbury. For all of Jocelin's acuity and humanity, he looks out from his monk's cowl upon a 'narrow section of the world' (10: 41); Jocelin's 'Editor' sees beyond Jocelin to the ends of the Kingdom. And in moments of privileged vision he appears to rise above the known world and glimpse another, beyond time and space:

For twenty generations, here was the earthly arena where painful living men worked out their life-wrestle,—looked at by Earth, by Heaven and Hell. Bells tolled to prayers; and men, of many humours, various thoughts, chanted vespers, matins;—and round the little islet of their life rolled forever (as round ours still rolls, though we are blind and deaf) the illimitable Ocean, tinting all things with *its* eternal hues and reflexes. . . .

(10: 49)

'The Ancient Monk' is studded with 'cosmic pastorals' of similar expansiveness and beauty. In 'Twelfth Century' we see the smoke rising above the Abbey kitchens, hear the daily chanting of matins and vespers, the clanging of the church bells, but the perspective broadens from a particular moment in time to Time itself, Past and Present:

Bells clang out: on great occasions, all the bells. We have Processions, Preachings, Festivals, Christmas Plays, *Mysteries* shown in the Churchyard, at which latter the Townsfolk sometimes quarrel. Time was, Time is, as Friar Bacon's Brass Head remarked; and withal Time will be. There are three Tenses, Tempora, or Times; and there is one Eternity; and as for us,

"We are such stuff as Dreams are made of!"

(10: 63)[18]

The 'three Tenses' and 'one Eternity' remind us that the title *Past and Present* tells only half the story: in the final Book—'Horoscope'—Carlyle moves from the 'past' of St Edmundsbury and the 'present' of Manchester to a prophecy of England's future. And in all four Books he puts us in mind of the 'illimitable Ocean' that rolls around the 'little islet' of Jocelin's time and our own.

Although Jocelin outlived Abbot Samson, the *Chronicle* abruptly ends eight years before Samson's death. Carlyle indicates the break in Jocelin's manuscript with a double-dash on his own page; into this void he crowds all of his art, ushering Jocelin out of existence as adroitly as he had summoned him into being one hundred pages earlier. He compresses into half a paragraph sixteen manuscript pages dealing with Samson's later years, for it suits his design to end with the miraculous exhumation, the 'culminating point of [Samson's] existence' (10: 125).[19] Jocelin's narrative has indeed been 'shorn-through by the scissors of Destiny', but Carlyle's further abbreviation of the *Chronicle* intensifies the shock of finding ourselves transported back into the nineteenth century, gazing with the picturesque tourists ('dilettanti') at the blackened ruin from the Middle Ages:

> [Samson] is sent for again, over sea, to advise King Richard. . . . The magnanimous Abbot makes preparation for departure; departs, and— —And Jocelin's Boswellean Narrative, suddenly shorn-through by the scissors of Destiny, *ends*. There are no words more; but a black line, and leaves of blank paper. Irremediable: the miraculous hand, that held all this theatric-machinery, suddenly quits hold; impenetrable Time-Curtains rush down; in the mind's eye all is again dark, void; with loud dinning in the mind's ear, our real-phantasmagory of St. Edmundsbury plunges into the bosom of the Twelfth Century again, and all is over. Monks, Abbot, Hero-worship, Government, Obedience, Coeur-de-Lion and St. Edmund's Shrine, vanish like Mirza's Vision; and there is nothing left but a mutilated black Ruin amid green botanic expanses, and oxen, sheep and dilettanti pasturing in their places.

> (10: 125)

*

A casual phrase describing life in St Edmundsbury—'We have Processions, Preachings, Festivals . . .' (10: 63)—comes to mind as we read 'Phenomena', the first chapter of Book III, which opens with three processions through the streets of modern London and Rome. The word *phenomenon*, from a Greek verb meaning *to show* or *appear*, has come to suggest an extraordinary or especially significant appearance, and Carlyle intends this later sense as he portrays three contemporary 'Phantasms riding with huge clatter along the streets . . .' (10: 137). A few sentences after the 'real-phantasmagory of St Edmundsbury'* plunges back into the twelfth century, we find

* The term 'phantasmagoria' was coined in 1802 to promote the first exhibition in London of 'magic lantern' projections by means of which moving figures appeared to grow rapidly in size, merge, advance, retreat, and vanish. Carlyle's enlisting of such illusionary devices in the service of metaphor reflects his larger preoccupation with the incongruities between appearance and reality, dress and substance. By clothing the

ourselves staring at the egregious phenomenon of a modern Pope made out of wood and baked hair:

> The old Pope of Rome, finding it laborious to kneel so long while they cart him through the streets to bless the people on *Corpus-Christi* Day, complains of rheumatism; whereupon his Cardinals consult;—construct him, after some study, a stuffed cloaked figure, of iron and wood, with wool or baked hair; and place it in a kneeling posture. Stuffed figure, or rump of a figure; to this stuffed rump he, sitting at his ease on a lower level, joins, by the aid of cloaks and drapery, his living head and outspread hands: the rump with its cloaks kneels, the Pope looks, and holds his hands spread; and so the two in concert bless the Roman population on *Corpus-Christi* Day, as well as they can.
>
> (10: 138)

Ten pages of print separate this stuffed effigy of a living Pope from the life-like body of the long-dead Saint. Carlyle never explicitly links the two figures, but the reader recognizes them as the embodiment of an idea stated at the start of 'Phenomena': 'We have quietly closed our eyes to the eternal Substance of things, and opened them only to the Shows and Shams of things' (10: 136). Hence this superlative illustration of what Carlyle calls 'the Scenic Theory of Worship' (10: 139), paraded on *Corpus-Christi* Day. Carlyle's grim humour twice plays over the italicized *body* in *Corpus-Christi*. A touch of Ovidian mockery colours the metamorphosis of this modern Pope on the Feast of the Eucharist: a transubstantiation not into the Sacred Body but into a stuffed rump.

Carlyle's second instance of a symbol frayed at the elbows is 'The Champion of England', the heraldic officer who rides into Westminster Hall in full armour to answer any challenge to the coronation of a new sovereign. On his last recorded appearance, this stout flower of a decadent aristocracy had to be hoisted into the saddle (10: 140). From these 'Shows and Shams' of modern church and state, Carlyle turns to the streets of commercial London and a gigantic seven-foot Hat. Again he writes what Emerson calls 'true contemporary his-

---

past in a reality as seemingly substantial as that of the present, the historian, like any writer, practises *trompe-l'œil*. Jocelin's *Chronicle*, in addition to being a 'magical speculum' and 'intermittent magic-mirror', is also a 'singular *camera lucida*' (10: 43), a device which projects the image of an external object onto a flat surface and by midcentury was made obsolete by the image-retentive *camera obscura*. The contradiction in the phrase 'real-phantasmagory' typifies the visual oxymorons that recur regularly in Carlyle's historical writings, like his portrait of the plumed and crimson spectre of King John. ' "Tout est optique" ', as Mercier remarks in *The French Revolution* (4: 103).

tory' by seizing 'on a fact as a symbol which was never a symbol before':*

Consider, for example, that great Hat seven-feet high, which now peram-
bulates London Streets; which my Friend Sauerteig regarded justly as . . .
"the topmost point as yet . . . to which English Puffery has been observed to
reach!"—The Hatter in the Strand of London, instead of making better felt-
hats than another, mounts a huge lath-and-plaster Hat, seven-feet high, upon
wheels; sends a man to drive it through the streets; hoping to be saved *thereby*.
He has not attempted to *make* better hats, as he was appointed by the
Universe to do, and as with this ingenuity of his he could very probably have
done; but his whole industry is turned to *persuade* us that he has made such!
He too knows that the Quack has become God.

(10: 141)

Early photographs in *The Victorian City: Images and Realities* depict
sandwich-board men dwarfed by their larger-than-life advertisements, and one photograph shows a huge, horse-drawn Boot that
rivals in scale the seven-foot Hat.[20] 'Signs of the Times', the biblical
title of Carlyle's first important essay, took on new meaning in the
years of *Past and Present*: vehicular traffic in the Strand was choked by
gargantuan mobile advertisements, like the Boot touting the 'Public
Benefit Boot & Shoe Company'; and the owners of the *Illustrated
London News*, to promote the birth of their paper in May 1842, packed
the streets of central London with two hundred sign-bearers, each
carrying a placard taller than himself.[21]

The oddity of the monster advertisements is that they look quite
ordinary within the larger, vibrantly grotesque setting of Victorian
London. 'Alas, that we natives note him little,' Carlyle writes of the
maker of the seven-foot Hat, 'that we view him as a thing of course,
is the very burden of the misery' (10: 142). In 'Tintern Abbey'
Wordsworth had written of the 'burthen of the mystery', but the

* From an unsigned review of *Past and Present* in the *Dial*, July 1843, rpt. in Seigel,
Heritage, pp. 220, 224-5. Emerson's comment on Carlyle's style deserves fuller quotation:

Carlyle is the first domestication of the modern system with its infinity of details into
style. We have been civilizing very fast, building London and Paris, and now planting New England and India, New Holland and Oregon,—and it has not appeared
in literature,—there has been no analogous expansion and recomposition in books.
Carlyle's style is the first emergence of all this wealth and labor, . . . How like an
air-balloon or bird of Jove does he seem to float over the continent, and stooping
here and there pounce on a fact as a symbol which was never a symbol before. This
is the first experiment; and something of rudeness and haste must be pardoned to so
great an achievement.

Wordsworthian mystery has become, for Carlyle, urban misery. A picturesque Tourist at the start of *Past and Present*, he now sees himself as a 'native' gazing at the exotic 'phenomena' of his own city, the human inhabitants metamorphosed into outlandish 'animations' scarcely regarded by the passers-by. The commercialization of life distressed Carlyle, but the alienation of human beings from each other and from their own humanity distressed him more. The stuffed Pope and perambulated Hat prod him into satire; the Irish Widow, crying 'I am your sister, bone of your bone . . . help me!' (10: 149), moves him to pity and to horror.

*

Carlyle intended *Past and Present* as an urgent call to action; we would be frivolous to admire its artistry but ignore its programme. He advocates strong, paternalistic government, along the lines of his hero, Abbot Samson. He attacks *laissez-faire* and utilitarianism. He calls for government regulation of mines, factories, and public health, including minimum housing standards and control of pollution; he proposes a guaranteed permanent wage, part-ownership of industry by the workers, a ministry of education, and free public schools (10: 264–7, 277, 282). Finally he dismisses political reform as mere tinkering with 'machinery' and opposes the spread of democracy as an invitation to anarchy.

Of this miscellany of attitudes and proposals, only Carlyle's views on authority and democracy invite controversy. In the vexing chapter on 'Democracy' in Book III, Carlyle argues that democracy was the extension into politics of the economic Liberalism that had for its end product the St Ives Workhouse, a view share by Engels in *The Condition of the Working Class in England*. In Raymond Williams's phrase, Carlyle saw democracy as merely a 'negative solution'.[22] It could defer but not prevent the kinds of protest that led in France to the Revolution and in England to the Peterloo Massacre.* Williams quotes a passage from *Chartism* that anticipates the later chapter on 'Democracy': 'In democracy can lie no finality . . . with the completest winning of democracy there is nothing yet won—except

* In Manchester on 16 August, 1819, a cavalry-charge killed thirteen in a crowd of 60,000 petitioning for repeal of the Corn Laws and reform of Parliament. The Massacre and the 'grim vengeance' it aroused figure early in *Past and Present* (10: 16–17).

emptiness, and the free chance to win.'[23] Williams writes that 'we have all learned to shout "fascist"' at such a position, yet it is 'a most relevant criticism of that kind of democracy which, for example, reached its climax in the Reform Bill of 1832.'[24] This was precisely the kind of democracy that Carlyle attacked in *Past and Present*—the democracy typified by the mill-owners and their Liberal spokesmen in Parliament who in 1844 defeated the Ten Hours Bill on the grounds that 'women and young persons are capable of making their own bargains'.[25] For the toiling millions, Carlyle writes, life has always been a struggle against hunger and injustice, yet never before

was the lot of those same dumb millions of toilers so entirely unbearable as it is even in the days now passing over us. It is not to die, or even to die of hunger, that makes a man wretched; many men have died; all men must die,—the last exit of us all is in a Fire-Chariot of Pain. But it is to live miserable we know not why; to work sore and yet gain nothing; to be heart-worn, weary, yet isolated, unrelated, girt-in with a cold universal Laissez-faire: it is to die slowly all our life long, imprisoned in a deaf, dead, Infinite Injustice, as in the accursed iron belly of a Phalaris' Bull! This is and remains forever intolerable to all men whom God has made. Do we wonder at French Revolutions, Chartisms, Revolts of Three Days?

(10: 210–11)

This is Carlyle at his compassionate, clear-sighted best. He knows that the Revolutionary clock cannot be turned back, that 'Democracy is everywhere the inexorable demand of these ages, swiftly fulfilling itself.'[26] But he also knows that for millions in England, a full half-century after the Revolution, the millennium had never seemed further away. As he saw it, a spurious liberty had been secured at the expense of community—the liberty to go hungry in a free market. This is the point of the notorious paragraph on Gurth and Cedric:

Gurth, born thrall of Cedric the Saxon, has been greatly pitied by Dryasdust and others. Gurth, with the brass collar round his neck, tending Cedric's pigs in the glades of the wood, is not what I call an exemplar of human felicity: but Gurth, with the sky above him, with the free air and tinted boscage and umbrage round him, and in him at least the certainty of supper and social lodging when he came home; Gurth to me seems happy, in comparison with many a Lancashire and Buckinghamshire man of these days, not born thrall of anybody! Gurth's brass collar did not gall him: Cedric *deserved* to be his master. The pigs were Cedric's, but Gurth too would get his parings of them. Gurth had the inexpressible satisfaction of feeling himself related indissolubly, though in a rude brass-collar way, to his fellow-mortals in this Earth.

He had superiors, inferiors, equals.—Gurth is now "emancipated" long since; has what we call "Liberty." Liberty, I am told, is a divine thing. Liberty when it becomes the "Liberty to die by starvation" is not so divine!

. . . O, if thou really art my *Senior*, Seigneur, my *Elder*, Presbyter or Priest,—if thou art in very deed my *Wiser*, may a beneficent instinct lead and impel thee to "conquer" me, to command me! If thou do know better than I what is good and right, I conjure thee in the name of God, force me to do it; . . . That I have been called, by all the Newspapers, a "free man" will avail me little, if my pilgrimage have ended in death and wreck. O that the Newspapers had called me slave, coward, fool, or what it pleased their sweet voices to name me, and I had attained not death, but life!—Liberty requires new definitions.

(10: 211–13)

The passage is calculated to enrage the reader. Carlyle cannot know that Gurth's collar did not gall him, and it is galling to be told so. That Cedric *deserved* to be Gurth's master is dangerous nonsense, italicized to offend the reader even further. The intolerable corollary to Cedric's mastership is that Gurth *deserved* to be a slave, fed on pig-parings. Carlyle is throwing the 'worst-case' in our faces, in order to show that even at its harshest the servitude of Gurth was less dehumanizing than the 'liberty' of the modern wage-slave. His indictment of *laissez-faire* is powerful and just; but if his diagnosis is correct, his proposed cure—the call for a 'beneficent' leader to 'command' us—has proved in our own century to be worse than the disease. The chapter on 'Democracy' marks one of the last moments when all that is most perceptive in Carlyle's social thought, and all that is most inflammatory, co-exist in fruitful tension. Even as we recall Whitman's remark that progressivism never had a worthier foe than Carlyle, we also see that he can be brutal and obtuse. The moving paragraph that ends, 'Liberty requires new definitions', is followed by another that begins with the bad joke, ' "Democracy . . . means despair of finding any Heroes to govern you . . ." ' (10: 215). Abbot Samson seems especially to appeal to Carlyle because he was *not* elected by universal suffrage. Without ballot-boxes or reform bills, Carlyle writes, the monks of St Edmundsbury 'contrived to accomplish the most important social feat a body of men can do, to winnow-out the man that is to govern them . . .' (10: 82). It never occurs to Carlyle that under certain procedures the winnowing will be more just than under others. He had little interest in political institutions, dismissed Parliament as 'our National Palaver' (10: 219), and derided all attempts at political reform as mere 'Morrison's Pills', a widely-advertised quack-remedy.[27] Convinced that the disease afflicting England was at bottom neither political nor economic but moral, he was uninterested in reforming the body-politic and sought instead to cure the 'soul-politic'. But his gospel of national salvation through Work, directed by 'Captains of Industry' who have seen the Carlylean light, is of more interest as a private fantasy than as public policy. More alarming, in the closing pages of *Past and Present* Carlyle sounds a note of racism that was to become more blatant in 'The Nigger Question'. He argues that English Christians had no business freeing West Indian Blacks while tolerating the wage-slavery of their White brothers at home: 'In one of those Lancashire Weavers, dying of hunger, there is more thought and heart, a greater arithmetical amount of misery and desperation, than in whole gangs of Quashees' (10: 278). Carlyle's contempt for Blacks blinds him to the perniciousness of an 'arithmetic' of comparative misery.

With the exceptions of 'Phenomena' and 'Democracy', Carlyle seems to have lost his way in the last two books of *Past and Present*. It is as if the 'Proem' and 'The Ancient Monk' had exhausted his fund of ideas but not his compulsion to write. In the final book, 'Horoscope', he seems by some trick of fate to have himself become 'enchanted'— the victim not of insulting the gods, like Midas, but of the delusion that he is privy to their purpose, perhaps that he has become one of them. A decade before Carlyle wrote *Past and Present*, an acquaintance was struck by his resemblance to a 'religious zealot',[28] a role he both played and mocked in *Sartor Resartus*. In *The French Revolution* he assumed the voice of an Old Testament prophet and, at the end, impersonated the mock-prophet Cagliostro. In 'Horoscope' the distance between self and mask disappears and the voice of the zealot Thomas Carlyle proclaims a new religion. He prophesies a millennium of fruitful industry when the old 'Epic' of '*Arms and the Man*' will be superseded by the new epoch of '*Tools and the Man*' (10: 250). Waste places will be cleared and chaos conquered in a kind of secular Second Coming led by the regenerate Captains of Industry (10: 297–8, 271–2). 'Plugson of Undershot' is their imperfect forerunner, Abbot Samson their perfected, pre-industrial type.[29] In this new dispensation the old 'Rituals, Liturgies, Credos, [and] Sinai Thunder' will be set aside as childish things, for 'I am grown to be a man now; and do not need the thunder and the terror any longer!' (10: 230). The 'I' of this passage is hard to place, coming seemingly from nowhere, until one realizes that Carlyle is speaking as a type of perfected mankind. Abbot Samson is the hero of Book II, but the prophet Thomas Carlyle is the thinly-veiled hero of 'Horoscope':

This man's life [is] . . . a battle and a march, a warfare with principalities and powers. . . . He walks among men; loves men, with inexpressible soft pity,—as they *cannot* love him: but his soul dwells in solitude, in the uttermost parts of Creation. . . .

(10: 291)

In his study of Victorian typology, Herbert Sussman argues that the new saviour in this passage is 'indistinguishable from Christ' and that Carlyle is writing about the Captains of Industry, former avatars of greed converted into exemplars of sacrifice.[30] But surely Carlyle is also describing himself. In *On Heroes* he had praised the 'Man of Letters' as 'our most important modern person', the age-of-print Hero whom older generations had named 'Prophet, Priest, Divinity' (5: 155–6). In *Past and Present* he virtually claims for himself this lonely and exalted role. The more celebrated he became, the more solitary he felt. The strange fruits of this imagined neglect first manifest themselves in his works during the decade of *Past and Present*. In 1840 he writes in his *Journal* of the 'baleful Nessus shirt of perpetual pain and isolation in which I am lamed, embated, and swathed as in enchantment till I quit this earth'.[31] At the end of the decade the imagined speaker of 'The Nigger Question'—clearly Carlyle—calls himself a 'minority of one' and taunts his hostile audience with the cry, ' "Crucify him! Crucify him!" ' (29: 360).

Never more powerful than in its opening pages, *Past and Present* begins to unravel as it nears its end. The interplay of sacred and secular history that lent such strength to *The French Revolution* still works in *Past and Present*, but after 'Phenomena' Carlyle's typological imagination operates not on the materials of history but on those of personal fantasy. Private mythologies are easier to invent than to propagate, and neither Carlyle's Captains of Industry nor Carlyle himself can serve us as the New Adam or move us to set aside our old Credos and Sinai-Thunders. Although *Past and Present* ends on a note of messianic hope, Carlyle's vision of the future is the product of present despair.

8

Cromwell Face to Face

Carlyle completed *Past and Present* in the spring of 1843, and in the autumn returned to his long-deferred history of Cromwell. He had made several false starts since the winter of 1838–9, when Mill invited him to contribute an essay on Cromwell to the *London and Westminster Review*.[1] The essay never materialized, although Mill sent Carlyle a 'huge hamper' of books on the Cromwell period, as he had done a decade earlier with books on the French Revolution. In November 1843 Mill must have seen the ghost of former flames: Carlyle wrote that he had burned the dozen or more bad beginnings he had so far managed to put onto paper.[2] He had already written about Cromwell in *On Heroes*, but his portrait of the Lord Protector in 'The Hero as King' is a brief sketch, not a history. He still could not find his way through the morass of materials on the Civil War or find the thread that would lend coherence to a life of Cromwell: 'No history in the strict sense can be made of that unspeakable puddle of time, all covered up with things entirely obsolete to us—a Golgotha of dead dogs.'[3] Just before setting the problem of *Cromwell* aside in favour of the sudden fluency of *Past and Present*, he complained of feeling as if he were 'sunk deep, fifty miles deep, below the region of articulation . . . .'.[4] The fear of being buried alive while trying to rescue Cromwell from two centuries of obloquy is the unstated subject of *Cromwell*, the dark side of Carlyle's attempt to wash Cromwell's 'natural face *clean*' (8: 127) of the accumulated filth of the ages.

When Carlyle returned to the long-delayed project, his solution was not to write a history of the Civil War or a biography of Cromwell, but to let Cromwell speak for himself through his own letters and speeches. The result is an uneven book, with moments of compelling vitality and tracts of barrenness that no healthy imagination can long endure. Of the success of Carlyle's stated intention—the rehabilitation of Cromwell as neither an ambitious fanatic nor a hypocrite—there can be no doubt. Bit by bit Cromwell comes to life, until the reader recognizes the very timbre of his voice. According to Froude, himself

an historian of some note, *Cromwell* is 'by far the most important con-
tribution to English history . . . in the present century. Carlyle was
the first . . . to make Cromwell and Cromwell's age again intelligible
to mankind.'[5] Historians much less sympathetic to Carlyle than
Froude share his high regard for *Cromwell*. Hugh Trevor-Roper
praises Carlyle's transformation of the received view of Cromwell as a
'permanent achievement',[6] and G. P. Gooch commends him for
having 'disinterred' Cromwell from 'the load of misrepresentation
and calumny' which had weighed upon him for nearly two
centuries.*

Gooch's choice of the word 'disinterred' is especially appropriate to
the opening of *Cromwell*, with its journey to the dank underworld of
archival research. Carlyle describes tons of Civil War pamphlets
buried in the British Museum, a 'mouldering dumb wilderness of
things once alive'. The features of the once-human past have etiolated
'into mouldy blank', human speech has lapsed into an 'inarticulate
slumberous mumblement . . .' (6: 3, 10). The opening of *Cromwell*
('Anti-Dryasdust') dramatizes the historian's struggle to 'voice' the
past; but Carlyle is also dramatizing a life-and-death struggle within
himself, from which he emerges deeply scarred. The battle is for his
soul as a writer, and it takes place between two antithetical aspects of
himself: the 'sacred Poet' who aspires to make of Cromwell's story 'a
modern *Iliad*', and 'Dryasdust', the ghoulish pedant who rummages
among the boneyards of the dead (6: 8). 'One wishes there were a
History of English Puritanism, the last of all our Heroisms', Carlyle
writes at the start of 'Anti-Dryasdust'; 'but [one] sees small prospect
of such a thing at present' (6: 1). Still fired by his old vision of history
as the proper subject of modern epic, he would have loved to write a
Cromwelliad and not *Oliver Cromwell's Letters and Speeches: with Elucidations by Thomas Carlyle*. The opening chapter of *Cromwell* is the tomb

* Although Gooch calls *Cromwell* 'a classic, fearing no rivalry', he decries Carlyle's
failure to appreciate Cromwell's commitment to democratic institutions and his reluc-
tance to assume supreme power. Gooch is also hard on Carlyle for being duped by
William Squire, the forger of thirty-five purported Cromwell letters that Carlyle
printed with a defence of their authenticity in *Fraser's Magazine* (December 1847) and
reprinted as an appendix to the third edition of *Cromwell*. See G. P. Gooch, 'Carlyle
and Froude', in *History and Historians in the Nineteenth Century*, 2nd edn. (Boston: Beacon
Press, 1959), pp. 306–7. As a sequel to this tangled tale, Carlyle compounded 'The
Squire Papers' hoax by anonymously co-authoring with John Forster a 'review' in
The Examiner that again asserted the authenticity of the letters and defended
'Mr. Carlyle's' publication of them in *Fraser's*. See K. J. Fielding, 'A New Review (of
Himself) by Carlyle: The Squire Forgeries, *Examiner* (15 January 1848)', *The Carlyle
Newsletter*, 3 (1981; dated on cover, October 1982).

in which Carlyle lays that ambition to rest. No English poet has written a more haunting elegy to the feared loss of his own powers, an elegy buried in a book that is now all but forgotten.

Most of the chapter is spoken by a nameless 'impatient friend', a 'well-known Writer' (6: 1, 3) whom Carlyle commiserates on his 'almost desperate enterprise' (6: 11) of trying to resuscitate the heroic age of English Puritanism. At the outset of his career Carlyle had dedicated himself to the 'high emprise' (28: 53) of writing historical epic; now in mid-career, he finds the old ambition desperate. At the end of the chapter, he wishes his friend more patience, bids him a sad farewell, and invites the reader 'to our own small enterprise, and solid despatch of business in plain prose!' (6: 12). Carlyle is of course incapable of plain prose, and the small enterprise turns out to be a tome of nearly fifteen hundred pages. But the self-mockery bears a darker meaning. Although *Cromwell* was a great success and its author 'admired, praised, and honoured by all England and America',[7] the writing had been an ordeal more costly than any he had previously known. His normally anxious letters written in the throes of composition take on a note of morbid panic. 'My thrice unfortunate Book on Cromwell', he writes to Emerson in January 1844, 'is a real descent to Hades, to Golgotha and Chaos! I feel oftenest as if it were possibler to die oneself than to bring it into life.'[8] Carlyle is never more articulate than on the feared drying up of the sacred fountain of speech. At the end of 'Anti-Dryasdust' the impatient friend asks, ' "Why has the living ventured thither, down from the cheerful light . . . to these baleful halls of Dis and the three-headed Dog?" ' (6: 10). Carlyle answers that the task of reviving the heroic past requires 'pious love in any "Orpheus" that will risk descending to the Gloomy Halls;— descending, it may be, and fronting Cerberus and Dis, to no purpose!' (6: 11). The descent took Carlyle seven years. He succeeded in washing clean the face of his beloved Cromwell, but he returned to the light an embittered Orpheus.

*

The contest between the sacred Poet and Dryasdust does not end with the first chapter but turns into a kind of guerrilla warfare that Carlyle continues to wage against his sources. The labour of love that he expends on restoring Cromwell to life is counterbalanced by the contempt he heaps upon the predecessors whose writings made the resuscitation possible. This polarization of emotion so characteristic of Carlyle is reflected in his portrait of Cromwell: 'What a rage, wide-sweeping, inexorable as Death, dwells in that heart;—close neighbour to pity, to trembling affection, and soft tears!' (7: 54). Pity for Cromwell, rage against his critics combine to arouse in Carlyle invectives of inexhaustible vitality, all directed against the Dryasdust that he fears to become. John Vicars, author of *God's Ark . . . or . . . the Parliamentary Chronicle*, is a 'poor human soul zealously prophesying as if through the organs of an ass' (6: 175). James Heath (always '*Carrion* Heath' in Carlyle's pages) is all but flayed alive before our eyes, along with his scurrilous compendium of lies, *Flagellum, or the Life and Death of O. Cromwell, the Late Usurper* (6: 14–15). When the fat-headed Bulstrode displays an unwonted 'poetic friskiness', it is 'as if the hippopotamus should show a tendency to dance' (8: 11). 'Chaos itself is Cosmos' (9: 20) compared to Somers's *Tracts*, debased by successive reprinting into 'such a Coagulum of Jargon as was never seen before in the world!' (9: 37). The reader should be grateful, Carlyle warns just before citing large chunks of the *Tracts*, that Somers's 'mere Dulness . . . is not Madness over and above. Let us all be patient; walk gently, swiftly, lest we awaken the sleeping Nightmares! We suppress, we abridge, we elucidate; struggle to make legible his Highness's words' (9: 38). There follow eighty-two interminable pages of debate in which Cromwell declines Parliament's preferred title of King (9: 38–119). The Nightmare Carlyle fears to revive is that of his own entombment, and it is his own grave that he walks over, 'gently, swiftly', lest it open to receive him.

Earlier he had described the unearthing of two long-buried Cromwell letters from the ruins of Hungerford Castle. The new steward of the Castle, while poking through heaps of rotting lumber, found the letters under 'masses of damp dust; unclean accumulation of beetle-and-spider exuviae' (8: 20). Apart from bearing Cromwell's signature, the letters are of no interest, yet Carlyle reprints one of them in full, and traces, with all the pedantry of Dryasdust, the history of the now-defunct Hungerford family. The letters and the family that received them quickly pass from the reader's mind, unlike the mounds of beetle and spider husks, remnants of Carlyle's mis-spent energies.

Traces of *exuviae* are scattered throughout *Cromwell*. Yet the reader's impatience yields to admiration for Carlyle's antiquarian zeal and his unexpected modesty in working as a mere day-labourer in the vineyards of history. Because he could find no reliable list of the members of the Long Parliament, he compiles a detailed biographical 'Supplement' of some five or six hundred names. Dryasdust laboured over the list, but only the poet Carlyle could describe it as an assemblage of 'ticketed shadows', a ghostly 'sanhedrim' that once sat in daily sight of Oliver Cromwell (8: 315–16).

The same zeal that led Carlyle to compile lists of shadows also impelled him to walk the battlefields of Naseby and Dunbar until every contour was fixed in his mind and even the burial mounds yielded up their secrets. He detects an error of a mile in the siting of the Naseby Battle Monument and writes of two molars recently excavated from one of the mounds, 'sound effectual grinders . . . which ate their breakfast on the fourteenth morning of June two hundred years ago, and except to be clenched once in grim battle, had never work to do more in this world!' (6: 212).* At the end of his account of the battle, he cites Cromwell's letter to Parliament written on the night of the victory. Carlyle possessed a printed version of the letter in Rushworth's *Historical Collections*, but he sought out the original in the British Museum and studied it with the same 'loving minuteness' of attention he had given to the dips and rises of the battlefield. 'I tried hard to find some shiver in the hair-strokes,' he wrote to his friend Edward Fitzgerald, exhumer and owner of the two ancient molars; 'some symptom that the man had been bearding Death all day; but there is nothing of that sort there; a quite composed letter, the hand-writing massive, steadfast, you would say almost firmer than usual.'[9]

* In May 1842 Carlyle toured Naseby with Dr Thomas Arnold. He visited Dunbar on 3 September of the following year, the anniversary of the battle and of Cromwell's death. 'I had the conviction that I stood on the very ground', he wrote to Jane the next day; 'I surveyed the old Castle, washed my feet in the sea—smoking the while—took an image of Dunbar with me as I could, and then set my face to the wind and the storm . . .' (Froude, *London*, 1: 217, 277–8). Between the visits to Naseby and Dunbar, Carlyle set out on horseback through East Anglia on the journey that led to *Past and Present* and to the superb topographic description of St Ives that opens Part I of *Cromwell*. 'I have *seen* the Cromwell country,' he wrote to his mother in September 1842, and hold 'an image of it in my mind for all time henceforth' (cited in Grace J. Calder, *The Writing of Past and Present* (New Haven: Yale University Press, 1949), pp. 39–40). Froude comments that of everyone he ever knew, Carlyle had 'the greatest power of taking in and remembering the minute particulars of what he saw and heard, and of then reproducing them in language' (*London*, 1: 221). Jane says the same thing in a livelier idiom: 'I know you *beat the world* for the quantity of even *correct* impressions which you bring away from what M'Diarmid would call the most "bird's-eye view" of any place—witness Bury St. Edmond's!' (cited in Calder, p. 40; letter of 7 Sept. 1846).

Cromwell's steady hand after the stress of battle figures importantly in Carlyle's 'reading' of the letter. Not content merely to reprint it, he displays the letter as a physical object and makes us privy to the special circumstances of its composition. We learn, for example, that the letter is now much worn, its leaves reinforced by paste, its red seal defaced; that Cromwell addresses it from 'Harborough, or "Haver-browe" as he calls it'; that the signature is strong and unwavering. By the time we read the letter, we have all but held its worn leaves up to the light. Carlyle's editorial *Elucidations* are thus much more than mere annotations: they are meant to be lesser mirrorings of the divine *fiat-lux*, sudden illuminations of what had long lain formless and dark. That Carlyle sees his editorial function as sacred and life-giving is everywhere evident in the imagery of *Cromwell*, from the Orphic journey of the opening to the luminous death-scene at the end. During his campaign in Ireland, Cromwell had issued an anti-Papal *'Declaration Of The Lord Lieutenant Of Ireland, For The Undeceiving Of Deluded And Seduced People . . .'*. In elucidating the *Declaration* Carlyle expresses the hope that animates all of his historical writing: 'if we could all completely *read* it, as an earnest Editor has had to try if he could do, till it became completely luminous again, and glowed with its old veracity and sacred zeal . . .' (7: 111).

When the effort succeeds, as with the Battle of Dunbar, the results are incomparable. Perhaps by virtue of temperament or place of origin, Carlyle writes best about dismal weather; he seems especially inspired by the hard soaking rains that drench Frederick the Great's Army as it slogs towards Glogau or that turn the battlefield of Dunbar into a floating bog. Cromwell's outnumbered Army is camped on the penninsula of Dunbar, 'one of those projecting rock-pro-montories with which that shore of the Firth of Forth is niched and vandyked, as far as the eye can reach' (7: 197). The easy genius of *vandyked* characterizes Carlyle's prose throughout the chapter. The reader all but sinks into the mushy ground separating David Lesley's army from Cromwell's, 'a place of plashes and rough bent-grass; terribly beaten by showery winds that day, so that your tent will hardly stand' (7: 201). Cromwell detects Lesley attempting to secure a strategic pass in advance of the battle and resolves to attack before dawn of the next day. His troops spend the wild, wet night of 2 September 1650 within quick reach of their arms; 'the Harvest Moon wades deep among clouds of sleet and hail. . . . The hoarse sea moans bodeful, swinging low and heavy against these whinstone bays

. . .' (7: 205). Just before dawn 'the Moon gleams out, hard and blue, riding among hail-clouds' (7: 206). *Riding* has the same quickening effect as *vandyked*, a moon not casually imagined but actually beheld scudding across the clouds. The trumpets sound in the pre-dawn darkness, the cannon are wheeled into line, and Cromwell's battle-cry—' "The Lord of Hosts! The Lord of Hosts!" '—bursts upon the astonished Scottish Army. Over three thousand Covenanters are killed by shot or trampled to death on the spot. ' "I never saw such a charge of foot and horse," says one; nor did I, . . .' adds Carlyle (7: 207). In any other narrative, 'nor did I' would seem absurd. Here it does not, for in a sense Carlyle can claim to have witnessed the battle. He has seen it by dint of the same exegetical effort he urges on his readers earlier in the chapter. There he takes us along a modern road that dips toward a ford in the river where the battle took place:

At this "pass," on and about the present London road, as you discover after long dreary dim examining, took place the brunt or essential agony of the Battle of Dunbar long ago. Read in the extinct old Pamphlets, and ever again obstinately read, till some light rise in them, look even with unmilitary eyes at the ground as it now is, you do at last obtain small glimmerings of distinct features here and there,—which gradually coalesce into a kind of image for you; and some spectrum of the Fact becomes visible; rises veritable, face to face, on you, grim and sad in the depths of the old dead Time.

(7: 203)

The ancient Fact rising upon us 'face to face' recalls the reader's 'face to face' sight of the twelfth century in *Past and Present*. Close in time of publication, *Cromwell* and *Past and Present* are also close in the exalted role they assign to historical exegesis. In the Introduction to *Cromwell* Carlyle promises that through his hero's own words we 'may first obtain some dim glimpse of the actual Cromwell, and see him darkly face to face' (6: 19). St Paul had stressed the disjunction between *now*, 'when we see through a glass, darkly', and *then*, when we will see 'face to face'. Carlyle's *Elucidations* attempt to bridge the two worlds. To see 'darkly face to face' is both to see and not to see, a Carlylean equivocation that glimpses the sacred world from the shores of historical time.

Cromwell's England invites such a double reading of events, as does Cromwell himself, who scrutinized his every act in the light of Scripture. After his victory at Dunbar, he was heard to sing out, in the words of the Psalmist, ' "Let God arise, and scattered/ Let all his enemies be; . . ." ' (7: 207). The enemy fled so fast that Cromwell's troops had to regroup before they could pursue. Carlyle virtually 'scores' the scene that follows, specifying the words, tune, and the extra beat given to *nati-ons*:

The Scotch Army is shivered to utter ruin; rushes in tumultuous wreck, hither, thither; to Belhaven, or, in their distraction, even to Dunbar; the chase goes as far as Haddington; led by Hacker. "The Lord General made a halt," says Hodgson, "and sang the Hundred-and-seventeenth Psalm," till our horse could gather for the chase. Hundred-and-seventeenth Psalm, at the foot of the Doon Hill; there we uplift it, to the tune of Bangor, or some still higher score, and roll it strong and great against the sky:

> O give ye praise unto the Lord,
> All nati-ons that be;
> Likewise ye people all, accord
> His name to magnify! . . .

(7: 207–8)

In this zealous world the opposing Puritan and Scottish armies exchanged volleys of religious tracts before raking each other with shot (7: 190–3). The hills and valleys were populated with religious enthusiasts like James Nayler, who believed he was a reincarnation of Christ and whose harsh punishment—whipping, branding, and the boring of a hole through his tongue—was decreed by Parliament (9: 17–18). Nayler figures in a passage of inspired *exuviae* that tells us little about Cromwell but much about the England over which he ruled:

Soon after this Letter [of Cromwell] "in the month of October 1655," there was seen a strange sight at Bristol in the West. A Procession of Eight Persons; one, a man on horseback, riding single; the others, men and women, partly riding double, partly on foot, in the muddiest highway, in the wettest weather; singing, all but the single-rider, at whose bridle splash and walk two women: "Hosannah! Holy, holy! Lord God of Sabaoth!" and other things, "in a buzzing tone," which the impartial hearer could not make out. The single-rider is a raw-boned male figure, "with lank hair reaching below his cheeks"; hat drawn close over his brows; "nose rising slightly in the middle"; of abstruse "down look," and large dangerous jaws strictly closed; he sings not; sits there covered, and is sung-to by the others bare. Amid pouring deluges, and mud knee-deep: "so that the rain ran in at their necks, and they vented it at their hose and breeches": a spectacle to the West of England and Posterity! Singing as above; answering no question except in song. From

Bedminster to Ratcliff Gate, along the streets, to the High Cross of Bristol: at the High Cross they are laid hold of by the Authorities.

(8: 223–4)

Carlyle is the 'impartial hearer' who stands at the roadside and strains to make out the snatches of song as Nayler passes in triumphal entry into Bristol, a deluded Saviour arrested at the foot of the true Cross. The same keen attention Carlyle gives to Nayler he focuses on every syllable of Cromwell's letters and speeches, until they yield up ' "the express image of the soul" ' that uttered them (8: 71). This capacity of Cromwell to be himself in ' "every fibre" ' (8: 71) of his utterance is the sign of his truth to the ' "Incarnate Word" ' (8: 72) within him. His style is in reality the rejection of style, a mode of 'composition like the structure of a block of oak-root,—as tortuous, unwedgeable, and as strong!' (6: 273). Study it, writes Carlyle, and the block of oak will begin to sing; the reader will hear 'the voice of a man risen justly into a kind of *chant* . . .' (6: 273). One hears little chant in Cromwell's many letters begging for money for the Army or for more spades, but it is audible elsewhere, as in the letter reporting to the Speaker of Parliament from the besieged town of Waterford. With a mixture of ferocity and compassion, Cromwell rejoices that the Lord has broken 'the enemies of His Church in pieces', yet he wonders why, 'if the Father of the family be so kind', there should be 'such jarrings and heart-burnings amongst the children? . . . Indeed, Sir, I was constrained in my bowels to write thus much' (7: 101). The reader grows fond of Cromwell's vigorous, metaphorical 'bowels', as in his celebrated plea to the Scottish clergy, ' "I beseech you, in the bowels of Christ, think it possible you may be mistaken" ' (7: 187). The same blunt economy marks his command to the Reverend Mr Hitch of Ely, who persisted in conducting a choir-service offensive to the Puritans: ' "Leave off your fooling, and come down, 'Sir!" said Oliver,* in a voice still audible to this Editor . . .' (6: 179). Most often we hear the voice of Cromwell the commander. But we also come to recognize the creaky charm of his letters to his daughter Bridget (' "I write not to thy Husband [because] one line of mine begets many of his, which . . . makes him sit up too late" ' (6: 254)) or the sudden eloquence of his plea to Parliament for national reconciliation: ' "And truly, Righteousness and Mercy must kiss each other. If we will have

* Throughout *Cromwell* Carlyle addresses his hero familiarly as *Oliver*. The effect is to turn a former bogey into a revered friend.

Peace without a worm in it, lay we the foundations of Justice and Righteousness . . ."' (9: 13).

*

Finally, in a way that no analysis can clarify, we learn to hear Cromwell's silences. 'There is, in these Letters,' Carlyle writes, 'a *silence* still more significant of Oliver to us than any speech they have' (6: 78). In the long course of the work, we become conscious of the 'features of an Intelligence' (6: 78) anterior to any of Cromwell's words and that is Cromwell's very self. Carlyle's 'elucidations' are ultimately not of Cromwell's text but of the living consciousness that fathered the text. More and more Carlyle interjects his own commentary into the letters and speeches, until editor and text, hero-worshipper and hero, become a community of one. Perhaps this accounts for the power of the final book, when the exhausted, care-worn Cromwell, near the end of his great national effort, and the exhausted Carlyle, near the end of his seven-year ordeal, seem to speak in the same voice. In one of his last speeches Cromwell exhorts Parliament to avoid the folly of further civil war; Carlyle's bracketed interpolation seems as much an encouragement to himself as to his hero: '[Courage, my brave one! Thou hast but some Seven Months more of it, and then the ugly coil is all over]' (9: 171).

A month before Cromwell's death his favourite daughter Elizabeth died after a long and harrowing illness. 'Identification' is too clinical a term for the overt sympathy Carlyle feels and expresses for the bereaved father. So, too, the serviceable term 'narrative glide', although apt, is too antiseptic for a scene in which Carlyle unabashedly adopts the role of father and chief mourner ('She is taken from me . . .'). To the objection that Carlyle presumes to describe what he cannot have observed, we answer that he presumes nothing. He clearly distinguishes between what he supposes to have happened in the sick-room ('we can *fancy* . . .') and what indeed occurred. Scrupulous in representing fact, he is free in expressing emotion. In a few lines he conjures up the room in Hampton Court, enters it as an anxious father, and exits as a mourner, pronouncing the burial service over Elizabeth's wasted body:

Hampton Court we can fancy once more, in those July days, a house of sorrow; pale Death knocking there, as at the door of the meanest hut. "She had great sufferings, great exercises of spirit." Yes.—and in the depths of the

old Centuries, we see a pale anxious Mother, anxious Husband, anxious
weeping Sisters, a poor young Frances weeping anew in her weeds. "For the
last fourteen days" his Highness has been by her bedside at Hampton Court,
unable to attend to any public business whatever. Be still, my Child; trust
thou yet in God: in the waves of the Dark River, there too is He a God of
help!—On the 6th day of August [1658] she lay dead; at rest forever. My
young, my beautiful, my brave! She is taken from me; I am left bereaved of
her. The Lord giveth, and the Lord taketh away; blessed be the Name of the
Lord!—

(9: 197)

Shortly after Elizabeth's death, Cromwell became ill, and in the
ten concluding pages Carlyle stages a death-scene that combines the
circumstantiality of eye-witness accounts with the freest rendering of
states of consciousness. George Fox visits Cromwell late in August
1658 and feels ' "a waft" (*whiff*) "of death go forth against him" '
(9: 199). Public prayer meetings are held up and down England in
apprehension of 'the exit of Oliver Cromwell and of English Puritanism; a great Light . . . going down now amid the clouds of Death'
(9: 201). On the morning of 30 August, four days before Cromwell's
death, a fierce windstorm arises and halts the stream of visitors
to Cromwell at Whitehall. The reader senses, without Carlyle's
underlining the connection that the wind that howls for the next four
days, penetrating even into the sick-room, is the same ' "waft of
death" ' George Fox detected when he saw Cromwell for the last time.
    Firmly anchored in time and place, footnoted in every detail, the
course of Cromwell's decline can be followed almost hourly. But
despite the weight of documentation, Carlyle also conveys a more
subjective, internalized notation of the scene that suggests Cromwell's
own slipping in and out of consciousness. The telling detail in the
following passage is its lack of all temporal orientation, as befits the
words of a man in transit out of time. The prayers are fragmentary,
and arise in seemingly random order:

Here also are ejaculations caught up at intervals, undated, in those final
days: "Lord, Thou knowest, if I do desire to live, it is to show forth Thy
praise and declare Thy works!" Once he was heard saying, "It is a fearful
thing to fall into the hands of the Living God!" "This was spoken three
times," says Harvey; "his repetitions usually being very weighty, and with
great vehemency of spirit" . . . "A fearful thing to fall into the hands of the
Living God!"——But again: "All the promises of God are in *Him*: yes, and
in Him Amen; . . ."

(9: 202–3)

This paragraph of trance-like fragments is followed by Cromwell's last prayer, which Carlyle transcribes from several sources as it was heard above 'the tumult of the winds' (9: 204). The reader who has come this far with Carlyle on his Orphic Journey seems to *hear* Cromwell intone the prayer in a voice that rises into a chant:

Lord, though I am a miserable and wretched creature, I am in Covenant with Thee through grace. And I may, I will, come to Thee, for Thy People. Thou hast made me, though very unworthy, a mean instrument to do them some good, and Thee service; and many of them have set too high a value upon me, though others wish and would be glad of my death; Lord, however Thou do dispose of me, continue and go on to do good for them. . . . Pardon such as desire to trample upon the dust of a poor worm, for they are Thy People too. And pardon the folly of this short Prayer:—Even for Jesus Christ's sake. . . . Amen.

(9: 204-5)

9

Demon-Cocks and *Latter-Day Pamphlets*

The 1840s should have been a triumphant decade for Carlyle, but what it brought him in fame it took away in inner certainty and direction. Perhaps prophets should not be honoured in their own countries, as Carlyle was after the publication of *Cromwell*. In October 1846, just after *Cromwell* had gone into a second edition, a group of admiring Americans arrived at Cheyne Row bearing greetings from Emerson. Among the visitors was the feminist and critic Margaret Fuller, who was 'carried away' with the musical quality of Carlyle's Scottish dialect, 'his way of singing his great full sentences so that each one was like the stanza of a narrative ballad'.[1] But soon after their first meeting she detected discords in the music: 'the habit and power of haranguing have increased very much upon him . . . To interrupt him is a physical impossibility.' She became alarmed over his political ideas, especially his 'defence of mere force' and of 'success [as] the test of right':

If people would not behave well, put collars round their necks. Find a hero, and let them be his slaves. It was very Titanic and Anticelestial. I wish the last evening had been more melodious. However, I bade Carlyle farewell with feelings of the warmest friendship and admiration. We cannot feel otherwise to a great and noble nature . . .[2]

Margaret Fuller exaggerates but does not grossly misrepresent Carlyle's authoritarianism,* the seeds of which are present in his earliest writings. Along with Mill and others, she detects in the

---

* But she does misrepresent Carlyle's position on 'might vs. right'. Carlyle nowhere defends 'mere force', but on the contrary argues that might without right on its side is ultimately impotent. His position may be pietistic but it is not vicious: 'In all battles, if you await the issue, each fighter has prospered according to his right. His right and his might, at the close of the account, were one and the same' (10: 12). The problem here is that, in Carlyle's eyes, the account is settled not at the end of a few encounters but over the long course of history, perhaps not until the dust clears from Armageddon. In the interim he can be too tolerant of bullying and injustice that is *not* righted until the end of time. In an important marginal note written in the third person, Carlyle corrects an early biographer who wrongly attributed to him the view 'that, basically, might was right':

Carlyle of the middle 1840s a hardening of the moral arteries. In 1849, just before the publication of *Latter-Day Pamphlets*, Matthew Arnold was to deplore the same fault: Carlyle had become a 'moral desperado'.[3] Margaret Fuller's response to Carlyle is more ambivalent than Arnold's. She finds his politics repugnant, but comes away from Cheyne Row enamoured of his 'great and noble nature'.[4] The fascination of 'late' Carlyle for the fair-minded reader lies in this co-presence of the repugnant and the noble, the prophetic and the blind. 'Sugar Islands, Spice Islands, Indias, Canadas,—these, by the real decree of Heaven, were ours' (20: 145), Carlyle asserts in *Latter-Day Pamphlets*, arguing from the absurd assumption that God is a jingo and Thomas Carlyle is His prophet. Yet in the same pamphlet ('The New Downing Street') Carlyle manifests the moral imagination that inspired Dickens's *Bleak House* and Ruskin's *Unto This Last* and contributed to the reformation of industrial capitalism: '. . . where there is a Pauper, there is a sin; to make one Pauper there go many sins. Pauperism is our Social Sin grown manifest' (20: 158).

A *Journal* entry Carlyle made in February 1848 takes us from the bluster of his public pronouncements to the bafflement that underlies much of what he wrote after *Cromwell*. The *Journal* is largely a blank for the previous four years—a sign of well-being—but in this anguished entry we overhear, in Froude's phrase, Carlyle's 'dialogues with his own heart':

For above two years now I have been as good as totally idle, composedly lying *fallow*. It is frightful to think of! After getting out of "Cromwell," my whole being seemed to say, more sulkily, more weariedly than ever before, "What good is it?" I am wearied and near heartbroken. Nobody on the whole "*believes* my report." The friendliest reviewers, I can see, regard me as a wonderful athlete, a ropedancer whose perilous somersets it is worth sixpence

---

What floods of nonsense have been and are spoken . . . about this poor maxim of Carlyle's! . . . No man who is not in the *right*, were he even a Napoleon I at the head of armed Europe, has any real *might* whatever, but will at last be found *might*less, and to have *done*, or settled as a fixity, nothing at all, except precisely so far as he was *not* in the wrong. Abolition and erosion awaits [*sic*] all "doings" of his, except just what part of them *was right* . . . & the salutary process of *expunction* goes on to the end, as fast as it can. So that *right* and *might* are identical, in the long run; glory to Heaven!—Upon which many men of weak judgment take to wondering, and not a few to exclaiming, "Ha, Carlyle thinks might is right, the scandalous fellow-mortal!" And hate the poor man, more or less; which is of no consequence. . . .

Written in 1866, the note appears in *Two Reminiscences of Thomas Carlyle*, ed. John Clubbe (Durham, NC: Duke University Press, 1974), pp. 98–9. Cf. a similar disavowal of 'might makes right' cited in Froude, *London*, 2: 360.

(paid to the Circulating Library) to *see*; or at most I seem to them a desperate half mad, if usefullish fireman, rushing along the ridge tiles in a frightful manner to quench the burning chimney. . . . Neither does Art, &c., in the smallest hold out with me. . . . I do not believe in "Art"—nay, I do believe it to be one of the deadliest *cants*; swallowing, it too, its hecatombs of souls. So that the world, daily growing more unspeakable is meaning to me, as well as daily more inarticulate, and I quite indisposed to *try* speaking to it, the result has been silence and fallow, which, unless I will go *mad*, must end. . . . Lonelier man is not in this world that I know of. . . . No deliverance from "confusion," from practical *uncertainty*, and all its sad train of miseries and waste, is to be looked for while one continues in this world. Life consists, as it were, in the sifting of huge rubbish-mounds. . . .[5]

One is struck by the unrelenting power of Carlyle's lament over his impotence and disgust. Continued silence, he believed, would result in madness; he could no more refrain from speaking out than from breathing, even if his only audience were himself. He articulates his griefs and pains with all the skills of a virtuoso, and when outward circumstance fails to justify the bitterness of the outcry, he invents his own ills. The words of no one in the English-speaking world were more widely followed, yet he complains, in Isaiah's phrase, that no one believes his report. Like a deaf man who fears he cannot be heard, he raises his voice to a shout and wonders at the startled looks he gets. Within another decade or two, a writer who felt alienated from a Philistine society could take refuge in the growing cult of Art, but for Carlyle '*Kunst*, so called',[6] was cant. Though he always stressed his 'message' and denigrated his medium, his own writings helped elevate discursive prose into a fine art. But he could not, like the Aesthetes who despised him, take refuge in the house he had built. Years earlier, when the design of *The French Revolution* had first clarified itself in his mind, his Puritan soul recoiled from the notion that he might create a work of beauty as well as of truth: 'Alas! . . . if this should be a *work of art*. Poor me!'[7]

Loneliness, fallowness, contempt for the 'rubbish mound' of the world, disgust with himself—this is the distemper of spirit that underlies 'The Nigger Question' and *Latter-Day Pamphlets*. Such acute distress does not excuse or even satisfactorily explain the ferocity of Carlyle's rancour, but it helps account for the reader's sense that he has stumbled into a mire or a madhouse or a menagerie. As a witness to the filth and blasphemies of modern life, Carlyle writes in 'The Present Time', he has seen men sink 'almost below the level of lowest humanity, and down towards the state of apehood and oxhood!' (20: 13). At the end of the pamphlet he depicts an abysmal landscape symbolic of the modern era, but the 'terrible *new* country' (20: 46) he describes seems more a portrait of Carlyle's private nightmares than of the England of Victoria and Albert. The landscape is void of human beings but teems with 'irrational flabby monsters . . . laughing hyaenas, predatory wolves', devils, haggard forests, and quaking bogs (20: 46–7). 'Stump-Orator' is a tedious harangue against political haranguing, easily forgotten except for a malodorous dead dog, decomposing in the ooze of a river and drifting with unexpected vivacity through one of Carlyle's paragraphs (20: 200–1). In 'Model Prisons' he inveighs against the 'pruriency of indiscriminate Philanthropism' (20: 51) that wastes itself on trying to rehabilitate hardened criminals while tolerating slums and starvation in the streets. He walks through a neighbourhood of cellar-tenements and dismal shops to Milbank Penitentiary, the 'ne-plus-ultra' of humane prisons. Within its walls Carlyle is shown spacious apartments where 'notable murderesses' sit in quiet pride, and revolutionaries enjoy the amenities of private quarters (20: 52–3). The visitor from Cheyne Row looks in growing amazement as ranks of unregenerate faces return his stare: 'ape-faces, imp-faces, angry dog-faces, heavy sullen ox-faces; degraded underfoot perverse creatures, . . . and other diabolic-animal specimens of humanity . . .' (20: 55–6). The *Pamphlets* are a bestiary of dogs, mice, owls, cats, apes, and 'hrumphing' pigs.[8] Reading the *Pamphlets*, with their obsessive repetitions, violence, tedium, and intermittent fascination, is strangely like reading pornography, only the sexuality has been transmuted into scatology and aggression, often directed against the reader. Herr Sauerteig, spokesman in 'Jesuitism' for Carlyle's disgust, propounds certain 'Pig Propositions', the first of which is that the Universe is one 'immeasurable Swine's-trough, consisting of solid and liquid . . .' (20: 316). Of course Carlyle is condemning, not espousing, the 'Pig Philosophy' of his contemporaries, but Sauerteig's anger has none of the distancing irony of Teufelsdröckh, and it is Carlyle himself who seems mired in what he hates.* In turning from the 'heroism' of Cromwell's England to what he takes to be the squalor of the mid-nineteenth century, he becomes an unwitting specimen of what he

---

* In a letter discussing the *Pamphlets* Carlyle describes himself as burning with rage, but also feeling as if he were immersed in 'a *continent* of foul liquid'. See Fred Kaplan, *Thomas Carlyle: A Biography* (Ithaca: Cornell University Press, 1983), p. 352.

calls the '*Scavenger Age*' (20: 163). In 'New Downing Street' his violent attack on government bureaucracy makes Dickens's 'Circumlocution Office' seem a model of antiseptic efficiency. The Home Office is a mountain of dung in which human cattle sprawl in 'insalubrious horror and abomination' (20: 164).

One cannot pay attention very long to a man who constantly shouts, especially if he shouts the same thing over and over. Yet it would be a loss to our literature if two of the pamphlets, 'Model Prisons' and 'Hudson's Statue', were to pass into oblivion. In 'Hudson's Statue', Carlyle argues that George Hudson, the famous 'Railway King', was a bloated scoundrel, and that the solid British citizens who had subscribed £25,000 to erect a statute in his honour were Mammonites and phallus-worshippers. The collapse of Hudson's financial empire in an orgy of speculation in 1849 aborted the plans to put up the statue, but the great brazen erection that Carlyle substitutes in its stead towers over any likeness that a grateful nation might otherwise have cast in bronze.

The essay opens with a contrast between the modest, belated memorial planned for Cromwell at St Ives and the colossus projected for Hudson. Had Hudson not fallen, the world would have seen an image of what England actually worships, suitably mounted on top of a Locomotive and 'garnished with Scrip-rolls proper; and raised aloft in some conspicuous place . . .' (20: 256). Detail by obscene detail, the statue that was never built rises before the reader's eyes. Carlyle's mock-heraldic Hudson, garnished with appendages of worthless shares, is the progenitor of John Ruskin's 'Goddess of Getting-on', with her thirty pockets for receiving pieces of silver.[9] Both Carlyle and Ruskin distinguish between the nominal religion of England to which the nation pays tithes, and the real religion, to which it devotes six-sevenths of its energies. In both 'Hudson's Statue' and Ruskin's essay on 'Traffic' popular taste serves as an index of national values. Hence Carlyle's dismay over the host of entrepreneurial images that dominate English cities—'the ugliest images, and . . . the strangest class of persons, ever set-up in this world' (20: 261–2), a brazen horde fit only to melt down into cheap candlesticks (20: 262). 'Are these your Pattern Men? *Great* Men?' Carlyle asks (20: 262). His answer has a sexual suggestiveness that by the end of the essay ripens into a certainty: they are not fit heroes but 'Gamblers swollen *big*' (20: 262), serpents 'lifted up . . . in the wilderness' (20: 275). At one point Carlyle's voracious imagination takes in all of England, town by town, and mourns with brooding pity over the ugly multitude of metal men rusting in the polluted rain:

> To me this populace of British Statues rises aloft over the Chaos of our affairs like the living symbol and consummate flower of said Chaos . . . Perhaps as strange a Pantheon of brass gods as was ever got together in this world. They stand there, poor wretches, gradually rusting in the sooty rain; black and dismal,—when one thinks of them in some haggard mood of the imagination,—like a set of grisly undertakers come to bury the dead spiritualisms of mankind.
>
> (20: 264)

As the essay nears its end, Carlyle's language becomes more savage and more comic. If the government outlaws indecent exposure or the piling up of excrement in the streets, then why does it not prohibit 'prurient stupidity' from erecting columns in honour of gamblers 'swollen to the edge of bursting . . . huge and abominable!' (20: 287). The brazen image of Hudson comes to resemble some Babylonian abomination too foul to name yet too gross to mistake, a huge unclean idol suited to a people whose new religion is the Cult of 'the Anti-Virgin' and whose literature is 'Desperation curiously conjoined with Phallus-Worship' (20: 289). Is it humane, Carlyle asks of his misguided friends, to erect

> this blotch of mismolten copper and zinc, out of which good warming-pans might be made? That all men should see this; innocent young creatures, still in arms, be taught to think this beautiful;—and perhaps women in an interesting situation look up to it as they pass. I put it to your religious feeling, to your principles as men and fathers of families!
>
> (20: 291)

Carlyle mimics the pieties of his audience while mocking their prudery. The innocent child would blush, the pregnant woman miscarry on the spot, at the sight of the 'Brazen Monster' (20: 291). Of course the 'catch' in all this indecent exposure is that Carlyle, and not England, has erected the obscenity. Hence his mock-horror in the closing paragraph is all the more outrageous: if certain benighted souls cannot control their perverse worship, let the Board of Sanitation or some Cleansing Committee build a high-walled joss-house, lit only by sky-lights, where 'your Monster' may be worshipped in secret and by the bellyful. 'Hudson's Statue' recalls but dwarfs the wood-and-wire Pope of *Past and Present*. It marks the furthest reach of

Carlyle's satiric imagination, an assault on Victorian propriety that everywhere risks, yet miraculously avoids, impropriety.

*

Latter-Day Pamphlets is a lonely book, its wit too barbarous and misanthropic for sustained laughter. In November 1849, three months before the publication of the first pamphlet, Carlyle looked into his own heart and saw stone:

> How lonely I am now grown in the world; how hard, many times as if I were made of stone! All the old tremulous affection lies in me, but it is as if frozen. So mocked, and scourged, and driven mad by contradictions, it has, as it were, lain down in a kind of iron sleep. . . . God help me! God soften me again. . . .[10]

For the rest of his life the prayer was often repeated but never answered. As Carlyle watched the Crystal Palace arising in London in a dazzling display of energy and optimism, his own mood bordered on the suicidal: 'My silence and isolation, my utter loneliness in this world, is complete. Never in my life did I feel so utterly-windbound, lame, bewildered. . . .'[11] Two sentences in a letter to Jane from Scotland, where he had gone to visit his ill and aged mother, recall the ape-and-imp faces, the angry dog-faces of the *Latter-Day Pamphlets*: 'Oh, I am sick of the stupidity of mankind—a *servum pecus*. I had no idea till late times what a bottomless fund of darkness there is in the human animal. . . .'[12] In the light of such virulence, Froude's claim that Carlyle was 'really the most tender-hearted of men' seems ludicrous—until one realizes that his misanthropy and his philanthropy, as in the similar instance of Swift, sprang from the same root. 'His savageness', Froude observes of Carlyle, 'was but affection turned sour.'[13] Embittered but not insensate, Carlyle felt his 'old tremulous affection' freeze within him, then turn to rage against the 'howling multitudes' (20: 32). The progression from love to stony indifference ('a kind of iron sleep') to the hatred that Carlyle manifests in middle life marks the return of that much earlier crisis he recounted in *Sartor Resartus* in the autobiographical chapters on 'The Everlasting No', 'The Centre of Indifference', and 'The Everlasting Yea'. But the second crisis, unlike the first, never ends; and it is not a replay but a reversal of the first, which began in defiance and ended in love (' "With other eyes . . . I now

look upon my fellow man: with an infinite Love, an infinite Pity" '
(1: 150)). From his early fifties until his death thirty-five years later,
Carlyle's life was a protracted 'No!'

The return of 'The Everlasting No' is not surprising, for the
resolution of the initial crisis was more costly and equivocal than
Carlyle himself ever realized. Of the three famous chapters, 'The
Everlasting No' contains the heart of the experience. 'The Centre of
Indifference' describes a psychological half-way house, the neutral
point between the opposite poles of denial and affirmation. 'The
Everlasting Yea', despite its title, is burdened with denial: ' " "It is
only with Renunciation (*Entsagen*) that Life, properly speaking, can
be said to begin' " ' (1: 153). The chapter ends with a chilling quotation from the Gospel of John more appropriate to a Calvinist fearing
Judgement than a natural-supernaturalist saluting the everlasting
yes: ' "Work while it is called Today; for the Night cometh, wherein
no man can work" ' (1: 157).

Perhaps the spiritual crisis Carlyle recounts in *Sartor Resartus* was
vital to so many Victorians because it allowed such wide scope to
doubt and fear while seeming to affirm a divine and benevolent
universe. 'The Everlasting Yea' easily slips from memory, but no
reader can forget Teufelsdröckh's horrific vision in 'The Everlasting
No' of a Universe void of life, of purpose, even of hostility, a 'huge,
dead, immeasurable Steam-engine' that threatens to grind Teufelsdröckh limb from limb (1: 133). Teufelsdröckh's defiance of this
mechanical monster is heroic, a shouting of 'No' in the very teeth of
Nullity, and his protest inspired a whole generation of anguished
doubters. But Teufelsdröckh's negation of negation is at bottom
equivocal. One re-reads 'The Everlasting No' with the conviction
that neither Teufelsdröckh nor Carlyle can live by ' "Protest . . .
Indignation and Defiance" ' alone (1: 135). In shutting out doubt,
Carlyle cut himself off from much more than doubt, and his cries of
loneliness in late middle life, stifled and self-pitying, seem to reach us
through walls he had built around himself in early manhood. John
Stuart Mill writes in his *Autobiography* of a similar period of suicidal
despair, but Mill's crisis follows a course very different from
Carlyle's, and in the long run was far more salutary. Mill's is a crisis
not of defiance but of reconciliation and growth, a breaking away
from earlier rigidities and the incorporation of a whole range of feeling that his father had taught him to despise. Belatedly, after the
hyper-rationality of his early education, he makes a spiritual home for

himself in his own century, the century of Wordsworth and Coleridge, yet he retains all that he still finds valid in the intellectual culture of his two eighteenth-century mentors, James Mill and Jeremy Bentham. Mill retains a remarkable athleticism of mind into old age; Carlyle's later writings cease to be works of exploration and discovery and become exercises in compulsive reiteration. The cause may be found in a letter of Carlyle's to Jane in 1835, the year after the publication of *Sartor Resartus*. Above all else, he writes, he must rid himself of 'Cants and formulas'. If only he can do that, he will then 'fear nothing. . . . It is a great misery however for a man to lie, even unconsciously, even to himself.'[14] In 'Dr. Francia' and much that follows, we detect the high cost of Carlyle's unconscious lies.

Carlyle was too conscious of his unconscious deceits for comfort, and the defensive walls he built around them in his twenties were in disrepair by the time he reached his fifties. With his sure instinct for seizing on symbols, he found it necessary to immure himself once again, only this time within real walls. The sound-proof study the Carlyles added onto their home in 1852–3 was, like the joss-house enclosing Hudson's statue, without windows and lit by a skylight. While the study was under construction and workmen came crashing through Jane's bedroom ceiling, Carlyle was trying with desperate unsuccess to begin his new book on Frederick the Great. The study was built to shut out all distractions, especially the horrid clarions of the 'demon cocks' belonging to the Carlyles' next-door neighbour.[15] Carlyle threatened to resolve 'the great cock question' by shooting the creatures, and he ordered Jane to borrow a gun from their friend Mazzini—a command she wisely ignored. Morning after morning the cocks trumpeted Carlyle into a sleepless frenzy, until Jane finally '*purchased*' them out of existence with a five-pound note and some diplomatic words with the neighbour.[16]

Neither the disappearance of the cocks nor the completion of the sound-proof study brought Carlyle any peace, for the discords that threatened to derange him arose, as Carlyle well knew, from within as well as without.[17] The plaster on the double-walls was scarcely dry when he complained that in the new setting he felt as if he were 'being placed on the point of a spear, and there bidden at once stand and write. . . . To work! Try to get some work done, or thou wilt go mad.'[18] Albert J. LaValley compares the building of the study to an escape into a second Craigenputtock that, unlike the retreat a quarter-century earlier, brought no new burst of creativity.[19] The comparison is especially apt in light of two *Journal* entries Carlyle made early in 1854, soon after the study was completed. In the first he writes of his utter incapacity to make headway with *Frederick* and complains of living 'a strange interior tomb life',[20] as if he had returned to the underworld of entombed creativity envisioned at the start of *Cromwell*. The second entry takes us inside a nightmare of Carlyle's set in the desolate landscape of Craigenputtock. The dream has no narrative content, or none that Carlyle chooses to record; it requires no interpretation but stands as the 'express symbol' of the anxious mind that dreamed it:

I dream horribly . . . waste scenes of solitary desolation, gathered from Craigenputtock, as I now perceive, but tenfold *intensated*; endless uplands of scraggy moors, with gnarls of lichened crag of a stern ugliness, for always I am quite a *hermit* there too—fit to go into Dante's "Inferno;" with other visions less speakable, of a similar type. Every vision, I find, is the express symbol . . . of the mood of mind then possessing me. Also, it is sometimes *weeks after* the actual dream . . . when some other analogous dream or circumstance first brings them to my waking recollection. . . . one always *dreams*, but . . . only in cases where the nerves are disturbed by bad health, which produces light, imperfect sleep, do they start into such relief—call it agony and antagony—as to force themselves on our waking consciousness.[21]

To an unusual degree even for an introspective writer, Carlyle is his own ultimate subject. But sometime during the 1840s, the centre of his creative life seems to shift away from his finished *Works* and into his notebooks and journals. As the books grow longer and less coherent, his autobiographical writing becomes more compelling, until one finds oneself reading Froude's excerpts from the *Journals* with more sustained interest than many of the twenty-one books of *Frederick*. One wishes that Carlyle had created, like Ruskin in *Fors Clavigera*, an autobiographical vehicle worthy of his troubled genius. But he failed to do so. As he had no faith in Art, so he could not conceive of the Self as a legitimate subject of his art, and his works become warped rather than strengthened by their hidden autobiographical content. In the New York Edition of Froude's *Life*, the completion of the sound-proof study, Carlyle's struggle to begin *Frederick*, and the Craigenputtock nightmare all appear on facing pages. The seeds of *Frederick* were planted on the craggy moors and desolate slopes of a nightmare; no book ever took root in less hospitable soil.

10

The Long Night of *Frederick the Great*

It is uncertain just when Carlyle began what he came to call 'that unutterable horror of a Prussian Book',[1] but in the autumn of 1852 his widening research led him to visit Berlin and the sites of Frederick's battles. Early in 1853 he made a halting start at the writing, and for over a decade he lived and worked as a virtual recluse. As Froude puts it, Carlyle had begun in his late fifties 'an enormous undertaking; nothing less than the entire history, secular and spiritual, of the eighteenth century'.[2] With the help of two research assistants—his neighbour Henry Larkin and Joseph Neuberg, a devoted admirer—he brought out the first two volumes in 1858, the middle volumes in 1862 and 1864, and the final two in 1865. For thirteen years he laboured and complained, complained and laboured: 'I haggle and struggle here all day, ride then in the twilight like a haunted ghost; speak to nobody; have nobody whom it gladdens me to speak to.'[3] With these words Carlyle closes his *Journal* for 1858, just after the first instalment of *Frederick* had been highly praised by the reviewers and the first two printings had been sold out.[4] But Carlyle admitted no pleasure in all this acclaim: 'Book . . . much babbled of in newspapers. No better to me than the barking of dogs.'[5] The ill-temper of *Latter-Day Pamphlets* continues to manifest itself in Carlyle's *Journal* and more than once ruffles the pages of *Frederick*. Only one bright touch of colour appears to lighten these years: in September 1858, on a second visit to the sites associated with Frederick, Carlyle plucked a wild pink from the battlefield of Prague and tucked it into a letter to Jane.[6]

Carlyle has always elicited extreme critical reactions, and response to *Frederick* has been especially divided, ranging from Macaulay's 'gibberish' to Emerson's 'the wittiest book that was ever written'.[7] More recently the consensus on *Frederick* has been negative, with the exception of a memorable essay by Morse Peckham.[8] Yet almost any judgement can be supported by the text, for within its vast and uneven bulk are whole bookfuls of some of the best and worst prose of the nineteenth century. One very much wants to say that *Frederick* is a work of genius (which it is), or that it is a colossal failure (which it is), but to assert both seems feckless or contradictory. To begin with the interminable, few readers will follow for hundreds of pointless pages Carlyle's account of the diplomatic manœuvrings over the projected double marriage of Frederick and his sister Wilhelmina to Princess Amelia of England and the Prince of Wales, a double-coupling neither half of which ever occurred. 'Courage, patience, good reader!' becomes a desperate refrain whenever we come to 'regions of Narrative, which seem to consist of murky Nothingness put on boil' (13: 2). Whole chapters of *Frederick* read like undigested notes or consist of obscure lists 'terrestrially interesting only to the spiders' (13: 30). At times Carlyle seems to sink under the sheer weight and inchoate bulk of his sources, a Dryasdust drowned in a sea of ' "things mad, chaotic and without ascertainable purpose or result" ', events which the abused human memory purges itself of by the happy alchemy of forgetfulness (15: 144). At times, when Dryasdust or Smelfungus seem about to crush Carlyle's very soul as a writer, he defends himself with Shandyesque self-mockery: '*Succinct History of the Spanish War, which began in 1739; and ended—When did it end?*' The point of this chapter-title is that the war, after flaring up, went mysteriously underground, like the River Niger, only to resurface and finally die out. Ever accurate to the last ascertainable detail, Carlyle describes Frederick's palace at Reinsberg or his New Opera House at Berlin with the exactitude of an architectural drawing. But when he tries to compute the cost of the Opera House, he cannot, for the 'sibylline leaf' on which he made his calculations has blown away upon the winds (15: 367). Wit serves as Carlyle's defence against the fear of failure, but the failure is as undeniable as the grim humour that accompanies it.

Frederick the Great is a book of too few ideas and too many ill-sorted facts. In the 'Proem' Carlyle asserts that ' "History is an imprisoned Epic" ' which ' "illuminate[s] the dark ways of God" ' (12: 17, 19). In *The French Revolution* he had given life to the idea of history as a theodicy through an intricate network of allusions, classical and biblical, and through a prophetic style. The world of *Frederick*, however, is largely void of the cosmic resonances of *The French Revolution* or of the sense, as in *Past and Present*, that an 'illimitable Ocean' (10: 49) swirls around our little lives in the here and now. *Frederick* is the most 'modern' of Carlyle's histories, vast in bulk but shrunken in implication and quite thoroughly secularized. The sceptical, flute-playing Frederick—a sexually enigmatic 'philosopher-king' as much at home concertizing at his all-male soirées as on his lightning marches into Silesia—is strangely miscast as an epic hero.* It is a distinction to have written so precisely and in such detail of Frederick's battles that the German General Staff used Carlyle's descriptions to instruct its officers, but such a distinction pertains to military science and not to literature.[9] Carlyle seems to have mistaken diligence for thought, believing that if only Dryasdust could dig deep enough, he would re-emerge as a 'sacred Poet' (6: 7) and piece together the epic of Frederick's shaping of modern Prussia. But while digging he forgets what he once knew: that history is a 'Prophetic Manuscript' (27: 90) and not a record of battles or of diplomatic intrigues.

Worse still, Carlyle begins to worship what he once decried: 'Our true Deity is Mechanism', he had written at the outset of his career; 'In all senses, we worship and follow after Power . . .' (27: 74, 79). That the puritanical, anti-mechanical Carlyle should end his career by praising the Prussian military machine, utterly efficient and utterly amoral, has all the irony of tragedy but none of its redemptive quality. In Raymond Williams's words, 'a genuine insight, a genuine vision' was corrupted by the same worship of power to which it was initially opposed, 'until a civilizing insight became in its operation barbarous . . .'.[10] Two scenes tell the whole story. The first is from *The French Revolution*; the second, from *Frederick*, takes us to the heart of the Carlylean darkness. In the first, four hundred priests are imprisoned in the suffocating confines of a river-barge. Each heavy pause in the punctuation, each detail of the narrative, down to the psalmist's closing cry of 'How long, O Lord!—calls to mind the choric refrain of *The French Revolution*: 'Pity them all; for it went hard with them all' (4: 120).

> Some Four-hundred Priests . . . ride at anchor "in the roads of the Isle of Aix," long months; looking out on misery, vacuity, waste Sands of Oleron and the ever-moaning brine. Ragged, sordid, hungry; wasted to shadows:

---

* John Clive writes in his edition of *Frederick*, 'There appears to be something almost bizarre about this self-appointed sage, this son of a pious Scottish peasant, this declared enemy of the Enlightenment, deciding to spend a major portion of his life in celebrating the achievements of an eighteenth-century enlightened and cynical despot in order to furnish an example of moral heroism for the Victorian middle classes' (Chicago: Chicago University Press, 1969), p. xxiii.

eating their unclean ration on deck, circularly, in parties of a dozen, with finger and thumb; beating their scandalous clothes between two stones; choked in horrible miasmata, closed under hatches, seventy of them in a berth, through night; so that the "aged Priest is found lying dead in the morning, in the attitude of prayer"!—How long, O Lord!

(4: 272-3)

In the aftermath of the bloodiest battle of the Seven Years War, at Zorndorf in August 1758, Frederick's cavalry entrapped four hundred Cossacks in a burning barn. The Prussians blocked all the exits: 'Not a devil of you [shall escape]! said the Hussars; and the whole four hundred perished there, choked, burnt, or slain by the Hussars,—and this poor Planet was at length rid of them!' (17: 392). The death on water and the death by fire are some thirty years apart in date of composition; in quality of moral awareness the distance is immeasurable. Compassion for human suffering yields to an obtuseness that borders on the pathological: Carlyle pities not the burning Russians but the 'poor Planet' that is 'at length rid' of such vermin.

Throughout *Frederick* the gargantuan and the grotesque displace the 'loving minuteness' of attention Carlyle had expended on people and events in *The French Revolution*. The reader misses the myriad humanizing reminders of ordinary life in the midst of the extraordinary, the labourers of Valmy sunning themselves on stone benches as the Berline races by, the thousands of Parisians snoring in their beds as the Abbé Sicard escapes on the shoulders of his cellmates. One remembers instead the stocky, half-mad Friedrich Wilhelm drilling his regiment of Potsdam Giants or ordering them to parade through his bedroom when gout kept him off his feet. Recruited from all over Europe, 'kidnapped' by secret agents, or shipped by Peter the Great as presents in annual batches of 100, these towering 'sons of Anak' made an arch of their outstretched arms under which the King's Carriage rode in review.[11] Cut from the same Brobdingnagian cloth as the Potsdam Giants is the vast military encampment at Radewitz, where 30,000 troops constructed a ten-square mile stage-set for a sham battle far greater in scale than 'the Siege of Troy'. Although Carlyle tells us that the historical significance of the camp at Radewitz is nil, he describes it in inordinate detail, capping the nullity with a monstrous Cake, drawn by a team of eight horses, on which the Army feasts at the end of its manœuvres (13: 248, 257-9).

Frederick has great 'scenes' but no coherent centre, a fatal flaw in a work of over 4,000 pages that opens with Henry the Fowler in 928 and ends with Frederick's death in 1786. The problem of gargantuan scale is related to the problem of coarsened feeling and uncertain direction. Carlyle is alienated both from his own book and from his audience. As he inches his dismal way across what Jane called 'the valley of the shadow of Frederick',[12] he feels 'withdrawn from all the world . . ., all the world withdrawing from me'.[13] Composed in such a temper, *Frederick* necessarily lacks the middle range of feeling and seeing. Carlyle's genius remained intact but, like Goya in the silence of his villa, he found himself painting only giants and monsters.

Frederick, then, is a failure, but the failure of a great writer can be vital even in its deformity. Friedrich Wilhelm and his Giants provide a case in point. Like the story of Carlyle and his demon-cocks, the story of the Potsdam Giants is almost impossible to tell badly, and Carlyle tells it very well. But he is more than merely amusing. For all I have said of his coarsened feeling, he sees the cruelty as well as the comedy of their situation. Like giants of fable, many of the Potsdam Grenadiers were slow-witted; some were splay-footed and their legs swelled with fluid. Once their usefulness as Footguards ended, those without pensions faced a future in all senses dim. Some found work as drudges, others as freaks in travelling circuses. On the night of his father's funeral, Frederick disbanded the whole troop of 4,000 Guards. Unemployed and, for the most part, unemployable, they clogged the highways and crossroads of Brandenburg, shambling misfits who haunt the reader's imagination long after they pass out of sight.

*

Carlyle's powers of realization remain intact in *Frederick*; his powers of synthesis do not. The result is a Cyclopean wall of a book, almost impossible to breach,* made up of irregular boulders somehow fitted together. Within the bulk of the work are three principal narratives. The first is the Oedipal conflict between Friedrich Wilhelm and his son, with the David-and-Jonathan sub-plot of Frederick and Lieutenant von Katte, his closest friend. The first narrative is generational and political. It comprises the first ten Books of *Frederick* and centres on two antipathetic temperaments locked in a love-hate

---

* Frederick is born on page 20 in volume 12 of the Centenary Edition; he reaches the age of 1 on page 319. In between come eight centuries of Wends, wolves, Albert the Bear, Intercalary Kaisers, and innumerable Hohenzollerns.

relationship. On the resolution of this conflict hangs the future of the Prussian state. The second narrative focuses on Frederick and Voltaire. They, too, are in a kind of father–son relationship, only the 'son' is the patron and holds the reigns of power, while the 'father', Frederick's literary tutor and nearly twenty years his senior, dances to the son's tune. Their correspondence, 'courtship' (the term is Carlyle's), quarrel and reconciliation is a comic replay of the deathly struggle between Friedrich Wilhelm and his son. The third narrative overlaps the second and centres on the solitary figure of Frederick in dialogue with himself. Opposed by the combined forces of France, Austria, Russia, Saxony, and Sweden, facing almost certain defeat, Frederick is also at war with himself, torn between hope and suicidal despair. The turn in his fortunes marks the climax of the book. Following the third narrative is a brief coda (Book XXI) into which Carlyle compresses Frederick's last two decades, quietly closing his hero's career and, without knowing it, his own.

In Friedrich Wilhelm, Carlyle creates one of the few credible monsters in modern literature. Had he written only of the tyrannical half-mad father* and the abused son, he would have created a work of great unity and power. Both the pious, bullying, 'Hyperborean Spartan' (12: 349) of a father and the disbelieving, sensitive son were deeply attractive to Carlyle, as if their conflict represented not only 'a perennial controversy in human life' (12: 427) but warring elements in his own nature. The rocky course of the relationship veers between farce and tragedy as 'the rugged Father has grown to hate the son . . .' (12: 427). Friedrich Wilhelm berates the young Frederick as an '*effeminirter Kerl*', beats and half-starves him, detests his verses, his flute, his long locks, and commands the court surgeon to crop him in public. The 'fountains of bitterness' flow ever wider, 'necessitating the proud Son to hypocrisies towards his terrible Father'.[14]

Throughout his appalling apprenticeship Frederick responds to murderous verbal and physical abuse with integrity and self-possession. ' "My conscience has not accused me of any the least thing with which I could reproach myself" ', he writes at the age of 16 to His Majesty. ' "But if I have, against my will and knowledge, done anything that has angered my dear Papa, I herewith most submissively beg forgiveness; and hope my dear Papa will lay aside that cruel

---

* Nancy Mitford writes that Friedrich Wilhelm suffered from porphyria, a hereditary metabolic disease that 'drives its victims mad with prolonged and terrible suffering . . .', in *Frederick the Great* (New York: Harper & Row, 1970), p. 17.

hatred which I cannot but notice in all his treatment of me" ' (13: 134). A year or two later the King discovers Frederick at a forbidden flute lesson, dressed in a brocaded gown, his hair redone in the French style. Lieutenant von Katte is in the room, along with Frederick's flute-master. The enraged King spares Frederick but burns the gown, con-fiscates Frederick's library of French books, and, presumably, comes to quick conclusions about the relationship between the two young officers (13: 187–9). The scene has its macabre comedy as the Franco-phobic Father (Friedrich Wilhelm ordered convicts dressed in French clothes before they were publicly hanged) terrorizes his Francophilic Son.

The final intrusion of Friedrich Wilhelm into the privacies of Frederick and von Katte is pure horror. In August 1730 they were arrested while plotting to escape into France (13: 300–1). Frederick was thrown into solitary confinement in the fortress at Cüstrin and the two were tried by court martial as deserters from the Prussian Army (13: 326–33). Lieutenant Katte was sentenced to life imprison-ment, which the King insisted be changed to death by beheading. The Crown Prince was sentenced to death. But the King yielded to the pleas of his wife, the world, and his own divided heart: the sentence was commuted to 'repentance, prostrate submission and amendment'.[15]

On the eve of his execution von Katte, aged 26, wrote last letters whose tone was 'like that of dirges borne on the wind' (13: 339). He was taken to Cüstrin, where the King ordered Frederick to witness the beheading, a barbarity his guards quietly ignored. Katte caught sight ' "of his beloved Jonathan" ', the two now dressed in identically drab prison garb: ' "*Pardonnez-moi, mon cher Katte!*" ' Frederick pleaded, to which Katte responded, ' "*La mort est douce pour un si aimable Prince*" ' (13: 341).[16]

In no other episode does Friedrich Wilhelm appear more purely monstrous or more deserving of the condemnation of history. As Trevor-Roper has written, the 'dreadful' King was a 'brutal, boorish tyrant [who] ruled his country by stick and gallows, hanged innocent men without compunction, and forced his eighteen-year-old son to witness the summary execution of his closest friend'.[17] Trevor-Roper here speaks for all right-thinking persons; but Carlyle is not a right-thinking person. He is less interested in judging Friedrich Wilhelm than in imagining what it was to *be* Friedrich Wilhelm. And so Carlyle re-creates him, as it were, from the inside out. Trevor-Roper is simply wrong to accuse Carlyle of idolizing Friedrich Wilhelm; he is guilty of the more intelligent sin of trying to understand him:

> Friedrich Wilhelm's conduct, looked at from without, appears that of a hideous royal ogre, or blind anthropophagous Polyphemus fallen mad. Looked at from within, where the Polyphemus has his reasons . . . and is not bent on man-eating, but on discipline in spite of difficulties,—it is a wild enough piece of humanity, not so much ludicrous as tragical.
>
> (13: 332)

From the execution of Katte to the death of the old King in 1740, Frederick gradually comes out from under the shadow of his father's anger. But he does not emerge unscathed. As a boy, his father compelled him to dress and undress as fast as humanly possible, unhelped and unseen by others (12: 397). As a young man he learns more subtle modes of concealment. He begins to dissemble, to make himself 'invisible', to live an outward life of obedience while taking his inner self elsewhere. By the time he completes his painful apprenticeship as Crown Prince, he has won his father's grudging admiration; and he has mastered 'the art of wearing among his fellow-creatures a polite cloak-of-darkness . . . impregnable to the intrusion of human curiosity; able to look cheerily into the very eyes of men . . . and yet continue intrinsically invisible to them' (13: 374). Friedrich Wilhelm is a known quantity; his son remains a fully-clothed enigma through twenty-one Books. The enigma is first played off against the boorish Friedrich Wilhelm, then against the cat-like Voltaire. ' "Am not I happy to have such a Son to leave behind me!" ' exclaims the dying father to his grieving son (14: 270). The last words of Friedrich Wilhelm that we remember, almost the last he speaks,* are addressed to his wife Sophie, to whom he remained tenaciously faithful throughout their marriage: ' "Feekin, O my Feekin, thou must rise this day, and help me what thou canst. This day I am going to die; thou wilt be with me this day!" ' (14: 271).

The first ten books of *Frederick* are a historical *Bildungsroman* and might be subtitled 'The Apprenticeship of a Prince'. The second narrative pairs Frederick not with a hostile father but with a flattering mentor. Voltaire and Frederick serve as foils, the 'sage Plato of the Eighteenth Century' who sparkles at the Court of 'his Tyrant Dionysius' (14: 193). Together they exemplify for Carlyle the mind

---

* His last recorded words are ' "Herr Jesu, to thee I live; Herr Jesu, to thee I die; in life and in death thou art my gain (*Du bist mein Gewinn*)" ' (14: 273).

of the eighteenth century, as Frederick and his father represent the embodied will of Prussia. ' "Voltaire was the spiritual complement of Friedrich" ', Sauerteig tells us. What little their ' "poor Century . . . *did*, we must call Friedrich; what little it *thought*, Voltaire. . . . They are, they for want of better, the two Original Men of their Century . . ." ' (14: 177). The first narrative begins in hostility and ends in reconciliation; the second begins in a flurry of mutual admiration and ends in estrangement. After Frederick and Voltaire quarrel, they write to one another like 'a pair of Lovers hopelessly estranged and divorced; and yet . . . unique and priceless to one another'. Voltaire parries Frederick's banter 'in a finer *treble* tone', always taking the 'female' part in their uneasy duet (18: 188).

Carlyle hated the eighteenth century with a personal animosity, as if it had knocked him to the ground and robbed him of his faith. Yet the detested century nowhere shines more brilliantly than in his pages on Voltaire's walking 'his minuet among the Morning Stars' of Frederick's Court (16: 270). The high point comes in 1750 during Voltaire's fifth and final visit to his royal patron. Voltaire shines serenely among Europe's princes at the newly-built Berlin Carrousel, where he receives the homage of the world. He stars in performances of his own plays at the palaces of royalty who take the lesser parts (16: 269–70). Frederick showers honours on Voltaire as Carlyle rivals the King's munificence with a burst of metaphor at once extravagant and faintly ludicrous: Voltaire is the 'Trismegistus of Human Intellects', a caged poet whom Frederick shows off 'as the Talking Bird, the Singing Tree and the Golden Water, of intelligent mankind' (16: 272). In the light of such spirited play, or of Carlyle's description of Frederick's interminable verses as a 'leakage' of the King's internal plumbing, an involuntary 'expectoration' of his psyche into verse (14: 239; 17: 239–40), Emerson's 'wittiest book ever written' seems not altogether hyperbolical.

*

The third narrative centres on Frederick in the isolation of imminent defeat. In the winter of 1759–60, with England his only ally, he faces a confluence of disasters on all fronts. After the Prussian defeats at Kunersdorf and Maxen, he confides to the Marquis D'Argens, 'I am so crushed-down by these incessant reverses and disasters, that I wish a thousand times I were dead. . . . Astonishment, sorrow, indignation, scorn, all blended together, lacerate my soul' (18: 162). But he must fight on to the end. On 18 January 1762, the day before he learns of the death of his chief enemy, Czarina Elizabeth, he hints darkly to D'Argens of committing suicide (18: 419). Ringed by hostile forces and caught up in an internal conflict between defiance and despair, Frederick becomes for Carlyle a Promethean hero whose struggle against adversity mirrors his own.

More and more in this climactic act of Frederick's drama, Carlyle seems to step out of the wings and speak in the person of the King. Frederick's endurance of the darkest years of the war emboldens Carlyle to hope that he, too, will endure the long ordeal of telling Frederick's story. The turn for the better in Frederick's fortunes occurs in Book XX. The previous Book ('Friedrich Like to Be Overwhelmed in the Seven-Years War') ends with a grim paragraph that marks the moment of closest identification between Carlyle and Frederick. The paragraph is not history but distraught autobiography. For as Carlyle laboured in the sound-proof study, it was he who felt besieged, 'drenched in misery, but . . . defiant', he who fronted the world with Promethean courage but was ignored by a human 'herd' too stupid to recognize its benefactor:

> The symptoms we decipher in these Letters . . . are those of a man drenched in misery; but used to his black element, unaffectedly defiant of it . . . occupied only to do his very utmost in it, with or without success, till the end come. . . . Prometheus and other Titans, now and then, have touched the soul of some Aeschylus, and drawn tones of melodious sympathy, far heard among mankind. But with this new Titan it is not so. . . . Friedrich does wonderfully without sympathy from almost anybody; and the indifference with which he walks along, under such a cloud of sulky stupidities, of mendacities and misconceptions from the herd of mankind, is decidedly admirable to me.
>
> (18: 215)

Into the final Book of *Frederick* Carlyle compresses the years between the end of the Seven Years War in 1763 and Frederick's death in 1786. The 'Hercules-labours' (19: 1) of the Warrior-King were largely over and the narrative centres on Frederick's rebuilding of Prussia's war-ravaged economy and institutions. Early in the first chapter Carlyle warns the reader that he has written not 'a finished Narrative' but 'a loose Appendix of Papers' (19: 6), and at times the description seems apt. But beneath the miscellany of Polish Partition and Bavarian Succession, empty dates and fleeting faces, lies another narrative of compelling power. Lit by a coldly beautiful winter sun, this second narrative is a double elegy to the twilight of Frederick's life and the waning of Carlyle's own powers.

More and more the final Book becomes a *memento mori* as Frederick mourns the passing of his friends. For several pages Carlyle tolls their names and death-dates, pausing to note the inscription on the tomb of Francesco Algarotti, whose monument the King erected in the Campo Santo of Pisa: ' "*Hic jacet Ovidii œmulus et Neutoni discipulus*" ' (19: 41). 'Is the world becoming all a Mausoleum?' Carlyle asks, speaking for himself as well as for Frederick; '[is] nothing of divine in it but the Tombs of vanished loved ones?' (19: 42).

These dirge-like pages immediately follow Carlyle's description of the *Neue Palais* Frederick built in the 1760s near *Sans-Souci* but rarely inhabited. The description is notable both for its vivacity and its in-utility, for it serves no more apparent function in Carlyle's book than it did in Frederick's life, other than to gratify an appetite for building palaces. The passage is notable, too, because Carlyle so prominently places himself within it, first as a 'recent Tourist' on the palace grounds, then less coyly as the 'I' who lingers over the almost-animate stones and lets his genius play over the rococo façade with a freedom of invention that rivals the architect's:

"This *Neue Palais*," says one recent Tourist, "is a pleasant quaint object, nowadays, to the stranger. It has the air *dégagé, pococurante*; pleasantly fine in aspect and in posture;—spacious expanses round it, not in a waste, but still less in a strict condition; and (in its deserted state) has a silence, especially a total absence of needless flunkies and of gaping fellow-loungers, which is charming. Stands mute there, in its solitude, in its stately silence and negligence, like some Tadmor of the Wilderness in small. The big square of Stables, Coach-houses near by, was locked up,—probably one sleeping groom in it. The very *Custos* of the grand Edifice (such the rarity of fees to him) I could not awaken without difficulty. In the grey autumn zephyrs, no sound whatever about this New Palace of King Friedrich's, except the rustle of the crisp brown leaves, and of any faded or fading memories you may have. .

"I should say," continues he, "it somehow reminds you of the City of Bath. It has the cut of a battered Beau of old date; Beau still extant, though in strangely other circumstances; something in him of pathetic dignity in that kind. It shows excellent sound masonries; which have an overtendency to jerk themselves into pinnacles, curvatures and graciosities; many statues atop,—three there are, in a kind of grouped or partnership attitude; 'These,' said diligent scandal, 'note them; these mean Maria Theresa, Pompadour and *Catin du Nord*' (mere Muses, I believe, or of the Nymph or Hamadryad kind, nothing of harm in them). In short, you may call it the stone Apotheosis of an old French Beau. Considerably weatherbeaten (the brown of lichens spreading visibly here and there, the firm-set ashlar telling you, 'I have stood a hundred years');—Beau old and weather-beaten, with his cocked-hat not in the fresh condition, all his gold-laces tarnished; and generally looking strange, and in a sort tragical, to find himself, fleeting creature, become a denizen of the Architectural Fixities, and earnest Eternities!"—

(19: 36-7)

I know nothing else of Carlyle's quite so free or joyous as this, so without kinks. Carlyle sets all the fountains of the English language at play and the effortlessness is breathtaking. 'The stone Apotheosis of an old French Beau' is perfect, the more so if we recall Frederick's long courtship of things French. Not a soul is present (the custodian is surely asleep once more) except Carlyle and the three stone Muses, not a sound is heard except the dead leaves rustling in the autumn winds. The deserted, untenanted Palace is the most haunting of the many tombs in *Frederick the Great*. It is an emblem of Carlyle's book itself—vast, brilliant, empty, and forgotten.

Frederick appears to age with almost visible speed in the closing chapters. Like his stoical father, he continues to oversee all departments of government despite age and illness. Like his father, he is afflicted with gout in the midst of other woes. At first onset the disease seems almost a friend, but soon proves to be 'the captain of a chaotic company of enemies' (19: 285). While reviewing his troops Frederick gets drenched, becomes feverish, and withdraws from *Sans-Souci* to the Palace at Potsdam (19: 284-6). There Mirabeau visits the ailing King in April 1786, and the worlds of *The French Revolution* and *Frederick the Great* briefly intersect. But Mirabeau appears strangely diminished and business-like, not the blazing Titan of the earlier work. Very near Frederick's death we see through his 'cloak of darkness' and catch 'half-glimpses of a great motionless interior lake of Sorrow, sadder than any tears or complainings' (19: 291). We are surely not mistaken in seeing Carlyle's own reflection in the surface of the great, still lake.*

Death comes at night in a scene of utmost austerity. The King is paralysed and only semi-conscious, the room cold and empty, except

---

* 'At the edge of his own strength, and certain that his own death was imminent, [Carlyle] could not help but accentuate the autobiographical impulse of all his writing and track himself toward the grave as he described Frederick's old age.' Kaplan, *Thomas Carlyle*, p. 457.

for one of Frederick's dogs and a valet-nurse, Strutzki. The dog shivers in the cold and Frederick orders it covered with a quilt. The King's lungs fill with fluid, and as he slumps in his chair, Strutzki takes him on his knee, cradling him in his arms, 'in which posture the faithful creature, for above two hours, sat motionless, till the end came. Within doors, all is silence, except this breathing; around it the dark earth silent, above it the silent stars. At 20 minutes past 2 [on 17 August 1786], the breathing paused,—wavered; ceased' (19: 298).

This secular pietà of the dying King, cradled in the arms of his faithful *Kammerhussar*, is touching in its very frigidity and finality. 'Hope for himself in Divine Justice, in Divine Providence,' Carlyle writes, 'he had not practically any' (19: 291). The silence indoors is echoed by the silence of 'the dark earth' and of the stars above. The Cosmic Ocean encircling our little lives has turned chill and barren.

The death-scene is 'stern and lonely' (19: 298), a clinical account of rasping breath and failing pulse. No breeze blows through the sickroom, as at Cromwell's passing; no answering prayer rises on the wind. There is no dipping of handkerchiefs in blood, as at Louis's martyrdom; no inconsolable national mourning, as at Mirabeau's funeral. Death, which had been a great public spectacle in *The French Revolution*, here becomes private, witnessed only by a valet in the dead of night, or hidden behind the fortress wall at Cüstrin. History, as Carlyle now writes it, has shed the many-coloured robes of typology and walks in drab modern dress. The funeral is silent, like the sickroom and the stars above it: 'universal silence as of midnight, nothing audible among the people but here and there a sob, and the murmur, "Ach, der gute König!"' (19: 299). The procession, scarcely described, ends at the Garnison-Kirche of Potsdam, where the King who did not sleep with his wife is laid beside his father (19: 300).

Adieu, good readers; bad also, adieu. The envoy to *Frederick* is an exhausted, ill-tempered remnant of the great farewell to the reader in *The French Revolution*. After the completion of *Frederick* in 1865 and Jane's death in the following year, Carlyle became the historian of his own grief and guilt. In a blank little journal-book of Jane's, he wrote his pained 'Reminiscence' of her life, an act of contrition and unconscious usurpation; the 'Reminiscence' ends as Carlyle covers with his compact script the last remaining space in Jane's book. As a final memorial, he edited the letters of the wife who had sacrificed her genius to nurture his own. He soon abandoned the sound-proof room but never emerged from 'the valley of the shadow of Frederick'. A 'spectre moving in a world of spectres',[18] he took to sleeping in Jane's bedroom and staring himself to sleep with a photograph of her tomb in Haddington Church, where she was buried beside her father, as Carlyle was to be buried beside his parents in the ancient kirkyard of Ecclefechan. A tremor in his right arm made writing increasingly difficult and attempts at dictation resulted in 'diluted moonshine'.[19] 'Work is done. Self am done', he noted in his *Journal* for March 1870.[20] The *therefore* linking the two clauses is missing but understood: Carlyle's writing *was* his self. He continued to live for another eleven years, but the night whose coming he always feared had already arrived.

Notes

Chapter 1

1. Joseph Slater, ed., *The Correspondence of Emerson and Carlyle* (New York: Columbia University Press, 1964), p. 97. In much of what follows I am indebted to Professor Slater's fine Introduction.

2. James Anthony Froude, *Thomas Carlyle: A History of the First Forty Years of His Life, 1795–1835* (New York: Charles Scribner, 1910), 2: 290.

3. Ibid.

4. Slater, *Correspondence*, p. 58.

5. Ibid., p. 14.

6. Ibid., p. 15.

7. Ibid., p. 14. Slater writes that on Emerson's departure Carlyle 'did not ride with his guest to the top of the hill, but "preferred to watch him mount and vanish like an angel"' (p. 14). In his *Journal* for 28 August, Carlyle refers to Emerson's arrival as 'a singular apparition' (*The Collected Letters of Thomas and Jane Welsh Carlyle*, Duke–Edinburgh Edition, ed. Charles Richard Sanders et al., 9 vols. (Durham, NC: Duke University Press, 1970–81), 6: 425).

8. Mrs [Mary] Gordon, *'Christopher North': A Memoir of John Wilson* (Edinburgh, 1862), 2: 151. Cited in G. B. Tennyson, *'Sartor' Called 'Resartus'* (Princeton: Princeton University Press, 1965), p. 128.

9. Sanders, *Collected Letters*, 5: 109; 3 June 1830 to Anna Montague.

10. Sanders, *Collected Letters*, 5: 437.

11. *The Works of Thomas Carlyle*, Centenary Edition, ed. H. D. Traill, 30 vols. (London: Chapman and Hall, 1896–1901), 1: 154. Unless otherwise specified, all subsequent citations from Carlyle's *Works* will be to this edition and appear parenthetically in the text.

12. Charles Frederick Harrold, introd. and ed., *Sartor Resartus* by Thomas Carlyle (New York: Odyssey, 1937), p. xiv.

13. Sanders, *Collected Letters*, 6: 319–20; 10 Feb. 1833. Two weeks later Carlyle wrote to a young disciple in London that he might soon leave Craigenputtoch and appear 'in Cockney-land, like some John Baptist . . . proclaiming anew with fierce Annandale intonation: "Repent ye, ye cursed scoundrels, for" &c &c . . .' (6: 334; 22 Feb. 1833 to William Glen).

14. Froude, *Forty*, 2: 386.

15. Sanders, *Collected Letters*, 7: 9; 1 Oct. 1833.

16. Froude, *Forty*, 2: 326.

17. Sanders, *Collected Letters*, 7: 6; 1 Oct. 1833 to John A. Carlyle.

18. Ibid. 6: 446; 24 Sept. 1833.

19. Ibid. 7: 245; 22 July 1834 to John A. Carlyle.
20. Slater, *Correspondence*, p. 105; 12 Aug. 1834.
21. Sanders, *Collected Letters*, 7: 83; 21 Jan. 1834.
22. Sanders, *Collected Letters*, 7: 134–5; 18 Apr. 1834. For Homer's 'incalculable influence' on Carlyle, see John Clubbe, 'Carlyle as Epic Historian', in *Victorian Literature and Society*, ed. James R. Kincaid and Albert J. Kuhn (Columbus: Ohio State University Press, 1984), pp. 119–45.
23. Froude, *Forty*, 2: 333.
24. Harrold, introd., *Sartor Resartus*, p. xxvi.
25. Froude, *Forty*, 2: 314, 385.
26. Sanders, *Collected Letters*, 7: 104. 25 Feb. 1834.
27. Froude, *Forty*, 2: 352; undated letter to Margaret Carlyle.
28. *Two Notebooks*, ed. Charles Eliot Norton (New York: Grolier Club, 1898) p. 187.
29. *Two Notebooks*, p. 188.
30. 'Thomas Carlyle', in *Nineteenth-Century Studies* (1949; rpt. New York: Harper & Row, 1966), p. 105.
31. Fred Kaplan, *Thomas Carlyle: A Biography* (Ithaca: Cornell University Press, 1983, p. 37.
32. Carlyle owed the idea of a third scripture to Jean Paul Friedrich Richter, who wrote that 'Die Geschichte ist . . . die dritte Bibel.' In the second of his essays on Richter (1830), Carlyle cites Jean Paul's assertion that through Nature and History, ' "the Infinite Spirit . . . as with letters, legibly writes to us. He who finds a God in the physical world will also find one in the moral, which is History. Nature forces on our heart a Creator; History a Providence." ' See 27: 113 and Charles Frederick Harrold, *Carlyle and German Thought: 1819–1834* (New Haven: Yale University Press, 1934), p. 164.
33. 'Tintern Abbey', ll. 98–9.
34. See 1: 4, 45, 116, 190–1, 202. Cf. Willey, p. 118.
35. I owe this linkage of 'The Everlasting No' and 'transcendental despair' to Richard Goodman's dissertation, 'Carlyle's Intellectual Development Through *The French Revolution*', Columbia University, 1977, pp. 692–3.

Chapter 2

1. *Reminiscences*, ed. Charles Eliot Norton (1932; rpt. London: J. M. Dent, 1972), p. 3.
2. Sanders, *Collected Letters*, 8: 67, fn. 1.
3. Cited in Louise Mervin Young, *Thomas Carlyle and the Art of History* (Philadelphia: University of Pennsylvania Press, 1939), p. 143.
4. 'Well said, old mole! Canst work i' th' earth so fast?' Hamlet exclaims (I. v. 162). His last words are, 'The rest is silence.'

5. 29 Aug. 1842. Joseph Slater, ed. *The Correspondence of Emerson and Carlyle* (New York: Columbia University Press, 1964), p. 328; cf. p. 357.

6. Young, p. 143.

7. James Anthony Froude, *Thomas Carlyle: A History of His Life in London, 1834–1881* (New York: Charles Scribner, 1910), 1: 60; Journal entry of 22 March 1836.

8. Slater, *Correspondence*, p. 278; 26 Sept. 1840.

9. Slater, p. 325; 19 July 1842.

10. Compare this manuscript fragment from an early draft of *Cromwell*:

> The past belongs to Hela the Death Goddess . . . overspread with pale horror, with dim brown oblivion. And who are these, evidently kinsmen of the death goddess, that stand as Janitors admit[t]ing you, under heavy fees, to some view of the matter here and there? They are the Historians. . . . What an indistinct mouldy Whiteness overspreads their faces, so that no human feature can be clear, discovered; the features all gone, as in long-buried men, into a merely damp-powdery, blank. . . .

K. J. Fielding and Rodger L. Tarr, eds., *Carlyle Past and Present* (New York: Barnes and Noble, 1976), p. 19.

11. The phrase is from 'My Heart Leaps Up', the last three lines of which Wordsworth used as the epigraph to the Immortality Ode:

> The Child is Father of the Man;
> And I could wish my days to be
> Bound each to each by natural piety.

The same note sounds again in 'On History':

> Well may we say that of our History the more important part is lost without recovery; and,—as thanksgivings were once wont to be offered "for unrecognised mercies,"—look with reverence into the dark untenanted places of the Past, where, in formless oblivion, our chief benefactors . . . lie entombed.
> (27: 87)

13. The best gloss on this important passage is Elliot L. Gilbert's '"A Wondrous Contiguity": Anachronism in Carlyle's Prophecy and Art', *PMLA* 87 (1972), 432–42.

14. In the same vein he writes to Emerson, 'There is no use in writing of things past, unless they can be made in fact things present . . . the dead ought to bury their dead, ought they not?' Slater, p. 325, Letter of 19 July 1842.

15. *Iliad*, 5: 58, the death of Skamandrios, in the Lattimore translation. The formula recurs with minor variations in dozens of instances.

16. For the *Journal* entry, see Froude, *Forty*, 2: 78. For the story of the bust and the 'motto' from *The Tempest*, see Charles Frederick Harrold, ed., *Sartor Resartus*, p. 267 n. 2. In the essay 'Jean Paul Friedrich Richter Again' (1830), Carlyle cites Richter's comment that '"The passage of Shakespeare *rounded with a sleep (mit schlaf umgeben)* . . . created whole books in me."' (27: 154).

17. Froude, *London*, 1: 172; 26 Dec. 1840.

18. Froude, *London*, 1: 45–6; Summer 1835. Cf. Psalm 120: 5.
19. Sanders, *Collected Letters*, 8: 209; 23 Sept. 1835 to John A. Carlyle.
20. Slater, pp. 144, 145; 29 Apr. 1836.
21. Sanders, *Collected Letters*, 8: 253–4; 2 Nov. 1835.
22. Sanders, *Collected Letters*, 9: 267–8; 28 July 1837.
23. Kaplan, *Carlyle*, p. 395.

Chapter 3

1. Letter of 4 June 1835, cited in *Sartor Resartus*, ed. Charles F. Harrold, pp. 316–17. For Sterling's critique of *Sartor Resartus*, see ibid., pp. 307–16. Compare Thackeray's characterization of Carlyle's style as 'stiff, short, and rugged . . . astonishing . . . to those who love history as it gracefully runs in Hume, or struts pompously in Gibbon' (Review of *The French Revolution* in *The Times* of 3 Aug. 1837, reprinted in *Thomas Carlyle: The Critical Heritage*, ed. Jules P. Seigel (New York: Barnes & Noble, 1971), p. 69).
2. Letter of 22 July 1836. Sanders, *Collected Letters*, 9: 15.
3. Gibbon describes the scene in his *Autobiography*. See *The Decline and Fall . . . and Other Selected Writings*, ed. H. R. Trevor-Roper (Chalfont St Giles, Bucks.: Sadler & Brown, 1966), p. 53.
4. Froude, *London*, 1: 72; Sanders, *Collected Letters*, 9: 116; 17 Jan. 1837 to John Sterling.
5. Compare Hannah Arendt's contention that 'theoretically, the most far-reaching consequence of the French Revolution was the birth of the modern concept of history' (*On Revolution* (New York: Viking, 1963), p. 45).
6. Bolingbroke attributes the aphorism to Dionysius of Halicarnassus, who in turn ascribes it to Thucydides. Macaulay refers to the aphorism early in his essay on 'History' (1828), and Carlyle frequently cites the definition only to refute it, as in his essays 'On History' (1830) and on 'Sir Walter Scott' (1838). Compare Carlyle's letter of 17 Dec. 1833 to John Stuart Mill:

   'The "dignity of History" has buckramed up poor History into a dead mummy. There are a thousand purposes which History should serve beyond "teaching by Experience": it is an Address (literally out of Heaven, for did not God order it all?) to our *whole* inner man; to every faculty of Head and Heart from the deepest to the slightest. . . . Now for *all* such purposes, high, low, ephemeral, eternal, the first indispensable condition of conditions, is that we *see* the things transacted, and picture them out wholly as if they stood before our eyes. . . .' (Sanders, *Collected Letters*, 7: 52.)
7. *Enquiry Concerning Human Understanding*, cited by Emery Neff, *The Poetry of History* (New York: Columbia University Press, 1947), p. 230.
8. 'Romantic Historicism: The Temporal Sublime', in *Images of Romanticism*, ed. Karl Kroeber and William Walling (New Haven: Yale Univer-

sity Press, 1978), pp. 150-1, 160. Kroeber's comment on the weather concludes a discussion of Gibbon and Carlyle to which I am indebted.

9. I am summarizing here the principles given classic formulation by Condorcet in the Introduction to his *Progress of the Human Mind*: 'Such is the aim of the work that I have undertaken . . . to show by appeal to reason and fact that nature has set no term to the perfection of human faculties; that the perfectibility of man is truly indefinite; and that the progress of this perfectibility . . . has no other limit than the duration of the globe upon which nature has cast us' (Trans. June Barraclough (London: Weidenfeld & Nicolson, 1955), p. 4).

10. *Voltaire* (London: Macmillan, 1923), p. 16.

11. Sanders, *Collected Letters*, 6: 449; 24 Sept. 1833.

12. Macaulay's essay on 'History' appeared two years before Carlyle's 'On History' and provided the occasion for the later essay. Macaulay argues that Scott employed vivid historical details that historians themselves had disdained to use: 'He has constructed out of their gleanings works which, even considered as histories, are scarcely less valuable than theirs.' A truly great historian would 'reclaim those materials which the novelist has appropriated' and create a work that combines political history with social history. (*The Varieties of History*, ed. and sel. Fritz Stern (London: Macmillan, 1970), p. 87.)

13. Trans. Hannah and Stanley Mitchell (London: Merlin, 1962), pp. 23-5.

14. Ibid., p. 19.

15. Notable modern analyses of Carlyle's influence on Victorian fiction appear in Kathleen Tillotson's *Novels of the Eighteen-Forties* (Oxford: Clarendon Press, 1954) and George Levine's *The Boundaries of Fiction: Carlyle, Macaulay, Newman* (Princeton: Princeton University Press, 1968). Michael Goldberg's and William Oddie's studies of Carlyle's impact on Dickens's development (see below, fnn. 19 and 20) appeared concurrently in 1972. U. C. Knoepflmacher's untitled essay review in *Nineteenth-Century Fiction*, 32 (June 1977), 73-80, is a succinct but wide-ranging survey of Carlyle's influence on Victorian imaginative prose, fictional and non-fictional. Knoepflmacher suggests that the time is ripe for a study of 'Carlyle, Carlylism, and the Carlylean in Fiction: from Thackeray to Lawrence'. See also Rodger L. Tarr, ' "Fictional High-Seriousness": Carlyle and the Victorian Novel', in *Lectures on Carlyle and His Era*, ed. Jerry D. James and Charles F. Fineman (Santa Cruz: The University Library, University of California, 1982), pp. 27-54.

16. The *Oxford English Dictionary* credits Carlyle with coining the first two words and giving the third its modern meaning. It cites *Sartor Resartus* (1833-4; misdated 1831 in *OED*), bk. 2, ch. 4 as the first occurrence of *industrialism*, and 'Early German Literature' (1831) as the first occurrence of *genetic*.

17. The word *environment* rang strangely in the intellectual ear of the early Victorians. In a critique of Carlyle's language in *Sartor Resartus*, John Sterling condemns a number of 'positively barbarous' coinages. Heading Sterling's list of barbarisms is *environment* (Letter of 29 May 1835, cited in *Sartor Resartus*, ed. Harrold, p. 310). In its modern example of *environment* the *OED* misdates Carlyle's 'Goethe' essay as 1827 instead of 1828.

18. *Commissioned Spirits* . . . (New Brunswick, NJ: Rutgers University Press, 1979), p. 126. See also p. 97. Arac gives as his source Leo Spitzer, 'Milieu and Ambiance', *Philosophy and Phenomenological Research*, 3 (1942), 1–42, 169–218.

19. Cited in Michael Goldberg's *Carlyle and Dickens* (Athens, Ga.: University of Georgia Press, 1972), p. 2. Goldberg studies exhaustively and sensitively Dickens's debt to Carlyle. When *The French Revolution* first appeared, 'Dickens carried a copy of it with him wherever he went' (Froude, *London*, 1: 80). Dickens later estimated that he read 'that wonderful book' nine times, and when beginning *Bleak House* claimed an even more hyperbolic '500th' reading (see Goldberg, p. 101; Arac, p. 117). Carlyle sent Dickens a number of books on the Revolution early in the course of Dickens's research for *A Tale of Two Cities*. This small library of much-travelled volumes doubtless contained titles that Mill, who had once planned to write a history of the French Revolution, had sent in 'barrowfuls' to Carlyle in 1833–4 (see Froude, *Forty*, 2: 263, 352). Mill thus played the unique role of inadvertently burning one manuscript on the French Revolution and indirectly fathering the most famous English history and novel on the subject.

20. See Goldberg, pp. 105–16, and William Oddie, *Dickens and Carlyle: The Question of Influence* (London: Centenary Press, 1972), pp. 61–85. For recent discussion of the Carlyle—Dickens connection, see the essays by Murray Baumgarten, Michael Timko, Carol Mackay, Chris Vanden Bosche, Michael Goldberg, Branwen Pratt, and Elliot Gilbert in *Dickens Studies Annual*, 12, ed. Michael Timko *et al.* (AMS Press, 1983), pp. 161–265.

21. Dickens refers to *The French Revolution* as 'Mr. Carlyle's wonderful book' in the Preface to the first edition of *A Tale of Two Cities*. Both Carlyle and Dickens claimed to be in a feverish state of possession while writing their books on the Revolution, as if having to experience—perhaps induce—in themselves the larger upheaval they were describing. Compare Carlyle's account of *The French Revolution* as 'a wild savage book' born hot out of his soul (see above, p. 31) with Dickens's similar claim in the Preface to *A Tale of Two Cities* that the writing 'has had complete possession of me; I have so far verified what is done and suffered in these pages, as that I have certainly done and suffered all myself.'

22. (Oxford: Clarendon Press, 1954), p. 154.

23. *Critical Heritage*, ed. Seigel, pp. 410–11.
24. Gordon S. Haight, *George Eliot: A Biography* (Oxford: Oxford University Press, 1968), p. 367.
25. 'The Formal Nature of Victorian Thinking', *PMLA* 90 (1975), 916, 905–6.
26. See paragraph 2 of the 'Finale'.
27. Teufelsdröckh's description of the modern poet's mission appears in the chapter on 'Symbols' in *Sartor Resartus* (1: 179). Compare Stephen's closing words in Joyce's *A Portrait of the Artist*.
28. For a very different evaluation of *Romola*, see Felicia Bonaparte's *The Triptych and the Cross: The Central Myths of George Eliot's Poetic Imagination* (New York: New York University Press, 1979). Professor Bonaparte reveals the epic and prophetic design of the novel with great clarity. Our disagreement is over whether or not George Eliot realizes that design in a successful work of fiction.
29. Passed on 17 September 1793, the law defined suspected persons so broadly as to make everyone a hostage of the Terror. 'Watch well your words,' Carlyle writes, 'watch well your looks: if Suspect of nothing else, you may grow, as came to be a saying "Suspect of being Suspect"! For are we not in a state of Revolution?' (4: 192).
30. George Eliot demystifies her demons and naturalizes her saints. At the novel's end, Romola heals her disillusioned spirit by ministering to the inhabitants of a plague-ridden village, where she is venerated as a kind of Madonna. Like the real-life Savonarola, the fictional Romola is about to become a legend. But in a paragraph of austere renunciation George Eliot desanctifies her own heroine: 'Many legends were later told about "the blessed Lady who came over the sea," but their essential meaning is that a good woman "had done beautiful loving deeds" ' (ch. 68). In this reverse transfiguration from blessed Lady to good woman, from legends to deeds, George Eliot effectually destroys the fifteenth-century historical fiction she has so painstakingly created.
31. George Eliot, 'Historical Imagination', in *Essays of George Eliot*, ed. Thomas Pinney (New York: Columbia University Press, 1963), pp. 446–7.
32. *Two Notebooks of Thomas Carlyle*, ed. Charles Eliot Norton (New York: Grolier Club, 1898), p. 124.
33. The phrase 'polycentric perspective' comes from a discussion of narrative techniques in *The French Revolution* in Philip Rosenberg's *The Seventh Hero* (Cambridge, Mass.: Harvard University Press, 1974), p. 76.
34. The *action* of the novel, that is, begins and ends with fragments of dialogue. The philosophical essay that Tolstoy appended to the novel and entitled 'Second Epilogue' is another matter.
35. Carlyle asserts in *On Heroes* and elsewhere that history is 'the Biography of Great Men', that the Hero shapes events, whereas Tolstoy argues in

War and Peace that events shape men, who are the product of their times. 'To study the laws of history,' Tolstoy contends in bk. XI, ch. 1, of *War and Peace*, 'we must completely change the subject of our observation, must leave aside kings, ministers, and generals, and study the common, infinitesimally small elements by which the masses are moved' (trans. Louise and Aylmer Maude, Norton Critical Edition, ed. George Gibian (New York: Norton, 1966), pp. 919–20). Yet Carlyle made the same point forty years earlier in 'On History': 'The Political Historian . . . too often . . . dwelt with disproportionate fondness in Senate-houses, in Battle-fields, nay, even in Kings' Ante-chambers; forgetting, that far away from such scenes, the mighty tide of Thought and Action was still rolling on . . .' (27: 91).

36. Bk. XI, ch. 1 (Norton edn., pp. 917–18). Tolstoy's comments on the 'absolute continuity of motion' suggest further comparison with Carlyle's assertion that history cannot be written without selection and compression, 'for Time, like Space, is *infinitely* divisible ('On History Again' (28: 172)).

37. (New Haven: Yale University Press, 1963), pp. 9–10, 22.

38. In the opening chapters of *Natural Supernaturalism*, M. H. Abrams makes the definitive case for *The Prelude* as an epic whose 'high argument' is the theodicy of self. From its opening paragraph onwards, *The Stones of Venice* is a Christian epic whose final volume—subtitled *The Fall*—completes the chronicle of a Gothic paradise lost. In the Preface to *London Labour and the London Poor*, Henry Mayhew uses the epic poet's trope of himself as a voyager into an 'undiscovered country'—in this case the vast, unexplored territory of the drifting poor who scavenge the London streets. Mayhew pioneers the documentary-epic; he is the first writer, as he puts it, 'to publish the history of a people, from the lips of the people themselves'. In Jules Michelet's passionate national epic, *Histoire de la Révolution Française* (1847–53), the people are the hero, as in the epics of Carlyle and Mayhew. The American historian William Prescott provides an illuminating parallel with Carlyle, for his conception of history as a prose epic is identical to Carlyle's and suggests how closely linked were British and American literary cultures during the Victorian period. Two years after the publication of Carlyle's *The French Revolution*, and fifty years to the day after the fall of the Bastille, the final shape of *The Conquest of Mexico* clarified itself in Prescott's mind. In his Notebook for 14 July 1839 he wrote, 'The true way of conceiving the subject is, not as a philosophical theme [not, that is, as 'Philosophy teaching by examples'] but as an *epic in prose* . . . borne onward on a tide of destiny, like that which broods over the fictions of the Grecian poets.' (See *The Literary Memoranda of William Hickling Prescott*, ed. C. Harvey Gardiner (Norman: University of Oklahoma Press, 1961), 2: 32.)

39 (Oxford, 1954; rpt. New York: Barnes & Noble, 1966), pp. 528, 530.

40. 1. 24; 9. 14-15. Cf. 1. 13-16, where Milton intends that his 'advent'rous Song' pursue 'Things unattempted yet in Prose or Rhyme'.
41. *The Recluse*, ll. 824, 793-4.
42. 3. 176, 184.
43. *Romantic Poets and Epic Tradition* (Madison: University of Wisconsin Press, 1965), p. 14.
44. From the concluding section, entitled 'Epics', of a long essay by Lowell on the New England poets. *New York Review of Books*, 21 Feb. 1980, p. 6. Thoreau's essay appeared in *Graham's Magazine* in 1847 and is reprinted in *The Critical Heritage*, ed. Seigel, p. 290. For Emerson's letter of 13 Sept. 1837 see Slater, *Correspondence*, p. 167.
45. Letter to John Carlyle of 21 Sept. 1834: 'The best news is that I have actually *begun* that French Revolution. . . . It shall be such a Book! Quite an Epic Poem of the Revolution: an Apotheosis of Sansculottism!' Sanders, *Collected Letters*, 7: 306.
46. Sanders, *Collected Letters*, 7: 6; 1 Oct. 1833, to John A. Carlyle.
47. Sanders, *Collected Letters*, 6: 446; 24 Sept. 1833. Cf. p. 5, above.
48. Slater, *Correspondence*, p. 105; 12 Aug. 1834.
49. The message is made less explicitly self-promotional by being put into the mouth of the oracular Herr Sauerteig. Only ' "by working more and more on REALITY," ' Sauerteig predicts, ' "will this high emprise [of the modern poet] be accomplished" ' (28: 53). In 'Biography' and its conclusion, 'Boswell's Life of Johnson', Carlyle first adumbrates his 'creed', expressed to Emerson two years later, 'that the only Poetry is History'. For an excellent analysis of *The French Revolution* as a modern epic, see Albert J. LaValley, *Carlyle and the Idea of the Modern* (New Haven: Yale University Press, 1968), pp. 139-59. See also Peter Allan Dale, *The Victorian Critic and the Idea of History* (Cambridge, Mass.: Harvard University Press, 1977), and Emery Neff, *The Poetry of History* (New York: Columbia University Press, 1947).
50. Cited in LaValley, p. 2, from Emerson's *Works* (Centenary edn., Boston, 1883), 12: 390.
51. Stephen E. Whicher, *Selections from Ralph Waldo Emerson* (Boston: Houghton Mifflin, 1957), p. 61. The passage occurs in Emerson's *Journal* for 29 March 1837. For a later version of this passage, see Seigel, *Critical Heritage*, pp. 224-5.
52. Hence in the Old Testament the Prophet is called rō eh or hōzeh, derived from roots meaning 'to see', and nābhī, from nābhā, meaning 'to announce'.
53. 20: 325; 27: 90; 12: 17; 1: 142.
54. *Hamlet*, V. ii. 10-11.
55. Whicher, *Selections*, p. 60. Cf. Frank Kermode's comments that the biblical 'exegete, the novelist and the historian are all doing their own things, and we easily see very sharp and obvious distinctions between

them; so we rarely think of them all together, rarely consider the remarkable and complicated resemblances' ('Novel, History, and Type', in *Novel: A Forum on Fiction*, i. (1968), 238). All three conjoin in the historical writings of Carlyle.

56. H. M. Leicester writes of this aspect of *The French Revolution* in 'The Dialectic of Romantic Historiography: Prospect and Retrospect in *The French Revolution*', *Victorian Studies*, 15 (Sept. 1971), 6–8.

57. See Dale, pp. 75–9.

58. In *Milton and the English Revolution* (London: Faber and Faber, 1977), Christopher Hill argues that *Paradise Lost* reflects Milton's struggle with the problems consequent on 'the failed revolution', the millennium that never came. See especially Part VI.

59. Cited in Seigel, *Critical Heritage*, p. 52, from *London and Westminster Review* of July 1837.

Chapter 4

1. Sanders, *Collected Letters*, 7: 306; 21 Sept. 1834.

2. Sanders, *Collected Letters*, 9: 15; 22 July 1836 to J. S. Mill. See above, p. 30.

3. Near the end of *The French Revolution*, Carlyle writes that 'the harvest of long centuries' has at last ripened and is now being 'reaped, in this Reign of Terror; and carried home, to Hades and the Pit! . . .' (4: 203).

4. Cf. Isaiah 46: 9–10 ('I *am* God, . . . Declaring the end from the beginning. . . .') and Revelation 21: 6 ('I am Alpha and Omega, the beginning and the end').

5. Carlyle refers to the painting in 4: 170.

6. 3: 181; 4: 110–11. Cf. Matthew 26: 26–9; 27: 35; Mark 14: 13–15, 22–4; Luke 22: 12–20; 23: 34; John 19: 23–30; 1 Corinthians 11: 23–6.

7. 'Truth, Fact, is the life of all things; Falsity, "fiction" or whatever it may call itself, is certain to be death . . .' (20: 322).

8. *The Flight to Varennes and Other Historical Essays* (London: Swan Sonnenschein, 1892), pp. 2, 36–7.

9. See Browning, p. 37 n. 1, and p. 74. C. R. L. Fletcher in his edition of 1902 (London: Methuen), and J. Holland Rose in his of 1913 (London: G. Bell & Sons) also give no source for the scene and annotate it as 'apocryphal' (Fletcher, 2: 122 n. 2; and Rose, 2: 213 n. 1).

10. *Relation du départ de Louis XVI le 20 juin 1791* (Paris: Baudouin Frères, 1822), p. 92.

11. John D. Rosenberg, ed., *The Genius of John Ruskin: Selections from his Writings* (New York: George Braziller, 1963), p. 514.

12. The City of London Light and Coke Company was founded in 1817, and in the 1820s gas lamps became 'a wonder in the streets'. (See Bernard Ash, *The Golden City: London Between the Fires, 1666–1941* (London: Dent,

1964), pp. 120, 148.) Carlyle's making of poetry from the latest technological advances brings to mind Wordsworth's remark that if 'Men of science should ever create any material revolution, direct or indirect, in our condition, and in the impressions which we habitually receive, the Poet . . . will be at his side, carrying sensation into the midst of the objects of science itself' ('Preface to Lyrical Ballads', 1800; *Selected Poems and Prefaces*, ed. Jack Stillinger (Boston: Houghton Mifflin, 1965), p. 456).

Chapter 5

1. *Essentials of English Grammar* (London: Allen and Unwin, 1933), p. 238. Cf. *A Modern English Grammar* . . . (Heidelberg: Carl Winters Universitätsbuchhandlung, 1931), 4: 19.

2. *The Handling of Words; and Other Studies in Literary Psychology* (London: John Lane, 1923), pp. 184–5. Lee transcribes, with omissions and a sizeable number of errors, the section of 'Charlotte Corday' beginning 'On the morrow . . .' and ending 'He that made him knows' (4: 167–9). See her brief, excellent essay on 'Carlyle and the Present Tense' in *The Handling of Words*.

3. Vernon Lee characterizes this narrative *persona* as looking 'down on the revolution from the skyey post of observation where *he* sits . . . a kind of cosmic, archangelic daemon, seeing the molehill-upsettings, the ants' processions and tumults of this world, and this world as but a tiny item of the swirling universe around him . . .' (ibid., p. 181).

4. *Joyce's Voices* (Berkeley: University of California Press, 1978), p. 71. Kenner's term for the phenomenon is 'the Uncle Charles Principle', named after the character in *A Portrait of the Artist* who, in the narrator's words, '*repaired* to the outhouse': ' "repaired" wears invisible quotation marks', as if Uncle Charles himself were narrating the story. According to Kenner, this fluctuating narrative idiom represents 'something new in fiction' (p. 17).

5. 28: 386. Cf. pp. 332 and 377, where the jeweller Boehmer and Mme de Lamotte address the narrator. Carlisle Moore comments on the volatile interaction between Carlyle and his characters in 'Carlyle's "Diamond Necklace" and Poetic History', *PMLA* 58 (1943), 547.

6. 2: 212. Compare the confrontation of the Sansculottes and the King in the Tuileries on 20 June, 1792, a 'spectacle, of Incongruity fronting Incongruity, and as it were recognising themselves incongruous. . . . Thus do the two Parties, brought face to face after long centuries, stare stupidly at one another, *This, verily, am I; but, good Heaven, is that Thou*?' (3: 261–3).

7. David DeLaura points out that the multiplicity of roles and attitudes Carlyle assumes in a particular work convinces us of 'the integrity of his own embodied personality, sensed as a single energizing force . . .'. This

constantly expanding ' "virtual" personality' constitutes the 'basis of the integrity of the work as a whole'. See 'Ishmael as Prophet: *Heroes and Hero-Worship* and the Self-Expressive Basis of Carlyle's Art', *Texas Studies in Literature and Language*, 11 (1969), 706–8. Morse Peckham writes of the many voices of the narrator in his essay on '*Frederick the Great*' in *Carlyle Past and Present*, ed. K. J. Fielding and Rodger L. Tarr (New York: Barnes and Noble, 1976), pp. 198–215. See especially his analysis of the 'dissolved narrator' on pp. 207–9. To this list I should add 'The Impulse Towards Fiction in Thomas Carlyle's *The French Revolution*', an unpublished essay by my former student, Barbara Cohen Weiss, and two studies of Carlyle's use of sources, both by Charles F. Harrold: 'The Translated Passages in Carlyle's *French Revolution*', *JEGP* 27 (1928), 51–66, and 'Carlyle's General Method in *The French Revolution*', *PMLA* 43 (1928), 1150–69. The latter is especially significant in showing that Carlyle often drew on a multitude of different sources in constructing a scene, at times citing a dozen accounts for a single paragraph, each phrase deriving from a different source. The episodic nature of Carlyle's narrative, Harrold demonstrates, 'reflects the episodic nature of his sources . . . a collection of memoirs, reminiscences, hastily-written histories, letters, and diaries, materials that were naturally deficient in coherence and perspective' (pp. 1152–3).

8. 2: 136, 235–6; 3: 16.

Chapter 6

1. In tracing the motif of cannibalism in *The French Revolution*, I am indebted to Lee Sterrenburg's essay, 'Psychoanalysis and the Iconography of Revolution', *Victorian Studies*, 19 (1975), 241–64. See especially pp. 249–50, 253–4.

2. Trans. James Strachey (New York: Norton, 1961), p. 58. Strachey attributes this phrase to Plautus, Asinaria, II. iv. 88.

3. See, for example, 3: 155, 4: 183, and cf. Carlyle's letter of 24 Sept. 1833 to John Stuart Mill, Sanders, *Collected Letters*, 6: 446.

4. *The Seventh Hero: Thomas Carlyle and the Theory of Radical Activism* (Cambridge, Mass.: Harvard University Press, 1974), pp. 102, 105.

5. 4: 24. Compare this similar assessment of the National Convention, whose acts 'became the astonishment and horror of mankind. . . . To hate this poor National Convention is easy; to praise and love it has not been found impossible. . . . To us, in these pages, be it as a fulginous fiery mystery, where Upper has met Nether, and in such alternate glare and blackness of darkness poor bedazzled mortals know not which is Upper, which is Nether . . .' (4: 70–1).

6. For Sansculottism as a chthonic, infantile monster, see pp. 65, 83, above, and 2: 212. Cf. Carlyle's personification of the proletariat as

'Rascality' that has 'slipped its muzzle; and now bays, three-throated, like the Dog of Erebus' (2: 281).

7. From an essay-review in the *London and Westminster Review*, October 1839, cited in Philip Rosenberg, p. 103. The essay, on balance highly favourable, is reprinted with omissions in Jules Seigel's *Thomas Carlyle: The Critical Heritage* (New York: Barnes and Noble, 1971), pp. 101–40.

8. 4: 121–2. Cf. 4: 249: 'Each man, enveloped in his ambient-atmosphere of revolutionary fanatic Madness, rushes on, impelled and impelling; and has become a blind brute Force. . . .'

9. *Research Studies*, 43 (Sept. 1975), 144.

10. Butwin, pp. 144, 149. See also Robespierre's speech to the Convention of 5 February 1794 describing the Revolution as a great struggle to shape 'the destiny of the world', with France 'the theatre of this fearsome contest', in Paul H. Beik, ed., *The French Revolution* (New York: Harper and Row, 1970), p. 283.

11. Cited in J. Holland Rose's edition of *The French Revolution: A History*, 3 vols. (London: G. Bell, 1913), 2: 169 n., from La Marck, *Correspondence*, 1: 259.

12. See C. R. L. Fletcher's edition of *The French Revolution: A History*, 3 vols. (London: Methuen, 1902), 3: 69, n. 3.

13. I owe to my student Edwin R. Smith the perception that Philippe Égalité's 'Last Breakfast' is a parody of Louis XVI's Last Supper.

14. See David Lloyd Dowd, *Pageant-Maker of the Republic: Jacques-Louis David and the French Revolution* (1948; rpt. Freeport, NY: Books for Libraries Press, 1969), pp. 1–23, and Walter F. Friedlaender, *David to Delacroix*, trans. Robert Goldwater (Cambridge, Mass.: Harvard University Press, 1952), pp. 18–19.

15. 'The Eighteenth Brumaire of Louis Bonaparte', in *Collected Works*, Vol. 11, 1851–3 (London: Lawrence and Wishart, 1979), pp. 103–4.

16. She was arrested on 17 June 1794, and died in prison the following year. See R. R. Palmer, *Twelve Who Ruled: The Year of the Terror in the French Revolution* (1941; rpt. Princeton: Princeton University Press, 1958), pp. 368, 377; Fletcher, 3: 193 n. 2; Georges Lefebvre, *The French Revolution*, Vol. 2: *From 1793 to 1799*, trans. John Hall Stewart and James Friguglietti (New York: Columbia University Press, 1964), p. 134. For Carlyle's account, see 4: 268, 273, 275.

17. 3: 216. Compare Carlyle's description of the fusillades at Lyons as 'butchery too horrible for speech' (4: 218).

18. See Luke 4: 1–2 and Matthew 26: 36.

19. It is possible, but quite unlikely, that Robespierre was shot by one of his guards. See Carlyle's footnote, 4: 284. Lefebvre assumes an attempted suicide: *The French Revolution*, 2: 135–6.

20. The chapter entitled 'The Gods are Athirst' ends, 'The Revolution, then, is verily devouring its own children? All Anarchy, by the

nature of it, is not only destructive but self-destructive' (4: 254). Cf. 4: 273.

21. 4: 284. Mark 15: 16–20.
22. See Matthew 27: 12, 14; Mark 15: 3–5; Luke 23: 9.
23. See Matthew 27: 28, 31; Mark 15: 17, 20.
24. Slater, *Correspondence*, p. 104; 12 Aug. 1834. Compare Carlyle's praise of Emerson's *The American Scholar* as a kind of sacred music:

> It was long decades of years that I heard nothing but the infinite jangling and jabbering and inarticulate twittering and screeching, and my soul had sunk down sorrowful, and said there is no articulate speaking then any more, and thou art solitary among stranger-creatures?—and lo, out of the West, comes a clear utterance, clearly recognisable as a m[an's] voice, and I *have* a kinsman and brother: God be thanked for it! I coul[d have] *wept* to read that speech; the clear high melody of it went tingling thro' my heart. . . . (Ibid, p. 173)

The antithesis of Emerson's 'clear high melody' is the inchoate jargon of Cagliostro:

> The man could not speak; [his Discourses are] only babble in long-winded diffusions, chaotic circumvolutions tending nowhither. He had no thought for speaking with; he had not even a language. . . . that tongue of his emits noises enough, but no speech. Let him begin the plainest story, his stream stagnates at the first stage; chafes, "ahem! ahem!" loses itself in the earth; or, bursting over, flies abroad without bank or channel,—into separate plashes. . . . what resemblance of thought he has, cannot deliver itself, except in gasps, blustering gushes, spasmodic refluences, which make bad worse. Bubble, bubble, toil and trouble: how thou bubblest, foolish "Bubblyjock"!
>
> (28: 293)

25. Matthew 27: 50; cf. Mark 15: 37; Luke 23: 46.
26. Carlyle has been criticized for ending his narrative too abruptly in 1795, but Georges Lefebvre sees the same finality as Carlyle in the quelling of the insurrection of 1 Prairial: 'This is the date which should be taken as the end of the Revolution. Its mainspring was now broken' (Lefebvre, 2: 145).
27. Sanders, *Collected Letters*, 7: 245; 22 July 1834 to John A. Carlyle.
28. *English Historians on the French Revolution*, p. ix.

Chapter 7

1. *On Heroes, Hero-Worship, and the Heroic in History* was first given as a series of lectures in London in the spring of 1840. 'They have nothing *new*, . . .' Carlyle complained when revising them for publication; 'the style of them requires to be low-pitched, as like talk as possible. The whole

business seems to me wearisome triviality. . . .' Apparently he took a less dim view of the book when he saw it in proof. See Froude, *Thomas Carlyle: A History of His Life in London*, 1.167, 176.

2. Froude, *London*, 2: 300; Journal entry for 3 Aug. 1867.

3. For Carlyle's influence on Engels, see Steven Marcus, *Engels, Manchester, and the Working Class* (New York: Random House, 1974), pp. 102–12, and G. Robert Stange, 'Refractions of *Past and Present*' in *Carlyle Past and Present*, ed. K. J. Fielding and Rodger L. Tarr (New York: Barnes and Noble, 1976), pp. 107–10. Engels read *Past and Present* almost immediately after its publication in April 1843, and his review in the following year is the first literary fruit of his association with Karl Marx. Marx and Engels later became highly critical of Carlyle.

4. Froude, *London*, 2: 58.

5. In Seigel, *Thomas Carlyle: The Critical Heritage*, p. 219.

6. Froude, *London*, 2: 240.

7. Cited in John Clive, ed., *History of Friedrich II of Prussia Called Frederick the Great* (Chicago: University of Chicago Press, 1969), pp. xvii–xviii. Clive quotes from a Journal entry of 1858, when only the first two volumes had appeared. Macaulay died before the later volumes were published.

8. See H. R. Trevor-Roper, *The Last Days of Hitler*, 3rd edn. (New York: Collier, 1962), pp. 159–60, and Clive, *Frederick*, p. xiii. The seeming miracle was the sudden death in 1762 of Frederick's adversary, Empress Elizabeth I of Russia. Trevor-Roper is not altogether clear whether *Frederick* was Hitler's or Goebbels's favourite book, but I follow Clive in assuming it to have been Hitler's.

9. Walt Whitman, *Specimen Days*, reprinted in Seigel, ed., *Thomas Carlyle: The Critical Heritage* (New York: Barnes and Noble, 1971), p. 462.

10. Elizabeth K. Helsinger points to the parallelism between the ruins of the Abbey and the 'discarded humans' of the Workhouse in a chapter on 'History as Criticism' in *Ruskin and the Art of the Beholder* (Cambridge: Harvard University Press, 1982), p. 154. See pp. 154–8 for discussion of the trope of the traveller in *Past and Present*.

11. Letter of 29 August 1842 in Slater, *Correspondence*, p. 328. Cf. Carlyle's letters to the same effect to his mother and to John Sterling in Froude, *London*, 1: 243–4.

12. See Richard D. Altick, ed., *Past and Present* (New York: New York University Press, 1977), p. vi, and Harold A. Boner, *Hungry Generations: The Nineteenth-Century Case against Malthusianism* (New York: King's Crown Press, 1955), pp. 125–6.

13. See Friedrich Engels, *The Condition of the Working Class in England in 1844*, trans. and ed. by W. O. Henderson and W. H. Challoner (Oxford: Basil Blackwell, 1958), pp. 161, 170, 278; John W. Dodds, *The Age of Paradox: A Biography of England 1841–1851* (New York: Rinehart, 1952), pp. 91–2, 157; Asa Briggs, *Victorian Cities* (Harmondsworth, Middlesex:

Penguin Books, 1968), p. 147; David Alec Wilson, *Carlyle on Cromwell and Others (1837–48)*, Vol. 3 of *Life of Thomas Carlyle* (New York: E. P. Dutton, 1925), p. 165; and Steven Marcus, *Engels*, p. 91.

14. Dodds, *Age of Paradox*, p. 158.
15. Engels, *Condition*, p. 322.
16. 'Who Is To Blame for the Condition of the People?' in *The Economist* (21 Nov. 1846), p. 1517.
17. Cited in '*Past and Present*: Topicality as Technique' by Richard D. Altick, in *Carlyle and His Contemporaries: Essays in Honor of Charles Richard Sanders*, ed. John Clubbe (Durham, NC: Duke University Press, 1976), p. 128.
18. Carlyle misquotes ('on', not 'of') the lines from *The Tempest* (IV. i. 156–7). The passage on the tenses should be compared to another on 'the LIFE-TREE IGDRASIL', which Carlyle describes at the beginning, middle, and end of *Past and Present*:

> For the Present holds in it both the whole Past and the whole Future;—as the LIFE-TREE IGDRASIL, wide-waving, many-toned, has its roots down deep in the Death-kingdoms, among the oldest dead dust of men, and with its boughs reaches always beyond the stars; and in all times and places is one and the same Life-tree!
>
> (10: 38; cf. 129, 250)

19. Linda Georgianna argues that 'the scissors which cut Jocelin's *Chronicle* short are Carlyle's, not Destiny's . . .' (p. 122). The case is overstated, but Georgianna's point that Jocelin gradually ceases to regard Samson as a 'hero', and that Carlyle ignores the change, is well taken. See 'Carlyle and Jocelin of Brakelond: A Chronicle Rechronicled', in *Browning Institute Studies*, 8 (1980), 103–27.
20. *The Victorian City: Images and Realities*, H. J. Dyos and Michael Wolff, eds., 2 vols. (London: Routledge & Kegan Paul, 1973), vol. 1, plate 17; vol. 2, plates 118, 151, 152.
21. See Altick, 'Topicality as Technique', pp. 117–18.
22. 'Thomas Carlyle' in *Culture and Society 1780–1950* (1958; rpt. New York: Harper & Row, 1966) p. 79.
23. Cited in *Culture and Society*, p. 79.
24. *Culture and Society*, p. 80.
25. From a speech by Lord Brougham cited in Dodds, *Age of Paradox*, p. 158.
26. John Clive aptly observes that 'what distinguishes Carlyle from so many of his contemporaries, who both feared and opposed the advent of democracy, was his profound awareness of the ineluctability of the historical process which was bringing about that advent.' See *Scott, Carlyle, and Democracy: A Centenary Lecture*, Carlyle Pamphlets, No. 3 (Publ. for *The Carlyle Newsletter*), p. 8.
27. For more on the dangers and fame of James Morison's [*sic*] 'vegetable universal medicine', see Richard D. Altick, ed., *Past and Present*,

p. 28 n. 1. See also Altick's 'Topicality as Technique', p. 118.

28. See Charles Frederick Harrold, ed., *Sartor Resartus* (New York: The Odyssey Press, 1937), p. xiv, and cf. above, p. 5.

29. For a fuller discussion of typology in *Past and Present*, see LaValley, *Carlyle and the Idea of the Modern*, pp. 213–20; and Herbert L. Sussman, *Fact into Figure: Typology in Carlyle, Ruskin, and the Pre-Raphaelite Brotherhood* (Columbus: Ohio State University Press, 1979), pp. 16–25.

30. Sussman, *Fact into Figure*, p. 17.

31. Froude, *London*, 1: 158; Journal entry of 3 June.

Chapter 8

1. See Froude, *London*, 1: 128. David Alec Wilson suggests that the invitation 'apparently' came from Mill's associate, John Robertson. Robertson subsequently withdrew the request, to Carlyle's great annoyance. See Wilson, *Carlyle on Cromwell and Others* (1837–48), Vol. 3 of *Life of Thomas Carlyle* (New York: E. P. Dutton, 1925), pp. 51–2.

2. Despite the conflagration, some six hundred pages of drafts and notes for *Cromwell* are now at the Victoria and Albert Museum, Yale University, and the University of California at Santa Cruz. These working papers, together with Carlyle's many letters concering *Cromwell*, constitute the fullest record of the composition of any of Carlyle's works. Professor K. J. Fielding and his student Dale Trela are currently studying this material, and I am indebted to Professor Fielding for calling it to my attention. Professor Fielding informs me in a letter of 26 June 1984 that this research may modify the accepted views of Carlyle's working habits as a historian and may suggest, in addition to Carlyle's uncertainty over form, a biographical basis for his confusion and delay over Cromwell. For Carlyle's burning of the early drafts, see Wilson, *Carlyle on Cromwell*, pp. 52 and 246.

3. Froude, *London*, 1: 170. Journal entry of 16 Nov. 1840.

4. Froude, *London*, 1: 238. Journal entry of 25 Oct. 1842.

5. Froude, *London*, 1: 305. Cf. A. J. P. Taylor: 'For almost two centuries the verdict of historians went unanimously against him: knave, hypocrite, fanatic; at best, in Clarendon's phrase, "a brave, bad man." Then Carlyle came to his rescue: "not a man of falsehoods, but a man of truths"'. 'Cromwell and the Historians', in *Essays in English History*, p. 23.

6. Hugh Trevor-Roper, 'Thomas Carlyle's Historical Philosophy', in *Times Literary Supplement* (26 June 1981), p. 733.

7. Froude, *London*, 1: 316.

8. Slater, *Correspondence*, p. 357, 31 Jan. 1844.

9. Alfred McKinley Terhune and Annabelle Burdick Terhune, *The Letters of Edward Fitzgerald* (Princeton: Princeton University Press, 1980), 1: 417; 9

Jan. 1844. Fitzgerald, whose family owned much of the battlefield, located the exact site of the battle and sent Carlyle informative amounts of his 'bone-rummaging'. See Terhune, 1: 28, 339–80.

Chapter 9

1. Froude, *London*, 1: 342–3.
2. Froude, *London*, 1: 343–4.
3. Howard Foster Lowry, ed. *The Letters of Matthew Arnold to Arthur Hugh Clough* (Oxford: Clarendon Press, 1968), p. 111, 23 Sept. 1849. Compare this comment of Edward Fitzgerald : 'Carlyle gets more wild, savage, and unreasonable every day; and, I do believe, will turn mad' (Terhune, *Letters of Fitzgerald*, 1: 534; 5 May 1846 to Bernard Barton).
4. Froude, *London*, 1: 344.
5. Froude, *London*, 1: 358–61; Journal entry of 9 Feb. 1848.
6. Froude, *London*, 1: 196.
7. Froude, *Forty*, 2: 359; Journal entry of 26 July 1834.
8. 20: 116, 141, 152, 315–18.
9. See Ruskin's essay on 'Traffic' in *The Crown of Wild Olive*. For the influence of 'Hudson's Statue' on Dickens's indictment of Mammonism in *Little Dorrit*, see Janet Larson, 'The Arts in These Latter Days: Carlylean Prophecy in *Little Dorrit*', in *Dickens Studies Annual*, 9, ed. Fred Kaplan *et al.* (AMS Press, 1980), pp. 139–96. See especially Professor Larson's comments on Merdle as an 'expansion' of 'Hudson's Statue', p. 186 n. 30. 'Hudson's Statue' is in turn an expansion of certain ideas in an unpublished manuscript in the Beinecke Library in which Carlyle deplores the current 'generation of the world, which has no marching standards but these two: a Phallus and a moneybag'. See Fred Kaplan, ' "Phallus Worship" (1848): Unpublished Manuscripts III . . .', in *The Carlyle Newsletter* 2 (1980), 19–23.
10. Froude, *London*, 2: 18–19; Journal entry of 11 Nov. 1849.
11. Froude, *London*, 2: 67, Journal entry of 3 May 1851.
12. Froude, *London*, 2: 70, Letter of 10 Sept. 1851.
13. Froude, *London*, 2: 25–6.
14. Sanders, *Collected Letters*, 8: 253; 2 Nov. 1835.
15. Froude, *London*, 2: 114–15; Thea Holme, *The Carlyles at Home* (London: Oxford University Press, 1965), p. 71.
16. Froude, *London*, 2: 114, 131.
17. 'Never in my life nearer *sunk* in the mud oceans that rage from without and within'; Froude, *London*, 2: 104; Journal entry of 9 Nov. 1852.
18. Froude, *London*, 2: 146; Journal entry of 16 Sept. 1854.
19. Albert J. LaValley, *Carlyle and the Idea of the Modern*, p. 270.
20. Froude, *London*, 2: 126; Journal entry of 28 Feb. 1854.
21. Froude, *London*, 2: 131–2; Journal entry of Apr. 1854.

Chapter 10

1. Letter to Marshall of 28 Nov. 1859, Egerton MS, cited in 'Frederick the Great: "That Unutterable Horror of a Prussian Book" ', by Arthur A. and Vonna H. Adrian, in *Carlyle: Past and Present*, K. J. Fielding and Rodger L. Tarr, eds. (New York: Barnes and Noble, 1976), p. 184.
2. Froude, *London*, 2: 73.
3. Froude, *London*, 2: 194. Journal entry of 28 Dec. 1858.
4. Froude, *London*, 2: 193.
5. Froude, *London*, 2: 194.
6. Froude, *London*, 2: 190.
7. See above, p. 117, and Froude, *London*, 2: 242.
8. '*Frederick the Great*', in *Carlyle: Past and Present*, pp. 198-215. In *Victorian Revolutionaries* Peckham argues that *Frederick* is Carlyle's 'masterpiece' and that, 'among other treasures, it offers in the portrait of . . . Frederick William the only literary portrait in English that can come close to challenging the portrait of Uncle Toby in Sterne's *Tristram Shandy* . . .' (New York: Braziller, 1970), p. 45. For another sympathetic reading of *Frederick*, see Myron C. Tuman, 'Heroic Failure in *Frederick the Great*', in *Prose Studies*, 3 (May 1980), 44-53.
9. Froude, *London*, 2: 193; G. P. Gooch, *History and Historians in the Nineteenth Century*, 2nd edn. (Boston: Beacon Press, 1959), p. 308.
10. Raymond Williams, 'Thomas Carlyle', in *Culture and Society 1780-1950* (1958; rpt. New York: Harper & Row, 1966), p. 77.
11. 12: 344, 384; 13: 45-50. See also Nancy Mitford, *Frederick the Great* (New York: Harper & Row, 1970), p. 21.
12. 26 Feb. 1863, to Mrs Austin, in *Letters and Memorials of Jane Welsh Carlyle*, ed. Froude (London: Longmans, 1883), 3: 155.
13. Cited in John Clive, ed., *History of Friedrich II of Prussia called Frederick the Great* by Thomas Carlyle (Chicago: University of Chicago Press, 1969), p. xxv, from Julian Symons, ed., *Carlyle: Selected Works, Reminiscences and Letters* (Cambridge, Mass., 1967), p. 655.
14. 12: 422-3, 429; 13: 169-70, 191, 309, 318.
15. This is Carlyle's summary of a much longer document; see 13: 346-7.
16. Carlyle's sources are Preuss's *Friedrich mit Freunden und Verwandten* and the *Mémoires* of Frederick's sister, Wilhelmina.
17. Hugh Trevor-Roper, 'Thomas Carlyle's Historical Philosophy', p. 733.
18. Froude, *London*, 2: 211; undated.
19. Froude, *London*, 2: 332-3, 356, 403.
20. Froude, *London*, 2: 334. For several more years Carlyle continued to write with a pencil. See 2: 333 n. 1.

Bibliography

Abrams, M. H. *Natural Supernaturalism*. New York: Norton, 1971.

Adrian, Arthur A. and Vonna H. 'Frederick the Great: "That Unutterable Horror of a Prussian Book"' in *Carlyle Past and Present*, ed. K. J. Fielding and Rodger L. Tarr. New York: Barnes and Noble, 1976; pp. 177–97.

Aimond, Charles. 'Varennes: L'Arrestation', in *L'Énigme de Varennes*. Paris: J. de Gigord, 1936; pp. 106–33.

Altick, Richard D. '*Past and Present*: Topicality as Technique', in *Carlyle and His Contemporaries: Essays in Honor of Charles Richard Sanders*, ed. John Clubbe. Durham, NC: Duke University Press, 1976; pp. 112–28.

Arac, Jonathan. *Commissioned Spirits: The Shaping of Social Motion in Dickens, Carlyle, Melville, and Hawthorne*. New Brunswick, NJ: Rutgers University Press, 1979.

Arendt, Hannah. *On Revolution*. New York: Viking, 1963.

Ash, Bernard. *The Golden City: London Between the Fires, 1666–1941*. London: Dent, 1964.

Beik, Paul H., ed. *The French Revolution*. New York: Harper and Row, 1970.

Ben-Israel, Hedva. 'Carlyle and the French Revolution', in *English Historians on the French Revolution*. Cambridge: Cambridge University Press, 1968; pp. 127–47.

Bonaparte, Felicia. *The Triptych and the Cross: The Central Myths of George Eliot's Poetic Imagination*. New York: New York University Press, 1979.

Boner, Harold A. *Hungry Generations: The Nineteenth-Century Case against Malthusianism*. New York: King's Crown Press, 1955.

Briggs, Asa. *Victorian Cities*. Harmondsworth, Middlesex: Penguin Books, 1968.

Browning, Oscar. *The Flight to Varennes and Other Historical Essays*. London: Swan Sonnenschein, 1892.

Bruns, Gerald L. 'The Formal Nature of Victorian Thinking.' *PMLA* 90 (1975), 904–18.

Buckler, William E. '*Past and Present* as Literary Experience: An Essay in the Epistemological Imagination.' *Prose Studies 1800–1900*, Vol. 1, No. 3 (1978), pp. 5–25.

Butwin, Joseph. 'The French Revolution as "Theatrum Mundi".' *Research Studies*, 43 (Sept. 1975), 141–52.

Calder, Grace J. *The Writing of* Past and Present: *A Study of Carlyle's Manuscripts*. New Haven: Yale University Press, 1949.

Carlyle, Thomas. *Works*, Centenary Edition, ed. Henry Duff Traill, 30 vols. London: Chapman and Hall, 1896–1901.

——. *The French Revolution: A History*, ed. C. R. L. Fletcher, 3 vols. London: Methuen, 1902.

——. *The French Revolution: A History*, ed. J. Holland Rose, 3 vols. London: G. Bell, 1913.

——. *Past and Present*, ed. Richard D. Altick. New York: New York University Press, 1977.

——. *Reminiscences*, ed. Charles Eliot Norton, introd. Ian Campbell. 1932; rpt. London: J. M. Dent, 1972.

——. *Sartor Resartus*, ed. Charles Frederick Harrold. New York: Odyssey, 1937.

——. *Two Notebooks*, ed. Charles Eliot Norton. New York: Grolier Club, 1898.

——. *Two Reminiscences*, ed. John Clubbe. Durham, NC: Duke University Press, 1974.

—— and Jane Welsh Carlyle. *Collected Letters*, Duke-Edinburgh Edition, ed. Charles Richard Sanders *et al.*, 9 vols. Durham, NC: Duke University Press, 1970–81.

Choiseul, Duc de. *Relation du départ de Louis XVI, le 20 juin 1791* . . . Paris: Baudouin Frères, 1822.

Clive, John. *Scott, Carlyle, and Democracy: A Centenary Lecture*, Carlyle Pamphlets, No. 3. Publ. for *The Carlyle Newsletter*.

——, introd. and ed. *History of Friedrich II of Prussia called Frederick the Great* by Thomas Carlyle. Chicago: University of Chicago Press, 1969.

Clubbe, John, ed. *Carlyle and His Contemporaries: Essays in Honor of Charles Richard Sanders*. Durham, NC: Duke University Press, 1976.

——, 'Carlyle as Epic Historian', in *Victorian Literature and Society*, ed. James R. Kincaid and Albert J. Kuhn. Columbus: Ohio State University Press, 1984; pp. 119–45.

Cohn, Norman. *The Pursuit of the Millennium*, 2nd edn. New York: Harper, 1961.

Collingwood, R. G. *The Idea of History*. Oxford: Clarendon Press, 1946;

Condorcet, Marquis de. *Progress of the Human Mind*, trans. June Barraclough. London: Weidenfeld and Nicolson, 1955.

Dale, Peter Allan. *The Victorian Critic and the Idea of History: Carlyle, Arnold, Pater*. Cambridge, Mass.: Harvard University Press, 1977.

DeLaura, David J. 'The Allegory of Life: The Autobiographical Impulse in Victorian Prose', in *Approaches to Victorian Autobiography*, ed. George P. Landow. Athens, Ohio: Ohio University Press, 1979; pp. 333–54.

——. 'Ishmael as Prophet: *Heroes and Hero-Worship* and the Self-Expressive Basis of Carlyle's Art', in *Texas Studies in Literature and Language*, 11 (1969), 705–32.

Dickens, Charles. *A Tale of Two Cities*. New York: Signet—New American Library, 1936.

Dodds, John W. *The Age of Paradox: A Biography of England 1841–1851*. New York: Rinehart, 1952.

Dowd, David Lloyd. *Pageant-Maker of the Republic: Jacques-Louis David and the French Revolution*. 1948; rpt. Freeport, NY: Books for Libraries Press, 1969.

Dyos, H. J. and Michael Wolff, eds. *The Victorian City: Images and Realities*, 2 vols. London: Routledge and Kegan Paul, 1973.

Eliot, George. 'Historical Imagination', in *Essays of George Eliot*, ed. Thomas Pinney. New York: Columbia University Press, 1963; pp. 446–7.

——. *Middlemarch*, ed. Gordon S. Haight. Cambridge, Mass.: Riverside—Houghton Mifflin, 1956.

——. *Romola*. Harmondsworth, Middlesex: Penguin Books, 1980.

Emerson, Ralph Waldo. *Selections*, ed. Stephen E. Whicher. Boston: Houghton Mifflin, 1957.

Engels, Friedrich. *The Condition of the Working Class in England in 1844*, trans. and ed. W. O. Henderson and W. H. Challoner. Oxford: Basil Blackwell, 1958.

Ferrières de Marsay, Charles Élie, Marquis de. *Mémoires*, ed. Berville and Barrière, 2nd edn., 3 vols. Paris: Baudouin Frères, 1822.

Fielding, K. J. 'A New Review (Of Himself) by Carlyle: The Squire Forgeries, *Examiner* (15 January 1848).' *The Carlyle Newsletter*, 3 (1981; dated on cover, Oct. 1982), 9–14.

—— and Rodger L. Tarr, eds. *Carlyle Past and Present*. New York: Barnes and Noble, 1976.

Flint, Helen C. 'Indications in Carlyle's *French Revolution* of the Influence of Homer and the Greek Tragedians'. *Classical Journal*, 5 (Jan. 1910), 118–26.

Freud, Sigmund. *Civilization and its Discontents*, trans. James Strachey. New York: Norton, 1961.

Friedlaender, Walter F. *David to Delacroix*, trans. Robert Goldwater. Cambridge, Mass.: Harvard University Press, 1952.

Froude, James Anthony. *Thomas Carlyle: A History of the First Forty Years of His Life, 1795–1835*, 2 vols. New York: Charles Scribner, 1910.

——. *Thomas Carlyle: A History of His Life in London, 1834–1881*, 2 vols. New York: Charles Scribner, 1910.

——, ed. *Letters and Memorials of Jane Welsh Carlyle*. London: Longmans, 1883.

Georgianna, Linda. 'Carlyle and Jocelin of Brakelond: A Chronicle Rechronicled.' *Browning Institute Studies*, 8 (1980), 103–27.

Gibbon, Edward. *The Decline and Fall of the Roman Empire and Other Selected Writings*, ed. H. R. Trevor-Roper. Chalfont St Giles: Sadler and Brown, 1966.

Gilbert, Elliot L. ' "A Wondrous Contiguity": Anachronism in Carlyle's Prophecy and Art.' *PMLA* 87 (1972), 432–42.

Goldberg, Michael. *Carlyle and Dickens*. Athens, Georgia: University of Georgia Press, 1972.

Gooch, G. P. *History and Historians in the Nineteenth Century*, 2nd edn. Boston: Beacon Press, 1959.

Goodman, Richard Allan. 'Carlyle's Intellectual Development through *The French Revolution.*' 2 vols. Dissertation, Columbia, 1977.

Greene, Thomas. *The Descent from Heaven: A Study in Epic Continuity*. New Haven: Yale University Press, 1963.

Haight, Gordon S. *George Eliot: A Biography*. Oxford: Oxford University Press, 1968.

Harrold, Charles Frederick. *Carlyle and German Thought, 1819–1834*. Yale Studies in English, No. 82. New Haven: Yale University Press, 1934.

——. 'The Translated Passages in Carlyle's *French Revolution.*' *JEGP* 27 (1928), 51–66.

——. 'Carlyle's General Method in *The French Revolution.*' *PMLA* 43 (1928), 1150–69.

Helsinger, Elizabeth K. *Ruskin and the Art of the Beholder*. Cambridge, Mass.: Harvard University Press, 1982.

Hill, John Edward Christopher. *Milton and the English Revolution*. London: Faber and Faber, 1977.

Holloway, John. *The Victorian Sage: Studies in Argument*. New York: Norton, 1953.

Jespersen, Otto. *Essentials of English Grammar*. London: Allen and Unwin, 1933.

——. *A Modern English Grammar on Historical Principles*, Vol. 4. Heidelberg: Carl Winters Universitätsbuchhandlung, 1931.

Jocelin of Brakelond. *The Chronicle of Jocelin of Brakelond*, trans. H. E. Butler. New York: Thomas Nelson, 1949.

Kaplan, Fred. ' "Phallus Worship" (1848): Unpublished Manuscripts III . . .', in *The Carlyle Newsletter* 2 (1980), 19–23.

——. *Thomas Carlyle: A Biography*. Ithaca: Cornell University Press, 1983.

Kenner, Hugh. *Joyce's Voices*. Berkeley: University of California Press, 1978.

Kermode, Frank. 'Novel, History, and Type.' *Novel: A Forum on Fiction*, 1 (1968), 231–8.

Knoepflmacher, U. C. Untitled Essay-Review on Carlyle, Carlylism, and the Carlylean in Fiction. *Nineteenth-Century Fiction*, 32 (June 1977), 73–80.

Kroeber, Karl. 'Romantic Historicism: The Temporal Sublime', in *Images of Romanticism: Verbal and Visual Affinities*, ed. Karl Kroeber and William Walling. New Haven: Yale University Press, 1978; pp. 149–65.

Larson, Janet. 'The Arts in These Latter Days: Carlylean Prophecy in *Little Dorrit*', in *Dickens Studies Annual*, 9, ed. Frank Kaplan *et al.* AMS Press, 1980; pp. 139–96.

LaValley, Albert J. *Carlyle and the Idea of the Modern*. New Haven: Yale University Press, 1968.

Lee, Vernon [Violet Paget]. *The Handling of Words; and Other Studies in Literary Psychology*. London: John Lane, 1923.

Lefebvre, Georges. *The French Revolution*. Vol. 1: *From Its Origins to 1793*, trans Elizabeth Moss Evanson. New York: Columbia University Press, 1962.

——. *The French Revolution*. Vol. 2: *From 1793 to 1799*, trans. John Hall Stewart and James Friguglietti. New York: Columbia University Press, 1964.

Leicester, H. M. 'The Dialectic of Romantic Historiography: Prospect and Retrospect in *The French Revolution*.' *Victorian Studies*, 15 (Sept. 1971), 5–17.

Levine, George. *The Boundaries of Fiction: Carlyle, Macaulay, Newman*. Princeton: Princeton University Press, 1968.

——. 'The Use and Abuse of Carlylese', in *The Art of Victorian Prose*, ed. George Levine and William Madden. New York: Oxford University Press, 1968; pp. 101–26.

Lowell, Robert. 'Epics.' *New York Review of Books*, 21 Feb. 1980; pp. 3–6.

Lowry, Howard Foster, ed. *The Letters of Matthew Arnold to Arthur Hugh Clough*. Oxford: Clarendon Press, 1968.

Lukács, Georg. *The Historical Novel*, trans. Hannah and Stanley Mitchell. London: Merlin Press, 1962.

Macaulay, Thomas Babbington. 'History' in *The Varieties of History: From Voltaire to the Present*, ed. Fritz Stern. London: Macmillan, 1970; pp. 71–89.

Marcus, Steven. *Engels, Manchester, and the Working Class*. New York: Random House, 1974.

Marx, Karl. 'The Eighteenth Brumaire of Louis Bonaparte', in *Collected Works*, Vol. 11 (1851–3). London: Lawrence and Wishart, 1979; pp. 99–197.

Mayhew, Henry. *London Labour and the London Poor*. London, 1861–62; rpt. New York: Dover Publications, Inc., 1968.

Mill, John Stuart. 'Review of *The French Revolution* in *London and Westminster Review*, 1837', in *Thomas Carlyle: The Critical Heritage*, ed. Jules Paul Seigel. New York: Barnes and Noble, 1971; pp. 52–68.

Mitford, Nancy. *Frederick the Great*. New York: Harper & Row, 1970.

Moore, Carlisle. 'Carlyle's "Diamond Necklace" and Poetic History.' *PMLA*, 58 (1943), 537–57.

——. 'Thomas Carlyle and Fiction: 1822–1834', in *Nineteenth-Century Studies*, ed. Herbert Davis, William C. DeVane, R. C. Bald. Ithaca, 1940; rpt. New York: Greenwood Press, 1968; pp. 131–77.

Morley, John. *Voltaire*. London: Macmillan, 1923.

Neff, Emery. *The Poetry of History*. New York: Columbia University Press, 1947.

Oddie, William. *Dickens and Carlyle: The Question of Influence*. London: Centenary Press, 1972.

Paget, Violet (see Vernon Lee).

Palmer, R. R. *Twelve Who Ruled: The Year of the Terror in the French Revolution*. 1941; rpt. Princeton: Princeton University Press, 1958.

Peckham, Morse. 'Frederick the Great', in *Carlyle Past and Present*, ed. K. J. Fielding and Rodger L. Tarr. New York: Barnes and Noble, 1976; pp. 198–215.

———. *Victorian Revolutionaries*. New York: George Braziller, 1970.

Prescott, William Hickling. *Literary Memoranda*, ed. C. Harvey Gardiner, 2 vols. Norman, Oklahoma: University of Oklahoma Press, 1961.

Rosenberg, Philip. *The Seventh Hero: Thomas Carlyle and the Theory of Radical Activism*. Cambridge, Mass.: Harvard University Press, 1974.

Ruskin, John. *The Genius of John Ruskin: Selections from His Writings*, ed. John D. Rosenberg. New York: George Braziller, 1963.

Seigel, Jules Paul, ed. *Thomas Carlyle: The Critical Heritage*. New York: Barnes and Noble, 1971.

Sharrock, Roger. 'Carlyle and the Sense of History', in *Essays and Studies*, Vol. 19. London: John Murray, 1966; pp. 74–91.

Shine, Hill. *Carlyle's Fusion of Poetry, History, and Religion by 1834*. Chapel Hill: University of North Carolina Press, 1938.

Slater, Joseph, ed. *The Correspondence of Emerson and Carlyle*. New York: Columbia University Press, 1964.

Stange, G. Robert. 'Refractions of *Past and Present*', in *Carlyle Past and Present*, ed. K. J. Fielding and Rodger L. Tarr. New York: Barnes and Noble, 1976; pp. 96–111.

Sterrenburg, Lee. 'Psychoanalysis and the Iconography of Revolution.' *Victorian Studies*, 19 (1975), 241–64.

Sussman, Herbert L. *Fact into Figure: Typology in Carlyle, Ruskin, and the Pre-Raphaelite Brotherhood*. Columbus: Ohio State University Press, 1979.

Tarr, Rodger L. ' "Fictional High-Seriousness": Carlyle and the Victorian Novel', in *Lectures on Carlyle and His Era*, ed. Jerry D. James and Charles F. Fineman. Santa Cruz: The University Library, University of California, 1982; pp. 27–54.

Taylor, A. J. P. 'Macaulay and Carlyle' and 'Cromwell and the Historians', in *Essays in English History*. Harmondsworth, Middlesex: Penguin Books, 1976.

Tennyson, G. B. *'Sartor' Called 'Resartus'*. Princeton: Princeton University Press, 1965.

———. 'Thomas Carlyle' in *Victorian Prose: A Guide to Research*, ed. David J. DeLaura. New York: Modern Language Assoc. of America, 1973; pp. 33–104.

Terhune, Alfred McKinley and Annabelle Burdick Terhune, eds. *The Letters of Edward Fitzgerald. Vol. 1: 1830–1850*. Princeton: Princeton University Press, 1978.

Thoreau, Henry David. 'From an Essay, *Graham's Magazine*, March and April 1847', in *Thomas Carlyle: The Critical Heritage*, ed. Jules Paul Seigel. New York: Barnes and Noble, 1971; pp. 277–301.

Tillotson, Kathleen. *Novels of the Eighteen-Forties*. Oxford: Clarendon Press, 1954.

Tillyard, E. M. W. *The English Epic and its Background*. Oxford, 1954; rpt. New York: Barnes and Noble, 1966.

Timko, Michael, *et al.*, ed. *Dickens Studies Annual*, 12 (AMS Press, 1983), pp. 161–265.

Tolstoy, Leo. *War and Peace*, trans. Louise and Aylmer Maude, ed. George Gibian. New York: Norton, 1966.

Tourzel, Duchesse de. *Mémoires*, ed. Jean Chalon. [France]: Mercure de France, 1969.

Trevor-Roper, H. R. *The Last Days of Hitler*, 3rd edn. New York: Collier, 1962.

——. 'Thomas Carlyle's Historical Philosophy.' *TLS* (26 June 1981), pp. 731–4.

Tuman, Myron C. 'Heroic Failure in *Frederick the Great*.' *Prose Studies*, 3 (May 1980), 44–53.

Wellek, René. 'Carlyle and the Philosophy of History' and 'Carlyle and German Romanticism', in *Confrontations*. Princeton: Princeton University Press, 1965, pp. 34–81 and 82–113.

White, Hayden. *Metahistory: The Historical Imagination in Nineteenth-Century Europe*. Baltimore: Johns Hopkins University Press, 1973.

Wilkie, Brian. *Romantic Poets and Epic Tradition*. Madison: University of Wisconsin Press, 1965.

Willey, Basil. 'Thomas Carlyle' in *Nineteenth-Century Studies*. 1949; rpt. New York: Harper & Row, 1966, pp. 102–31.

Williams, Raymond. 'Thomas Carlyle' in *Culture and Society 1780–1950*. 1958; rpt. New York: Harper & Row, 1966, pp. 71–86.

Wilson, David Alec. *Carlyle on Cromwell and Others (1837–48)*, Vol. 3 of *Life of Thomas Carlyle*. New York: E. P. Dutton, 1925.

Wilson, Edmund. *To the Finland Station: A Study in the Writing and Acting of History*. New York: Farrar, Straus, and Giroux, 1972.

Wordsworth, William. *Selected Poems and Prefaces*, ed. Jack Stillinger. Boston: Houghton Mifflin, 1965.

Young, Louise Mervin. *Thomas Carlyle and the Art of History*. Philadelphia: University of Pennsylvania Press, 1939.

Index

'On History' 31, 34, 43-4, 175 n. 11,
176 n. 6, 177 n. 12, 180 n. 35
'On History Again' 18-19, 180 n. 36
'On the Sinking of the *Vengeur*' 41 n.
Past and Present (*PP*) 17, 69, 115-35,
141 n., 143
 advertising, evils of 131
 alienation 122-3, 132-4
 allusions to: Bible 123, 126, 135;
  Dante 118, 121-2
 cash nexus and wage-slavery 36,
  122, 134-5
 characters and events: Abbot
  Samson 21, 118, 123-4, 127-9,
  132, 134-6; Captains of Industry
  135-6; Champion of England
  130; England (1200) 20, 24;
  Gurth and Cedric 133-4;
  Henry II 127; Irish Widow 36,
  39, 122-3, 132; John, King
  21-4, 126, 130; John of Dice
  124; London processions 130-2;
  Manchester Insurrection 119;
  Morison's pills 135; Saint
  Edmund, exhumation of 118,
  120-1, 123, 126-7, 129-30;
  Saint Ives Workhouse 118,
  121, 132; Seven-foot Hat 130-
  2; Stockport murders 121-2;
  stuffed Pope 130, 132, 154;
  Tree Igdrasil 18, 188 n. 18
 child labour 119, 133
 compared to: *Bleak House* 36-7;
  Condition of the Working Class
  117, 119, 132, 187 n. 3; *Metamorphoses* 120, 125, 126 n.
 composition of 118
 democracy 132-5
 'Hungry Forties' 118-20
 laissez-faire 118-20
 narrative techniques: 'circuitous
  way' 121 n., 122, 124; narrative
  glides 22-3, 126; narrative
  personae of: brother 122,
  Carlyle-Jocelin 22-3, 126,
  editor-exegete 126-8; omniscience 128, 'picturesque
  Tourist' 118, 120, 121 n., 132,
  TC as prophet-hero 135-6;
  self-reflexiveness 124; shifts
  in perspective 124, 128
 organicism 36, 123
 social programme 132

style: 'cosmic pastorals' 128, 160;
  dramatic monologue 22;
  Emerson on 117, 121, 126,
  129-31; ending, weakness of
  135-6; flux of names and times
  125; 'immortal newspaper',
  121-2, 126; influence on
  novel 35; Latin interpolations
  126; metaphors of: disease 36-
  7, 122-4, enchantment 120-2;
  mock-psychotic idiom 122;
  symbolism 121, 129-31; time
  and tenses 128; typology 136,
  189 n. 29
'Phallus-worship' 190 n. 9
'The Present Time' (*LDP*) 151-2
Reminiscences 15, 115, 171
Sartor Resartus (*SR*) 3-9, 115-16,
  155, 157, 177 n. 16, 179 n. 27
 autobiographical crisis in 11-13,
  39, 155-7
 'Centre of Indifference' 155-6
 Emerson and 4
 'Everlasting No' 11-12, 39,
  155-6
 'Everlasting Yea' 12-13, 39,
  155-6
 influence on novel 35
 madness, analysis of 13-14, 17,
  33
 'Natural Supernaturalism' 4,
  9-11, 49-50, 74, 116
 'Organic Filaments' 36, 39
 relation to *FR* 10-13, 93, 107
 Romanticism in 10
 solitude of 6-7
 style: 'barbarisms', Mill and Sterling on 30; 'cosmic pastorals'
  14; innovations 30, 48, 178 n.
  17; narrative personae: Editor
  10, poet and anti-poet 7, 10,
  135, Teufelsdröckh 7, 10-13,
  18 n., 40, 127, 152, 158, 179 n.
  27
'Shooting Niagara: and After?' 115
'Signs of the Times' 35, 49
'Sir Walter Scott' 34, 176 n. 6
'Stump-Orator' (*LDP*) 152
Two Reminiscences of Thomas Carlyle
  150 n.
Cheyne Row 6, 31
Choiseul C. A. G., Duc de 71
Clive, John 161 n., 187 n. 8, 188 n. 26